Critical Essays on Anthony Burgess

Critical Essays on Anthony Burgess

Geoffrey Aggeler

G. K. Hall & Co. · Boston, Massachusetts

Copyright © 1986 by Geoffrey Aggeler
All Rights Reserved

Library of Congress Cataloging in Publication Data

Main entry under title:
Critical essays on Anthony Burgess.

(Critical essays on modern British literature)
Includes index.
1. Burgess, Anthony, 1917-   — Criticism and interpretation —
Addresses, essays, lectures.
I. Aggeler, Geoffrey, 1939-   . II. Series.

PR6052.U638Z58 1986   823'.914   85-27319
ISBN 0-8161-8757-6

This publication is printed on permanent/durable acid-free paper
MANUFACTURED IN THE UNITED STATES OF AMERICA

CRITICAL ESSAYS ON MODERN BRITISH LITERATURE

The critical essays series on modern British literature provides a variety of approaches to both the modern classical writers of Britain and Ireland, and the best contemporary authors. The formats of the volumes in the series vary with the thematic designs of individual editors, and with the amount and nature of existing reviews, criticism, and scholarship. In general, the series represents the best in published criticism, augmented, where appropriate, by original essays by recognized authorities. It is hoped that each volume will be unique in developing a new overall perspective on its particular author.

Geoffrey Aggeler's collection includes important critical treatments of Anthony Burgess' best novels, with due attention to Burgess' linguistic pyrotechnics, and his interest in and indebtedness to both James Joyce and music. A long and revealing *Paris Review* interview complements Aggeler's informative introduction, which surveys Burgess' literary career and the initial critical reception of his books, and then proceeds to a more detailed discussion of his major works and their critics. Aggeler writes with ease, assurance and balance; his analysis of both Burgess and his critics is succinct and perceptive.

ZACK BOWEN, GENERAL EDITOR

University of Delaware

For Sondra

CONTENTS

INTRODUCTION

The literary career of John Anthony Burgess Wilson began in Malaya, where he served as an education officer with the British Colonial Service from 1954 until the coming of independence in 1957. In 1949 he had written a fictional account of his wartime experiences in Gibraltar, but this did not appear as *A Vision of Battlements* until 1965. He began writing fiction during his Malayan years, "as a sort of gentlemanly hobby, because I knew there wasn't any money in it."[1] *Time for a Tiger*, his first published novel, appeared in 1956 under his nom de plume, which consists of his confirmation name, Anthony, and his mother's maiden name. He used a nom de plume because it was regarded as indiscreet for one in his position to publish realistic fictional portrayals of actual events and personalities under one's own name, and besides, as he says, there were "already enough Wilsons writing."[2] Some years later, having observed the Laborite government of Prime Minister Harold Wilson, he became even less attached to his surname and considered abandoning it legally.

Time for a Tiger (1956) is the first part of a trilogy dealing with life in Malaya as Burgess saw it in the mid and late fifties. The British were still engaged in a long, bloody, ultimately successful campaign against communist guerrillas, but the long day of British colonial domination was clearly waning. The *Malayan Trilogy*, subsequently published in one volume entitled *The Long Day Wanes*, encompasses not only the actual passing of the British raj a year before it occurred but some of the less happy events that were to follow the birth of Malaysian independence. The trilogy is unified by Malaya itself and by the presence of Victor Crabbe, a young British schoolmaster who has come to the Far East in search of a new life. *Time for a Tiger* concerns the hilarious trials and adventures of one of Crabbe's most remarkable acquaintances, a gigantic colonial police lieutenant named Nabby Adams, for whom "Tiger" beer is a *raison d'être*, hence the title.

Reviewing *Time for a Tiger*, Peter Quennell found it "remarkably entertaining . . . one of the most enjoyable first novels I have read for many months."[3] A reviewer for the *Times Literary Supplement* was less enthusiastic, noting a lack of "the tenser conflicts that make a powerful story" and the

1

appearance of artificial contriving. While the novel "provides a number of amusing incidents . . . there is too much drifting, drinking and droning . . . although Mr. Burgess is at his best in the drinking scenes."[4]

In *The Enemy in the Blanket* (1958) Burgess dealt somewhat more seriously than he had in his first novel with the problems of adjustment to a darker civilization. One of the protagonists, Rupert Hardman, an albinoid lawyer, becomes, albeit reluctantly, absorbed into Malaya's Islamic culture, and his case reveals how Islam might lose its enchantment for an Englishman, as it once did for Burgess himself, who had actually considered becoming a Muslim. Victor Crabbe, the trilogy's linking protagonist, loses his wife to a Malayan but contents himself with the hope of being a spokesman for sound Western "values" as Malaya moves toward independence. Just how little effect such well-meaning efforts are going to have is suggested by the disquieting glimpses of the future provided by scenes depicting representatives of the various dominant races — Tamils, Sikhs, Malays, Chinese — who despise each other and are united only in their hatred of the common enemy, the British.

The Enemy in the Blanket was well received by reviewers, one of whom remarked that "there's more meat here than in half a dozen average novels."[5] In the *Times Literary Supplement* it was given a comparative review with *Knives*, a novel by Emmanuel Robles which also depicts a country in transition. The reviewer was able to perceive the seriousness underlying the wit and comedy of *The Enemy in the Blanket*: "In situations that M. Robles would take with extreme seriousness Mr. Burgess is often unashamedly flippant. Nevertheless there is a serious slant to his work which penetrates well below the surface. If some of his funny men, notably a pair of Sikhs performing as comic policemen, are not as funny as they might be, or presumably as they are intended to be, his disillusioned English, less tragic, less intense, more open to compromise than the idealistic Pierre Mayen, are convincingly, and at moments, movingly, portrayed."[6]

Encouraged by the reviews of his first two novels and by his publisher, Burgess completed the trilogy with *Beds in the East* (1959). This novel begins with a description of a Malay family arising for one of the last days of British rule and concludes with a description of a lovely Tamil girl wiping away a tear for Victor Crabbe, who has drowned miserably in a river upcountry. Most of the novel is concerned with native Malayans, members of groups Burgess introduced briefly in the first two books, and, as anticipated, the only change accompanying the "dawn of freedom" is an intensifying of interracial hostilities. The book is unquestionably pessimistic, and one reviewer objected that there was "too little sympathy" in it.[7] Other critics appreciated its "brilliant comedy" and skillful writing.[8]

Shortly after Malaya gained her independence, all British expatriates were forced to leave the country. Burgess soon found another teaching post in Brunei, Borneo. The favorable reception of his Malayan books notwithstanding, he did not view himself primarily as a novelist, but as a professional teacher who simply wrote novels "as a kind of hobby."[9] He was an English-Language Specialist in Brunei from 1957 until 1960, when, like Edwin Spindrift in *The Doctor is Sick*, he suddenly collapsed on the floor of a classroom. Immediately, he was loaded aboard a jet airliner for England, where doctors at the National Hospital for Nervous Diseases diagnosed his ailment as a brain tumor.

Initially the doctors considered removing the tumor, and Burgess was apprehensive, lest "they hit my talent instead of my tumor," but then they decided that removal was impossible. Burgess was told that he would probably be dead within the year, but that if he managed to live through the year, he could infer that the prognosis had been excessively pessimistic and that he would live. His situation was extremely dismal in that he had no pension, was unable to get a job, and saw no way of providing for his prospective widow. However, instead of moping about in self-pitying depression, he began writing novels, chiefly to secure posthumous royalties for his wife. Surprisingly, he felt more exhilarated than depressed, and his "last year on earth" was one of the most productive he has ever known. The five novels he produced—*Inside Mr. Enderby, The Wanting Seed, The Doctor Is Sick, The Worm and the Ring*, and *One Hand Clapping*—include some of his best work, and they were not the only things he wrote. Thus he launched himself as a professional novelist under much less than favorable and indeed quite accidental circumstances. But, as he says, "most writers who actually do become novelists do so by accident. If a man deliberately sets out to become a novelist, he usually winds up as a critic, which is, I think, something less."[10]

His productivity astonished the critics and, paradoxically, alarmed his publisher. The fecundity of writers such as Dickens, Trollope, and Henry James had long been forgotten in England, where it was generally thought that writers of quality followed the example of E. M. Forster and produced a canon of perhaps four or five books over a period of eighty to ninety years. Fecundity, Burgess found, was looked upon as a kind of literary disease. His publisher suggested that he conceal the malady by taking another pseudonym, and so it happened that *Inside Mr. Enderby* and *One Hand Clapping* were published under the name Joseph Kell.

Burgess intended *Inside Mr. Enderby* to be a "kind of trumpet blast on behalf of the besieged poet of today—the man who tries to be independent, tries to write his poetry not on the campus, but in the smallest room in the house," the lavatory, where he can have some privacy.[11] His hero, Mr. F. X. Enderby, is a shy, harmless, flatulent little poet whose misadventures reveal the condition of poetry and the poet in the 1960s. The novel was destined to have several sequels. Burgess followed it in 1968 with *Enderby Outside*, and the two books were published together the same year in America as a single novel entitled *Enderby*. A third Enderby novel, *The Clockwork Testament* appeared in 1975, and still another one, *Enderby's Dark Lady*, is scheduled to appear in 1985.[12]

The first Enderby novel was well received by the critics. Frederic Raphael in the *Sunday Times* called it "a brilliantly fly piece of work," and remarked that "Mr. Kell's narrative crackles with witticisms."[13] The *Spectator* termed it, rightly, "a little masterpiece," and it also received high praise in *TLS* and the *Listener*.[14] However, neither *Inside Mr. Enderby* nor *One Hand Clapping* sold very well, mainly because no one had ever heard of Joseph Kell. *One Hand Clapping* is a clever tour de force, a parable of life in Modern England narrated by a twenty-three-year-old wife of a used car salesman. Although it is not one of Burgess's best books, not on a level with *Inside Mr. Enderby*, it was reissued profitably under the name Anthony Burgess in 1972. A comical result of the Kell business was that Burgess was asked to review one of his own novels. The editor who sent him the book did not know he was Joseph Kell. Appreciating what he took to be the editor's sense of humor, Burgess wrote the review — and was never again allowed to write for that journal.[15]

As the novels came out, his health improved steadily, and he began to take on various nonfiction-writing chores as well. For a time, he was both music critic for *Queen* — a British glossy read in the United States — and drama critic for the *Spectator*. One of the trials of this dual role was being dogged by spies assigned "to see whether I really saw an opera and a play on the same night."[16] He also wrote a number of television scripts, including one on Martinů, one on Shelley and Byron in Switzerland, and one on Joyce. Other projects included a play written at the request of the Phoenix Theatre, London, another one for the BBC, and still another for Independent TV, as well as a new translation of Berlioz's *Enfance du Christ*. In addition, he was becoming more and more in demand as a book reviewer, and his average yearly output in reviews alone was estimated by one reporter at 150,000 words.[17]

But Burgess was and is primarily a writer of fiction, and most of his boundless energy during the early sixties went into the writing of novels. He also wrote some short fiction and, although he finds the short story a constricting form, contributed several to the *Hudson Review*, *Argosy*, *Rutgers Review*, and other periodicals. He also contributed verse to a number of periodicals, including the *Transatlantic Review*, *Arts and Letters*, and the *New York Times*, which commissioned him to write a poem on the landing of Apollo II.

He has never, however, remained rooted to his writer's chair. Always restless, he has traveled a great deal, and so far as his fiction is concerned, one of his most productive trips was a visit to Leningrad in 1961. His purpose in going "was to experience life in Leningrad without benefit of Intourist — i.e., as one of the crowd." Before the trip, he spent about six weeks reviving his Russian, acquired during the war; his use of the language enabled him to gain a great deal from the experience. One of his first discoveries in Russia was that it was possible to enter the country without a passport. One simply left the ship long after everyone else, after the immigration officials had gone off duty. If one were really willing to live dangerously, one could also reap a tidy profit selling smuggled Western goods. One could smuggle a man out of the country by securing a deluxe cabin with a bathroom in which he could be hidden. Burgess actually did some of these things himself or heard about others who had succeeded in doing them. On top of all this, he found that one could get to know the secret police on a friendly basis. Late one evening, these stock villains of Western spy thrillers were kind enough to take Burgess home, drunk, in one of their cars. This and other experiences finally led him to conclude that "the Russian soul is all right; it's the state that's wrong."

One of the fruits of this hair-raising "research" was *Honey for the Bears* (1963), a hilarious entertainment in which an unconsciously homosexual ("gomosexual") British antique dealer goes to Russia to sell smuggled dresses and in the process loses his wife to a lesbian. Another product was *A Clockwork Orange* (1962), a seriously philosophical picaresque tale narrated by a demonic young hoodlum who could be either Russian or English or both. Burgess and his wife encountered some of his prototypes late one evening outside a Leningrad restaurant. As they were finishing their meal, they were startled to hear loud hammering at the door. Having been filled with the usual western propaganda, they immediately had the terrifying thought that the hammerers were after them, the capitalist enemy. In fact, these hardfisted young toughs, called "stilyagi," were after different prey. When the Burgesses wanted to leave the restaurant, the stilyagi courteously stepped aside, allowed them to pass, and then resumed their hammering. Burgess was struck by the "Nabokovian quality" of the incident, the way in which their conduct reflected the "chess mind": "Even lawless violence must follow rules and ritual." He was also struck by their resemblance to the English teddy boys of the 1950s whom they were indeed copying, and he went home with an even sturdier conviction that "Russians are human."

In the same year he went to Russia, 1961, his novels *Devil of a State* and *The Worm and the Ring* appeared and were fairly well received critically, though the entire first edition of the latter book was withdrawn and pulped up because of a purely coincidental resemblance of events and characters, and his publisher was obliged to pay £100 in damages in an out of court settlement.

The Worm and the Ring was based upon Burgess's experiences as a grammar school teacher in Banbury, Oxfordshire. It is a kind of mock epic, or, more exactly, a mock opera, a burlesque of Wagner's *Der Ring des Nibelungen*. Wagner's allegorical tale of a struggle for power between Nibelung dwarfs, giants, and gods is translated into a struggle for the control of a grammar school in a little English borough. The protagonist, Christopher Howarth, an ineffectual Siegfried, is a thirty-nine-year-old assistant master who teaches German and leads an ungratifying existence. For one thing, his relationship with his wife is tense, partly because of their poverty, but mainly because of her submission to the rules of the Catholic

Church. The wretchedness of Howarth's poverty, the stupid tyranny of mindless Catholic orthodoxy, and the philistinism of the English borough are all presented with angry force. But Burgess's anger does not cause him to present any of his criticisms simplistically. If the society is drifting toward philistinism, it is not entirely due to the strength or cunning of philistine "giants." The liberal humanism of the headmaster, his unshakable faith in human goodness, gives him excuses to shirk responsibility and ignore the community's demands for stability. Burgess's balanced critical treatment of the extreme of rule based on liberal idealism versus the extreme of cynical autocracy agrees with his other novels. As in his dystopian books, *The Wanting Seed* and *A Clockwork Orange*, Burgess exposes the inadequacies and dangers of both as governing philosophies. Reviewing the novel, one critic praised the treatment of Howarth's private life and the terrible dilemma of his son, who must reconcile his love of God and the Catholic Church with love for his father. The reviewer also remarked that Burgess "has a gift for near-caricature which makes the damp grey atmosphere of his Midland town almost bearable."[18]

Devil of a State was a Book Society choice when it first appeared in 1961, but, like so many of Burgess's novels, it had a mixed critical response. A *New Statesman* reviewer observed that its comic devices would have been more effective "if Mr. Burgess hadn't been Scooped long ago."[19] He and others had noted that the book seems to echo Evelyn Waugh's early satires, *Scoop* and *Black Mischief*. Indeed, the African setting and the sardonic detachment with which Burgess presents the chaos of life in a newly emergent state are liable to give a reader of the Waugh satires a sense of déjà vu. Certainly Burgess has acknowledged a general indebtedness to Waugh, as well as to Joyce, Sterne, and Nabokov. But the book is essentially Burgess's own vision of life in such a state, and he quite likely saw the same sorts of things in the Far East that Waugh saw in Africa. "Dunia," the imaginary caliphate in *Devil of a State*, is, Burgess tells us, "a kind of fantasticated Zanzibar,"[20] but one senses that the real setting may be Borneo, just as one senses the Caribbean island of "Castita" in *MF* may actually be Malta.

The novel's protagonist, Lydgate, like backward-looking Victor Crabbe in the *Malayan Trilogy*, progresses toward a terrible reckoning with his past, and his progress, like Crabbe's, is set against the chaotic progress of a former British colony toward independence. But while it is possible to become involved with Crabbe and the Malaya he loves, in *Devil of a State* Burgess does not permit involvement with Lydgate and Dunia. He compels instead sardonic detachment from the horribly comic spectacle of irresponsibility and its fruits both on the individual and on the state level. The book is both farce and parable. Like the satire of Swift, it points in many directions and sustains its irony throughout.

In the same year that these two novels were published in England, another novel, *The Right to an Answer*, was published in America, and Burgess's reputation across the Atlantic began to grow. Like *The Worm and the Ring*, this novel focuses on the decadence of modern England. The narrator-protagonist, Mr. J. W. Denham, is a plump, balding middle-aged businessman who takes what he can out of life in pleasure and novel experiences. After living in the Far East, he feels alienated, but he is troubled more by the spectacle of "irresponsibility" and "instability" in "hideous, TV-haunted England." What he has seen of life in East and West has given him a Hobbesian view of human affairs. He values stability more than freedom and is convinced that "you definitely can't have both."

The brief glimpses of dreary or sordid suburban life in a "rather large smug Midland city" are a prelude to the entrance of Mr. Raj, a Ceylonese gentleman who provides yet another view of England from the vantage point of Far Eastern experience. He has come to England to carry out research for a thesis on "Popular Conceptions of Racial Differentiation." He tries to bridge some gaps between East and West by attempting to have an affair with a woman who has been involved in the game of wife-swapping, and the results are tragic.

The range of subjects treated in *The Right to an Answer* — from culture clashes to love and moral responsibility — is considerable; yet the relevance of each subject to the others is clearly evident. The nature of the subjects themselves may have been one reason why British reviewers were not enthusiastic when the novel appeared in 1960. It received a rather tepid review in *TLS* from a critic who wondered "whether the experiences recounted add up to anything of much importance."[21] Critics in America had fewer doubts in this regard. Naomi Bliven, in a long review essay in the *New Yorker*, had this to say:

> Mr. Burgess has invented complex, varying people, and he has moved them well, giving them much to suffer and to do. The reader cannot outguess the plot, though he can believe in it. As a bonus, in the closing pages, Burgess has crackle and sparkle in a gloriously funny surprise. Then, after a few pages of modulation, the book ends with a wistful, unfinished essay in which Raj, just before his death, is attempting to find an answer. It is a fitting close, for although Mr. Burgess jokes all the way through, the book is not a joke but a nicely controlled examination of some human predicaments that is cunningly disguised as entertainment.[22]

Margharita Laski, a British reviewer reading it for the *Saturday Review*, was a little less enthusiastic, calling it "an odd, rag-tag-and-bobtail of a novel, which starts with a distinctly nasty flavor and ends, surprisingly, with a sweet taste in the mouth." Overall, however, her assessment was favorable, and she praised its originality: "It's also great fun, not *very* good but *rather* good, and, for all its depressing beginning, a book made out of the author's own head and not from other Zeitgeist books."[23]

In 1962 the British edition of what was to become his best known novel, *A Clockwork Orange*, appeared. Based partly upon his experience during his trip to Leningrad, it is a proleptic nightmare in the Orwellian vein narrated by a fifteen-year-old protagonist, Alex, who is one of the most vicious creations in recent fiction. His language, a teenage patois called *nadsat* (a Russian suffix for "teen") reflects a fusion of eastern and western cultures. The novel itself is a kind of sermon on choice written partly in response to a suggestion in Parliament that modern British youth should be conditioned to be respectful toward the modern British state. Burgess's novel argues, in effect, that the modern state has no right to tamper with human nature and reduce man to a well-behaved mechanism. In the original British edition, there is an additional chapter, not in the subsequent American edition, in which the protagonist is shown deciding to reform himself, having survived both the imposition of "goodness" by behavioral engineers and the restoration of his former viciousness by other engineers in the service of a government embarrassed by the failure of its conditioning scheme. The message of this chapter appears to be that if there is any hope for man, it is in the capacity of individuals to grow and learn by suffering and error. Suffering, fallen human beings, not behavioral technology or the revolutionary schemes of idealists, bring "goodness" into the world.

Even before Stanley Kubrick made his film version of *A Clockwork Orange* in 1971, *A Clockwork Orange* was becoming Burgess's most widely read and frequently discussed novel. This does not altogether please Burgess, who considers some of his other novels, notably the *Enderby* books, much more significant. The earliest reviews of *A Clockwork Orange* did not generally suggest that it should be regarded as a work of major significance. A *Library Journal* reviewer found that "the ideas presented are thought-provoking" but insufficiently developed and moreover the invented language "will act as a barrier to the general reader."[24] Another reviewer cited examples of the author's "questionable taste" and accused him of using "a serious social challenge for frivolous purposes" while staying "neutral" himself.[25] More perceptive than either of these critics was Daniel Talbot: "*A Clockwork Orange* is a gruesome fable. Its poisonous culture has obvious roots in our own. It is a nightmare world, made terrifyingly real through Burgess' extraordinary use of language. . . . Burgess combines an acute ear for the onomatopoeic aspects of language with an intuitive sense of the ambiguity of words, and his artificial slang has an emotional impact which transcends specific word meanings. Like the music which rouses Alex to passion, Burgess' language echoes deeply within the reader's psyche to stir the mind, the eye and the ear with profound impact."[26]

Most of the numerous subsequent critical discussions of *A Clockwork Orange* appeared after Kubrick's film version was released. Though Burgess was depressed by a sense of being demoted to the level of "a mere provider of raw material for a great filmmaker," a sense of being a lowly hod carrier, as it were, for creative genius, it would seem that the book itself received so much attention at least partly because of the film. The film, incidentally, follows the truncated American edition, concluding with Alex's "self," his moral nature restored, along with his concomitant appetites for Beethoven and throat cutting. Burgess tends to agree with his American publisher with regard to the superiority of the truncated version, which ends the book "on a tough and violent note."[27]

Several articles have focused on *A Clockwork Orange* both as novel and film, but most of them deal only with the novel—its language, themes, and relations to various literary traditions—and one gathers that whatever Burgess himself thinks of the book, its place as a classic of the dystopian subgenre is generally accepted and secure.

Appearing the same year as *A Clockwork Orange*, Burgess's *The Wanting Seed* is the most explicit treatment of a theme that is ubiquitous in his fiction, the conflict between "Pelagian" and "Augustinian" views of the human condition. In the novel history itself is shown to be a perpetual oscillation or "waltz" between "Pelagian" and "Augustinian" phases. This theory of history is one Burgess had partially formulated in *A Vision of Battlements*. In that novel an American officer describes how the Pelagian denial of Original Sin had spawned "the two big modern heresies—material progress as a sacred goal; the State as God Almighty." The former has produced "Americanism" and the latter, "the Socialist process." In *The Wanting Seed* all government history is seen to be an oscillation between Pelagian and Augustianian philosophies. When a government is functioning in its Pelagian phase, or "Pelphase," it is socialistic and committed to a Wellsian liberal belief in man and his ability to achieve perfection through his own efforts. Inevitably man fails to fulfill the liberal expectation, and the ensuing "disappointment" causes a chaotic "Interphase," during which terrorist police strive to maintain order by force and brutality. Finally, the government, appalled by its own excesses, lessens the brutality but continues to enforce its will on the citizenry on the assumption that man is an inherently sinful creature from whom no good may be expected. This pessimistic phase is appropriately named for the saint whose preoccupation with the problems of evil led him, like Burgess, into Manicheism. During "Gusphase" there is a capitalist economy but very little real freedom for the individual. What Burgess appears to be suggesting is that a Godless society which accepts Augustine's view of unregenerate human nature is apt to be a Fascist dictatorship.

The Wanting Seed was less pleasing to most critics than *A Clockwork Orange*. Brigid Brophy was especially harsh, calling it "half-baked" and observing that Burgess "gets neither down to the atmospheric details of his new world nor up to an intellectual height from which to survey its structure."[28] A reviewer for the *Library Journal* considered the satire "heavy-handed" but found the book nonetheless "frightening" as a "warning to us to do whatever must be done to plan a sound future world. . . . Not entertaining fiction, but good reading."[29] A *TLS* reviewer saw the book very differently: "The whole thing is wildly and fantastically funny, for all the bitter aftertaste of many incidents. Here too is all the usual rich exuberance of Mr. Burgess's vocabulary, his love of quotations and literary allusions . . .

his fantastic dream and nightmare sequences, and his little digs at other literary figures . . . This, then, is a remarkable and brilliantly imaginative novel, vital and inventive."[30] Subsequent critical evaluations have been generally closer to this review, and one of the more perceptive exegeses is included in this volume.

1964 was the year of the Shakespeare quadricentennial, and Burgess commemorated it with what some critics regard as his finest achievement in the novel, *Nothing Like the Sun*, subtitled "A Story of Shakespeare's Love-Life." Confusing to some readers is the fact that the novel maintains simultaneously two settings, Elizabethan England and a classroom in twentieth-century Borneo. The narrator, as Burgess states in the prologue, is "Mr. Burgess," who has just been "given the sack" by his headmaster, and it is time to bid his students farewell. His farewell speech, a last lecture, will be primarily for the benefit of those "who complained that Shakespeare had nothing to give to the East." It is a long discourse, but he is well fortified with a potent Chinese rice spirit called *samsu*, a parting gift from his students. The *samsu* and his considerable knowledge of Shakespeare enable him to transport himself and his class back into sixteenth-century England. In a sense, however, he also brings Shakespeare forward into the twentieth century through identification with himself. As his lecture progresses, accompanied by much *samsu* swigging, the identification becomes stronger and stronger until finally, in the epilogue, we are able to hear the voice of a Shakespeare-Burgess composite hero.

The lecture begins with a vision of an adolescent Master Shakespeare at home in Stratford. The youth dreams of a "goddess," a dark lady who is his muse, his ideal of beauty, and his forbidden fruit. He finds her literally embodied in various dark-complexioned country maidens, and occasionally she inspires verse. Next we see "WS the married man," who has been trapped into marriage with fair-complexioned Anne Hathaway, and Burgess reveals how she might have served as a model for Regan in *King Lear*, Lady Ann in *Richard III*, and Gertrude in *Hamlet*.

Later, as he rises to prominence as both playwright and poet, WS is drawn on by occasional glimpses of his goddess, and when he catches a glimpse of Fatimah, more commonly known as Lucy Negro, a brown-gold girl from the East Indies, the old yearning to know his goddess fully in the flesh overwhelms him again. His conquest of this dark lady is a long and arduous process, but he finally succeeds and finds himself in a state of desperate sexual bondage. His deliverance from this enchantment is painful and disillusioning. His two "angels" (as he describes them in Sonnett 144) meet each other, and knowing their natures, he must ere long "guess one angel in another's hell." Eventually he is reconciled with the dark lady, whose relationship with "Mr. W. H." (Henry Wriosthesley, Third Earl of Southampton) has been terminated by a pregnancy for which WS is probably responsible. The golden son she bears is to be raised as a gentleman and sent to her homeland in the Far East, and the poet is exhilarated by the thought that "his blood would, after all, flow to the East." Unfortunately, she also bears within her "hell" the fatal spirochete, a gift of Mr. W. H., which will have a profound influence on the development of Shakespeare's art.

With the poet's discovery that he is syphilitic, Mr. Burgess is near the end of both his lecture and the *samsu*. In the "Epilogue," the voice of the poet merges completely with that of the writer-lecturer, and, although the latter is not himself syphilitic, he describes how the disease molded "his" art even as it ravaged his body.

Predictably, the critical responses to this novel were varied. D. J. Enright found it reminiscent of Mann's *Doctor Faustus* in a "smaller and more sensational way."[31] While praising it as a "clever, tightly constructed . . . tour de force," Enright remarked cryptically that "a little too much force has been applied, in the wrong places." It would seem that he objected mainly to the "horrific and grotesque" presentation of WS's sexual history. Another reviewer, while allowing that such a novel would inevitably be "long on lechery and short on the more reflective and philosophical aspects of Shakespeare's mind," objected that even a story of Shakespeare's love-life should be "informed with his developing ideas about the ambiguities of the human condition."[32] Since this is in fact one of Burgess's main focuses in the novel, one can only infer that this critic's reading was rather hasty. A more appreciative appraisal was that of Eileen Pippet in the *Saturday Review* who commented that "Nothing (in the novel) is dragged in for cheap effect; everything is relevant. The more you know about the plays and the period the more you will appreciate the subtle touches that give verisimilitude to the tale."

In 1966, after Burgess had published his fifteenth novel, William H. Pritchard published the first extended appraisal of Burgess's achievement in fiction. Pritchard's article is still one of the most perceptive and illuminating pieces on Burgess's fiction, and it has been included in the present volume. It focuses on five books representing what Pritchard considered Burgess's best "early" and "later" work, including *The Long Day Wanes, The Right to an Answer, A Clockwork Orange, The Wanting Seed*, and *Honey for the Bears*. Pritchard likened Burgess's art to the "theatrical" art of Dickens, delighting the reader by "the showman's ability energetically to command a large and various number of acts by an inexhaustibly creative language."[33] While appreciating Burgess's verbal showmanship, Pritchard shrewdly pointed out some problems that arise in *The Long Day Wanes* and *The Right to an Answer* because of the narrative points of view. His judgment of *A Clockwork Orange* was that "within its odd but carefully observed limits the book is entirely consistent, successful and even pleasing, Burgess' most eye and ear-catching performance." Quite rightly, I believe, Pritchard regarded the inclusion of the glossary in the American edition as a "mistake," because "it short-circuits the unmistakable rhythms of speech by which the sentences almost insensibly assume meaning."[34] He concludes his appraisal with high praise that would become more clearly deserved with the subsequent growth of the Burgess canon: "After Nabokov there is no other . . . ."[35]

Burgess's next novel, *Tremor of Intent* (1966), was in some ways an even more startling tour de force than *Nothing Like the Sun*. It is a spy-thriller, and upon the well-worn framework of Ian Fleming's James Bond formula Burgess has fleshed out and molded a tale of intrigue intended to fire the senses of even the most Bond-weary aficionado of the spy-thriller. The typical Bond feats of appetite are duplicated and surpassed, sometimes to a ridiculous extent. The protagonist, Denis Hillier, has bedroom adventures that make Bond's conquests seem as crude and unfulfilling as an adolescent's evening affair with an issue of *Playboy*. His gastronomic awareness is such that Bond is by comparison an epicurean tyro. In addition, Hillier possesses a mind that is good for something besides devising booby traps and playing games with supervillains.

In the course of carrying out his last mission for Her Majesty's Secret Service, Hillier encounters an obese supervillain by the name of Theodorescu, who exemplifies the state of self-serving "neutrality" that Burgess himself regards as the most contemptible and evil moral attitude a human being can assume. He agrees with Dante that such human beings are unworthy of the dignity of damnation. His protagonist, Hillier, discovers that the world is full of such "neutrals," and his mission for his government, which is dominated by bureaucratic neutrals, becomes a search for a way to make a meaningful commitment of himself against evil in the modern world. He is assisted in his spiritual progress by two women, who represent stages in a Dantesque progress through Hell into Heaven. One of them, an Indian woman named Miss Devi, is herself a "hell," in the Elizabethan sense of a locus of sexual excitement. The other, a young girl named Clara, becomes for him a Beatrice figure. Eventually Hillier finds his way back into the Catholic church, which he left as a youth because of its puritanical view of the flesh. Only the Church can satisfy his craving for commitment in the great conflict between the forces of "God and Notgod" that dominates the universe. Like other Burgess protagonists, he has become a Manichee.

Burgess's technical verbal brilliance in this novel was generally recognized, but some critics had difficulty accepting the fusion of eschatology and espionage. One suggested that Burgess's passion for words may be "his Achilles heel as a novelist . . . [He] determinedly produces a whole series of 'entertainments,' superbly done but always suggesting the enormous waste of Olivier performing in vaudeville."[36] Since that time, *Tremor of Intent* has received closer scrutiny as one of Burgess's more important novels, and this volume includes two recent critical exegeses.

In his next novel, *Enderby Outside* (1968) Burgess reconsidered the formidable question of what it is that makes a poet, a question that had exercised him in *Nothing Like the Sun* and in the first Enderby novel. In *Inside Mr. Enderby* the question of whether or not Enderby and others like him have what it takes to write significant poetry is left in the air. It is answered unequivocally in *Enderby Outside* by a mysterious young girl, who seems to be either Enderby's Muse or her representative. She tells Enderby that he lacks courage and that "Poetry isn't a silly little hobby to be practised in the smallest room of the house." However, after this devastating indictment, she tries to rescue him for poetry, offering herself as a delectable golden avenue to the commitment he needs to make in order to achieve anything truly great. But Enderby, visualizing himself "puffing in his slack whiteness," is paralyzed with fear. The episode effectively defines his limitations: "Minor poet," she said. "We know now where we stand, don't we? Never mind. Be thankful for what you've got. Don't ask too much, that's all." Great poetry, then, cannot be expected from fearful little men who have "opted to live without love."

Burgess also focuses on other claimants to the title of "poet" that flourished in the 1960s. Yod Crewsy and the Crewsy-fixers are representative of the rock singers who received critical acclaim at that time both as poets and musicians. Framed for shooting Crewsy, Enderby flees from England to Tangier where he comes in contact with another type of singer, the poet spawned by the so-called psychedelic revolution. Though he is unimpressed by their "verse," Enderby is led into searching questions concerning the status of his art in the 1960s. He wonders if perhaps these acid-inspired makers are not closer to the truth of art than he is: "Was it right that art should mirror chaos?" He wonders if Marshall McLuhan's widely accepted pronouncements on media and the universe have not made the whole business of putting words together in an ordered meaningful relationship a pointless exercise.

Burgess's own point of view on these questions is hard to perceive, but it is, I believe, clarified somewhat by one of the original essays written for this volume, Michael Rudick's "Enderbyan Poetics: the Word in the Fallen World," which illuminates, among other things, his (Burgess's) problematic relationship to literary modernism.

Frank Kermode, whom Burgess regards as one of the most perceptive critics of his fiction, felt that *Enderby Outside* suffered "in some measure the ordinary fate of sequels," a loss of charming and witty effects that accompanies the repetition of devices and motifs. On the other hand, he did not perceive any evidence of diminishing talent. Indeed, "Burgess is always on duty, building bits of plot to bear the meanings, prodigal of linguistic resources, be the need a Lancashire cook or an Arab sodomite. Enderby, a poet-grandson of Bloom, is surrounded by language which Bloom's maker would not have despised."[37]

Enderby Outside first appeared in America as part of a single novel entitled *Enderby*, which also included *Inside Mr. Enderby*. It was enthusiastically received, and the reviews reflected the growth of Burgess's critical reputation on this side of the Atlantic. According to Guy Davenport, "It is now widely known that Anthony Burgess is no ordinary novelist. There are novelists who could have created Enderby; there are fewer novelists who could have written Enderby's poetry for him — poetry that we aren't quite certain is parody; there are very few novelists who could have topped this and invented a Muse who reels off top-notch textual criticism of the densest of Enderby's poems. . . . Add to this Mr. Burgess' rolling prose rhythms and his uncanny aptitude for languages . . . and the category in which we can place Mr. Burgess seems to contain Mr. Burgess alone."[38]

Burgess's next novel, *MF* (1971) was less enthusiastically received. One critic remarked that Burgess's "bookish side has all but stifled the novelist in him. The prose is still fine, even spectacular in patches, but for the most part, *MF* is a ragbag of murky linguistic riddles about incest uttered by a dessicated sphinx to a trivial Oedipus."[39] Another critic observed that it "is not Burgess's best book because it is rather too schematic. The effort of dragging his mythic story into the 20th century has left the author with too little chance to flesh out his hero."[40] Other reviewers, however, were a good deal more impressed. Paul West warned readers against looking for "a rerun of Galsworthy, Waugh, and Amis, or even of . . . previous Burgess offerings." On the other hand, "anyone looking for a prose adventure should dive in, prepared for just a little suffocation: for here word-obsession, the speculative intelligence infatuated with analogies, and a prankish serendipity come together in the hands of a mosaic-maker."[41] Frank Kermode was even more lavish in his praise, concluding his review with this summation: "Perhaps all one ought to do is to characterize this book as a riddling Sphinx and abstain from guessing further, but it should be added that it is a work of astonishing narrative and intellectual energy, and that everybody who thinks the English novel lacking in those qualities should read it, twice."[42]

The novel that generated these radically differing critical responses is one that uses an Algonquin-Greek mythic framework to encompass much of Western culture and especially those branches that seemed to be flowering in North America during the late 1960s. The title, *MF*, derives in part from the initials of the narrator-protagonist, Miles Faber. It also stands for "male / female," a valid classification that the book implicitly contrasts with various false taxonomies, and it has another reference to the all-encompassing theme of incest, especially when certain racial factors, bases of false taxonomies, are revealed in the conclusion. While the obscenity "motherfucker" has a wide range of usages in the North American black idiom, Burgess reveals that the range can be widened further to encompass all the maladies currently afflicting Western culture — the breakdown of order, the collapse of communication, the irresponsible cultivation of chaos in the name of art, and, above all, racial consciousness. One of the "alembicated morals" that Faber offers the reader is "that my race, or your race must start thinking in terms of the human totality and cease weaving its own fancied achievements or miseries into a banner. Black is beauty, yes, BUT ONLY WITH ANNA SEWELL PRODUCTS."

MF has not received much critical attention since it first appeared, and this is regrettable. The critical selection included in this volume will alert readers to the mythic framework and the ideas of Claude Lévi-Strauss that inform the novel. It is certainly not an exhaustive treatment of *MF*, but one hopes it will encourage further exegeses.

In the same year that *MF* appeared, Carol M. Dix published a pamphlet for the British Council assessing Burgess's achievement up to that time. Her discussion is divided into three sections: the first dealing with novels of social realism and satire; the second with the more philosophical novels, and the third "with the novels which display his interest in language and the art of creation from words."[43] Under the first heading she considers the Malayan Trilogy, *The Worm and the Ring*, and *The Right to an Answer*. Philosophical novels include *A Clockwork Orange*, *Tremor of Intent*, and *The Wanting Seed*, which, she remarks, "contains some of Burgess's most imaginative work." Her discussion of *Tremor of Intent* includes some interesting parallels of Burgess with Norman Mailer: "Indeed, Burgess shares with Norman Mailer a hatred of totalitarianism, a fear that this is where today's passivity will lead, and a belief in the romantic nature of violence, on the grounds that it is symbolic of commitment and assertion."

Ms. Dix's discussion of novels concerned with language focuses on the *Enderby* novels, *Nothing Like the Sun*, and, very briefly, *MF*, which she regards as "not particularly successful as a novel of conventional standards . . . more a work of, shall we say, comprehensive literariness," and she concludes her pamphlet with some misgivings aroused by this novel: "Burgess may be letting down his ordinary reader, in *MF*, no longer making those witty and comic comments on our society which make his great body of writing such a gift to contemporary English literature."

Another critical appraisal of Burgess's fiction, *The Consolations of Ambiguity: An Essay on the Novels of Anthony Burgess* by Robert K. Morris, also appeared in 1971. This is an important monograph which focuses on *A Vision of Battlements*, *Tremor of Intent*, the Malayan Trilogy, *Devil of a State*, *The Right to an Answer*, *Honey for the Bears*, *A Clockwork Orange*, *The Wanting Seed*, and *Enderby*. The discussions of *A Vision of Battlements* and *Tremor of Intent* are especially stimulating. He compares the latter novel with Graham Greene's *The Confidential Agent* and points out how "both writers have activated Christian myth to question Christian belief."[44] His discussion of the Malayan Trilogy is a reduced version of an essay that appeared in *Continuance and Change*, his book on the contemporary British novel sequence. The longer version, "The Futility of History," is included in this volume.

The first book length critical evaluation of Burgess's fiction, *Anthony Burgess* by A. A. DeVitis, appeared the following year. It is a useful introduction to seventeen of Burgess's novels, alerting readers to thematic motifs that recur frequently and link novels that appear to have little in common. Burgess's religious themes especially—the attractions of Manichaeanism and Pelagianism, the concept of the "gangster-God," salvation through commitment and others — are given considerable attention. Occasionally, DeVitis becomes carried away in his eagerness to discern such motifs, as when, for instance, he inflates the significance of the Christmas party at the end of *Time for a Tiger* with this rather cryptic remark: "The partaking of food assumes sacramental aspects, reinforcing the subterranean meaning of the novel."[45] But Burgess himself is so intensely preoccupied with religious themes that a critic's readiness to find them anywhere in his fiction is understandable, and some of DeVitis's observations in this regard can greatly enrich a reader's experience. It would not occur to most readers, for instance, that a drinking scene in *The Right to an Answer* amounts to a parody of the Mass, but as DeVitis points out, this view of it is heavily supported by the narrator's comments and allusions as well as the conversation of the drinkers.

DeVitis could have provided even more helpful illumination of these same themes if he had discussed more fully the conflicts between "Pelagians" and "Augustinians" that are everywhere in Burgess's fiction. At times he seems to confuse Augustinianism with Manichaeanism (e.g., "If Manichaenism keeps reminding men of their sinful origin and prevents the creation of beauty, then it is its opposite — Pelagianism — that encourages men to persist in the attempt to achieve perfection").[46] This same confusion is not found in Burgess's fiction. Burgess, like Augustine, is a firm believer in the doctrine of Original Sin, and, like Augustine, he is attracted to Manichaeanism. Indeed, he is quoted in *Contemporary Authors* as declaring himself to be a Manichee, but this should not lead to a blurring of distinctions. Unfortunately, DeVitis says little about "Augustinism" except in connection with *The Wanting Seed* where it is used to label a phase in an historical cycle. Actually, though Burgess does not use the label "Augustinian" elsewhere, it is not hard to discern Augustinian premises underlying the thinking of many of his protagonists, including Hillier in *Tremor of Intent*, WS in *Nothing Like the Sun*, and Gardner in *The Worm and the Ring*. And the main conflict in *A Clockwork Orange* is between a government functioning in a detheologized Augustinian repressive phase and revolutionaries committed to a Pelagian faith in "Man, a creature of growth and capable of sweetness."

DeVitis is at his best when he is drawing upon his considerable knowledge of the twentieth-century writers to whom Burgess is most indebted — Nabokov, Waugh, Graham Greene, and Joyce — and comparing Burgess's handling of the antihero with that of other contemporary British writers such as John Braine and John Osborne. He also makes some provocative suggestions concerning the origins of the antihero, tracing him back to Stendahl's Julien Sorel. While I would trace him back much further, to the lowborn upstarts of Marlowe's tragedies, I think DeVitis makes a good case. On the whole, DeVitis's book is a useful attempt to define Burgess as a particular kind of novelist, but its analyses of individual novels and major themes leave out a good deal.

Burgess's next major novel after *MF* was an attempt to fuse his two major interests, the novel and music. *Napoleon Symphony* (1974) presents the life of Napoleon Bonaparte, from his marriage to Josephine until his death, in the "shape" of Beethoven's *Eroica* Symphony. What this means is that Burgess has deliberately matched the proportions of four "movements" within the novel to each of the four movements within the symphony. He began the project by playing the symphony on the phonograph and timing the movements; then he worked out a proportionate correspondence of pages to seconds of playing time. Working with the score of the *Eroica* in front of him, he made sections within his prose movements match sections within the *Eroica*; thus a passage of so many pages corresponds to a passage of so many bars. Beyond this, he sought to incorporate the actual dynamics of the symphony, the same moods and tempo.

The Allegro of *Napoleon Symphony* finds the hero in Italy and Egypt, writing passionate letters to the adulterous Josephine. The Funeral March is the retreat from Moscow. Because the scherzo and the finale of the *Eroica* both seem to deal with Prometheus, Burgess was left with the task of writing a set of variations on a Promethean theme. After his death on St. Helena, Burgess's Napoleon turns into a Promethean character in the last two "movements" of the novel, and there is a posthumous resurgence of the triumphant mood of the earlier movements, with Napoleon being crowned for having, despite all obstacles, at least partly fulfilled his dream of a united Europe.

Reviews of *Napoleon Symphony* were generally favorable. One reviewer chided Burgess for "simplistically relating Napoleon's military adventures to his amorous ones" and his anachronistic references to gas chambers, secret police, and other elements of 20th-century tyranny.[47] Another praised his realistic depiction of the historical characters, the retreat from Moscow, and the exile on St. Helena, and concluded: "The novel is massive and innovative in plan, and though the execution is not wholly successful, it fails on a level far higher than most novels ever attain."[48] It is unquestionably one of Burgess's major achievements in the novel, and I have included two recent critical articles on it in this volume.

Napoleon Symphony was followed by *The Clockwork Testament*, which outraged many New Yorkers, and two novellas, *Beard's Roman Woman* and *ABBA ABBA*. The latter two works represent, Burgess says, "a sort of farewell-to-Rome phase." In *Beard's Roman Women*, he draws upon his experiences as a scriptwriter and, as he does in *The Clockwork Testament*, puts cinematic art in its proper place, well below literature, in the hierarchy of artistic achievement. *ABBA ABBA* is primarily a collection of sonnets by the blasphemous dialect poet Giuseppe Giocchino Belli (1791–1863), which Burgess translated, maintaining the Petrarchan rhyme scheme, ABBA ABBA CDC CDC. The collection, seventy-two of Belli's nearly three thousand poems, is introduced by a brief novella about John

Keats's death in Rome and his possible meeting there with Belli in 1820 or 1821. Another poetic exercise for Burgess, written at about the same time as *ABBA ABBA*, is a long original poem in free verse entitled *Moses*. As he explains, the poem was actually the "source" of the script for the television epic *Moses the Lawgiver*, starring Burt Lancaster, which in turn became a film for the movies: "I was trying to get a rhythm and a dialogue style, and verse-writing helped."[49]

In 1979, my own book, *Anthony Burgess: The Artist as Novelist*, appeared. It contains a biographical essay and critical analyses of twenty-one of Burgess's novels in roughly chronological order. I group the novels according to thematic concerns which stem principally from Burgess's Manichean vision and preoccupation with the role of the artist. My chapter on the dystopian novels includes a comprehensive discussion of the "nadsat" language of *A Clockwork Orange* and an assessment of Burgess's application of Pelagius and Augustine which animates the historical dialectics of *The Wanting Seed*. The concluding chapter is an attempt to read the "musical" score of *Napoleon Symphony* alongside its Beethoven original. Burgess himself read and commented upon each part of the book as it was completed, and provided me with interesting background information to assist the reader's understanding.

In December 1980 Burgess published what many regard as his masterpiece, *Earthly Powers*. It is a long book, about the length of *Ulysses*, and it took Burgess nearly a decade to complete it. The novel's original title was "The Affairs of Men." Then it became "The Prince of the Powers of the Air" and finally *Earthly Powers*.[50] The second title was taken from Thomas Hobbes's description of Satan and his kingdom in Part IV of *Leviathan*.

The protagonist, Don Carlo Campanatti, is modeled on the late Pope John XXIII, a pontiff whom Burgess neither revered nor admired. He has referred to him as a "Pelagian heretic" and an "emissary of the devil" who caused the Church enormous damage by raising unrealistic hopes that there would be radical doctrinal changes to accommodate the pressures of twentieth-century life. His character Don Carlo is a Faustian figure who makes a bargain with the devil in return for the earthly powers of the papacy. My essay on the novel, "Faust in the Labyrinth," is included in this volume.

Earthly Powers has been generally praised by critics, and it was a Book of the Month Club choice. Enormous in scope, encompassing much of twentieth-century social, literary, and political history, it inevitably has some flaws; parts of the book are wearisome, and the language is occasionally pedantic. These flaws are, however, minor and unavoidable in a work so large and ambitious. Overall it is a magnificent performance.

Another recent novel, *1985* (1978) was less well-received by critics than *Earthly Powers*. Originally conceived as an introduction to George Orwell, it begins with a 106-page discussion of *1984* which suggests, among other things, that Orwell's vision of England in 1984 was shaped essentially by his vision of England in 1948. The remaining 166 pages present Burgess's own proleptic vision, one that differs markedly from that of *A Clockwork Orange* and *The Wanting Seed*, as well as that of *1984*. One of Burgess's more sympathetic critics has argued convincingly that this latter section of *1985*, Burgess's fiction, is intended as an ironic counterpoint to *1984*, one that presents a near future that is "harrowing but not horrific."[51] The England of Burgess's *1985* has left behind any belief in moral absolutes, is populated almost entirely by small people who are moral neutrals. What makes it such a bad place is the all-pervasive dullness that is the end result of social impulses carried too far, thus leveling intelligence, taste, and knowledge.

Burgess's most recent novel, *The End of the World News*, appeared in 1982. It deals with a dying Sigmund Freud being hustled out of Vienna into exile, a Broadway musical on the subject of Trotsky in New York, and the last throes of the planet Earth in A.D. 2000. One critic called it "a brilliant extravaganza . . . a continuous firework display . . . a feast for the reader."[52] Another was moved to wonder at the enormous Burgess energy: "The man is a powerhouse whose prose transmits an almost radioactive quality."[53]

It seems clear that Burgess's revels are nowhere near an end and equally clear that his critical reputation is secure. As D. W. Nichol observes, "In terms of language and innovation, Burgess is Joyce's most prolific inheritor and certainly deserves to be highly placed in the still unsettled tradition of twentieth-century British fiction."[54] The critical selections in this volume represent what I regard as the most significant and perceptive exegeses of his fiction. In making my selection, I found that there was a considerable body of good Burgess criticism. I also realized, however, that a great deal needs to be done. There is plenty of room for more articles and additional book length studies, and it is to be hoped that this collection will encourage future Burgess scholarship.

GEOFFREY AGGELER

University of Utah

Notes

1. Interview with Geoffrey Aggeler in Stratford, Ontario, 30 July 1969.
2. *Ibid.*
3. Peter Quennell, *Daily Mail*, 27 September 1956.
4. *Times Literary Supplement*, 9 November 1956.
5. *Sunday Times*, 7 February 1958.
6. *Times Literary Supplement*, 14 February 1958.
7. *Times Literary Supplement*, 1 May 1959.
8. *New Statesman*, 24 April 1959; *Daily Express*, 5 May 1959.

9. Interview with Geoffrey Aggeler, 30 July 1969.

10. Taped lecture at Simon Fraser University, Vancouver, B.C., 5 March 1969.

11. *Ibid.*

12. Letter to Geoffrey Aggeler, 4 January 1984.

13. Frederic Raphael, *Sunday Times*, 26 September 1960.

14. *Times Literary Supplement*, 29 September 1960; Jocelyn Brooke, *Listener*, September 1960.

15. Letter to Geoffrey Aggeler, 10 September 1969.

16. *Ibid.*

17. Dick Adler, *Sunday Times*, (London), Color Supplement, 2 April 1967.

18. *Times Literary Supplement*, 7 July 1961, p. 421.

19. John Gross, *New Statesman*, 24 November 1961, p. 28.

20. Anthony Burgess, *The Novel Now* (London: Faber & Faber, 1967), 212.

21. *Times Literary Supplement*, 3 June 1960.

22. Naomi Bliven, "Ordeals and Orgies," *New Yorker* 37 (8 April 1961):169.

23. Margharita Laski, "Morality with Heart," *Saturday Review* 44 (28 January 1961):17.

24. J. F. Moran, *Library Journal* 88 (15 February 1963):793.

25. *Times Literary Supplement*, 25 May 1962, p. 377.

26. Daniel Talbot, *New York Herald Tribune Books*, 14 April 1963, p. 7.

27. Interview with George Malko, *Penthouse*, June 1972, p. 115.

28. Brigid Brophy, *Book Week* (3 November 1963) p. 6.

29. R. F. Clayton, *Library Journal* 88 (1 October 1963) p. 3641.

30. *Times Literary Supplement*, 5 October 1962, p. 773.

31. D. J. Enright, *New Statesman* 67 (24 April 1964) p. 642.

32. Peter Buitenhuis, *New York Times Book Review* (13 September 1964) p. 5.

33. William H. Pritchard, "The Novels of Anthony Burgess," *Massachusetts Review* 7 (1966) p. 527.

34. *Ibid.*, p. 533.

35. *Ibid.*, p. 539.

36. Eric Moon, *Book Week*, 9 October 1966, p. 2.

37. Frank Kermode, "Poetry and Borborygms," *Listener*, 6 June 1968, pp. 735–6.

38. Guy Davenport, *National Review* 20 (18 June 1968) p. 613.

39. R.A.S., *Newsweek* 77 (19 April 1971) p. 120.

40. Martha Duffy, *Time* 97 (22 March 1971) p. 80.

41. Paul West, *Book Week* (15 March 1971) p. 7.

42. Frank Kermode, "The Algonquin Oedipus," *Listener* (17 June 1971) p. 791.

43. Carol M. Dix, *Anthony Burgess*. Writers and Their Work. Ed. Ian Scott-Kilvert. (London: Longmans, for the British Council, 1971)

44. Robert K. Morris, *The Consolation of Ambiguity An Essay on the Novels of Anthony Burgess* (Columbia: Univ. of Missouri Press, 1971) p. 23.

45. A. A. DeVitis, *Anthony Burgess* (New York: Twayne, 1972) p. 26.

46. *Ibid.*, p. 34.

47. Roderick Nordell, *Christian Science Monitor*, 29 May 1974, p. F5.

48. Robb McKenzie, *Library Journal* 99 (15 May 1974) p. 1406.

49. Letter to Geoffrey Aggeler, 22 April 1977.

50. Letters to Geoffrey Aggeler: 2 November 1971; 22 April 1977; 11 July 1979.

51. John J. Stinson, "Better to be hot or cold: *1985* and the Dynamic of the Manichaean Duoverse," *Modern Fiction Studies* 27 (1981) p. 509.

52. *The Guardian*, 7 April 1982, p. 19.

53. *Daily Express*, 20 April 1982, p. 11.

54. D. W. Nichol, "In Joyce's Wake," *Times Literary Supplement*, 23 May 1980.

ARTICLES AND ESSAYS

Interview with Anthony Burgess   John Cullinan*

INTERVIEWER

Are you at all bothered by the charges that you are too prolific or that your novels are too allusive?

BURGESS

It has been a sin to be prolific only since the Bloomsbury group — particularly Forster — made it a point of good manners to produce, as it were, costively. I've been annoyed less by sneers at my alleged over-production than by the imputation that to write much means to write badly. I've always written with great care and even some slowness. I've just put in rather more hours a day at the task than some writers seem able to. As for allusiveness — meaning, I suppose, literary allusiveness — that's surely in the tradition. Any book has behind it all the other books that have been written. The author's aware of them; the reader ought to be aware too.

INTERVIEWER

At what time of day do you usually work?

BURGESS

I don't think it matters much; I work in the morning, but I think the afternoon is a good time to work. Most people sleep in the afternoon. I've always found it a good time, especially if one doesn't have much lunch. It's a quiet time. It's a time when one's body is not at its sharpest, not at its most receptive — the body is quiescent, somnolent; but the brain can be quite sharp. I think also at the same time that the unconscious mind has a habit of asserting itself in the afternoon. The morning is the conscious time, but the afternoon is a time in which we should deal much more with the hinterland of the consciousness.

*From *Paris Review* 56 (1973):118–163. © 1973 by *The Paris Review*. Reprinted with permission.

That's very interesting. Thomas Mann, on the other hand, wrote religiously virtually every day from nine to one, as though he were punching a time clock.

Yes. One can work from nine to one, I think it's ideal; but I find that the afternoon must be used. The afternoon has always been a good time for me. I think it began in Malaya when I was writing. I was working all morning. Most of us slept in the afternoon; it was very quiet. Even the servants were sleeping, even the dogs were asleep. One could work quietly away under the sun until dusk fell and one was ready for the events of the evening. I do most of my work in the afternoon.

Do you imagine an ideal reader for your books?

The ideal reader of my novels is a lapsed Catholic and failed musician, short-sighted, color-blind, auditorily biased, who has read the books that I have read. He should also be about my age.

A very special reader indeed. Are you writing, then, for a limited, highly educated audience?

Where would Shakespeare have got if he had thought only of a specialized audience? What he did was to attempt to appeal on all levels, with something for the most rarefied intellectuals (who had read Montaigne) and very much more for those who could appreciate only sex and blood. I like to devise a plot that can have a moderately wide appeal. But take Eliot's *The Waste Land*, very erudite, which, probably through its more popular elements and its basic rhetorical appeal, appealed to those who did not at first understand it but made themselves understand it: the poem, a terminus of Eliot's polymathic travels, became a starting point for other people's erudition. I think every author wants to *make* his audience. But it's in his own image and his primary audience is a mirror.

Do you care about what the critics think?

I get angry at the stupidity of critics who wilfully refuse to see what my books are really about. I'm aware of malevolence, especially in England. A bad review by a man I admire hurts terribly.

INTERVIEWER

Would you ever change the drift of a book — or any literary project — because of a critic's comments?

BURGESS

I don't think — with the exception of the excision of that whole final chapter of *A Clockwork Orange* — I've ever been asked to make any changes in what I've written. I do feel that the author has to know best about what he's writing — from the viewpoint of structure, intention and so on. The critic has the job of explaining deep-level elements which the author couldn't know about. As for saying where — technically, in matters of taste and so on — a writer is going wrong, the critic rarely says what the author doesn't know already.

INTERVIEWER

You've mentioned the possibility of working with Stanley Kubrick on a film version of Napoleon's life. Can you remain completely independent in devising the novel you're currently writing about Napoleon?

BURGESS

The Napoleon project, which began with Kubrick, has now got beyond Kubrick. I found myself interested in the subject in a way that didn't suggest a film adaptation and am now working on something Kubrick couldn't use. It's a pity about the money and so on, but otherwise I'm glad to feel free, nobody looking over my shoulder.

INTERVIEWER

Has working as a professional reviewer either helped or hindered the writing of your novels?

BURGESS

It did no harm. It didn't stop me writing novels. It gave facility. It forced me into areas that I wouldn't have voluntarily entered. It paid the bills, which novels rarely do.

INTERVIEWER

Did it bring you involuntarily to any new subjects or books that have become important to you?

BURGESS

It's good for a writer to review books he is not supposed to know anything about or be interested in. Doing reviewing for magazines like *Country Life* (which smells more of horses than of calfskin bindings) means doing a fine heterogeneous batch which often does open areas of some value in one's creative work. For instance, I had to review books on stable management, embroidery, car engines—very useful solid stuff, the very stuff of novels. Reviewing Lévi-Strauss' little lecture on anthropology (which nobody else wanted to review) was the beginning of the process which led me to write the novel *MF*.

INTERVIEWER

You've stressed the importance of punctuality to a good reviewer. Do you find that a creative writer need stick to a strict work schedule too?

BURGESS

The practice of being on time with commissioned work is an aspect of politeness. I don't like being late for appointments; I don't like craving indulgence from editors in the matter of missed deadlines. Good journalistic manners tend to lead to a kind of self-discipline in creative work. It's important that a novel be approached with some urgency. Spend too long on it, or have great gaps between writing sessions, and the unity of the work tends to be lost. This is one of the troubles with *Ulysses*. The ending is different from the beginning. Technique changes halfway through. Joyce spent too long on the book.

INTERVIEWER

Are you suggesting that Molly Bloom's soliloquy is an inappropriate ending because it's technically different from the opening three chapters devoted to Stephen Dedalus?

BURGESS

I don't mean the very end of *Ulysses*. I mean that from the Cyclops episode on, Joyce decides to lengthen his chapters to make the reading time correspond with the imagined time of enactment. In that sense the book is technically not so much a unity as people like to think. Compare the Aeolus episode with the Oxen of the Sun and you'll see what I mean.

INTERVIEWER

Considering the length of time that Proust spent on his novel and that Mann devoted to *Joseph and his Brothers*, is seven years really so long for a work as great as *Ulysses*? What, then, about the seventeen years Joyce frittered away on *Finnegans Wake*?

BURGESS

Time spent on a book is perhaps no concern of the reader's really (*Madame Bovary*, a comparatively short book, took longer to write, surely, than the *Joseph* sequence). The whole question is whether the writer can be the same person, with the same aims and approach to technique, over a long stretch of time. *Ulysses*, being innovative, had to go on being more and more innovative as it was written, and this makes it a sort of disunity. *Finnegans Wake*, though it took much longer, got its essential technique established pretty early.

INTERVIEWER

Your new book, *Joysprick*, is coming out soon. I understand. How does it differ in emphasis from *Re: Joyce?*

BURGESS

It covers a little of the same ground but not very much. It's an attempt to examine the nature of Joyce's language, not from a strictly linguistic point of view, but from a point of view which may be said to be exactly halfway between literary criticism and linguistics; it doesn't use many technical terms. It makes a phonetic analysis of Joyce's language; there aren't many linguists who can do this nowadays. Phonetics is rather old hat. But it does examine the dialects of *Ulysses*, the importance of establishing a pronunciation in *Finnegans Wake*, an analysis of the way Joyce constructs a sentence. It is not a profound book; it is meant to be a beginner's guide to the language of Joyce, and the real work of probing into Joyce's linguistic method must be left to a more scholarly person than myself.

INTERVIEWER

You say that you are taking what you call an old-fashioned phonetic approach to Joyce's language; and yet in *MF* you make use of Lévi-Strauss' structuralism. Are you at all interested in considering Joyce from the point of view of structural linguistics?

BURGESS

I don't think that's my line; I think this has to be left to a scholar. I think somebody has to be in a university, has to be not engaged as I am in the production of books and teaching and lecturing and living a pretty varied "show-biz" life; this is a job for a cool scholar. I don't think I qualify to do it. I'm interested in what sounds Joyce is hearing when he is writing down the speech of Molly Bloom and Leopold Bloom and the minor characters. It's a matter of great literary import, I would suggest, because the final monologue of Molly Bloom inclines a particular way of speech which is not consonant with her declared background. Here in Joyce there is something very implausible about the fact that Molly Bloom is the daughter of a major, brought up in the Gibraltar garrison, coming to Dublin speaking and thinking like any low Dublin fishwife. This seems to be totally inconsistent, and the point has not even been made before. I know Gibraltar better than Joyce did and better than most Joyce scholars. I'm trying to examine this.

INTERVIEWER

If Molly's monologue is too elegant, isn't it one of Joyce's points to have the poetic emerge from the demotic?

BURGESS

It's not elegant enough. I mean the fact that she uses Irish locutions like "Pshaw." She would not use any such term, she would not.

INTERVIEWER

There's a geographical thing.

BURGESS

There's a pattern implied. There's a social thing. In a very small garrison town like Gibraltar with this man, Major Tweedy, whose previous wife is Spanish, his half-Spanish daughter would speak either Spanish as a first language (and not with the usual grammar) or English as a first language—but certainly both languages, in the first instance in an Andalusian way, and in the second instance in a totally class-conscious, pseudo-patrician way. She would not come back to Dublin and suddenly start speaking like a Dublin fishwife.

INTERVIEWER

So Molly's language is probably closer in terms of social background to that of Nora Barnacle.

BURGESS

It is indeed; this final image is an image of Nora Barnacle and not of Molly at all. And as we know from Nora's letters, Joyce must have studied the letters and learned from them how to set down this warm womanly pattern of speech. Nora wrote the letters totally without punctuation, and sometimes it is hard to distinguish between a chunk of one of Nora's letters and a chunk of Molly's final monologue.

INTERVIEWER

I'm looking forward to this book. Have you thought of writing a long expansive novel?

BURGESS

I have in mind two long novels—one on a theatrical family from the middle ages till today, the other on a great British composer. The projects are so big that I'm scared of starting on them.

INTERVIEWER

Could you begin with a few excerpts in the form of short stories?

BURGESS

I can't write short stories, not easily anyway, and I'd rather keep my novel dark until it's ready for the light. I made the mistake once of publishing a chapter of an emergent novel in the *Transatlantic Review* and the sight of the extract in cold print turned me against the project. This is my one unfinished novel.

INTERVIEWER

Do you still hope to write a novel about Theseus' encounter with the Minotaur, or has Rawcliffe's scenario in *Enderby* disposed of that project?

BURGESS

As for the Minotaur idea, I have thought of publishing a volume of all Enderby's poems, and they would include *The Pet Beast* (which has become, incidentally, the title of the Italian version of *Enderby — La Dolce Bestia*). I can see the sense of pretending that someone else has written your book for you, especially your book of poems. It frees you of responsibility — "Look, I know this is bad but I didn't write it — one of my characters wrote it." *Don Quixote, Lolita, Ada* — it's an old and still lively tradition. I don't get writing blocks, except from the stationer, but I do feel so sickened by what I write that I don't want to go on.

INTERVIEWER

Do you write the big scenes first, as Joyce Cary did?

BURGESS

I start at the beginning, go on to the end, then stop.

INTERVIEWER

Is each book charted completely in advance?

BURGESS

I chart a little first — list of names, rough synopsis of chapters and so on. But one daren't overplan; so many things are generated by the sheer act of writing.

INTERVIEWER

Do you write non-fiction any differently?

BURGESS

The process is the same.

INTERVIEWER

Is the finished product much influenced by the fact that you do the first draft on the typewriter?

BURGESS

I don't write drafts. I do Page One many, many times and move on to Page Two. I pile up sheet after sheet, each in its final state, and at length I have a novel that doesn't—in my view—need any revision.

INTERVIEWER

Then you don't revise at all?

BURGESS

Revising, as I said, is done with each page, not with each chapter or the whole book. Re-writing a whole book would bore me.

INTERVIEWER

Why did you decide to continue *Inside Mr. Enderby*, the first half of *Enderby*, after several years?

BURGESS

I planned the work as the long book that came out in America, but— since I was approaching the end of the one year that the doctors had given me to live—I was not able to do more than the first half in 1959-60. Unwillingness of the publishers to publish *Inside Mr. Enderby*—as Part I was called in England—made me delay the writing of Part II. But I had it all in my mind right at the start.

INTERVIEWER

After the doctors had diagnosed a brain tumor following your collapse in a Brunei classroom, why did you choose to write during that "terminal year" rather than travel, say? Were you confined in semi-invalid status?

BURGESS

I was no semi-invalid. I was very fit and active (this made me doubt the truth of the diagnosis). But to travel the world one needs money and this I didn't have. It's only in fiction that "terminal year" men have something tucked away. The fact is that my wife and I needed to eat and so on, and the only job I could do (who would employ me?) was writing. I wrote much because I was paid little. I had no great desire to leave a literary name behind me.

INTERVIEWER

Did your style change at all during that year, possibly as a result of your feeling under sentence?

BURGESS

I don't think so. I was old enough to have established some kind of narrative style; but the real business of working on style, of course, came later. The novels written in this so-called quasi-terminal year — pseduo-terminal year — were not written with, you know, excessive speed; it was just a matter of working hard every day, working very hard every day — and *all* day — including the evenings. A good deal of care went into the works, and what people look for in what seems an excessive amount of production is evidence of carelessness. There may be a little of that; but it's not because of the speed or apparent speed, but because of flaws in my own make-up. I don't think it is possible to say that a particular work is obviously written during the terminal year. I don't think there is any qualitative difference between the various novels; and certainly I was not aware of any influence on style, on way of writing, caused by this knowledge.

INTERVIEWER

Several of your novels contain poetry written by various characters. Have you thought of writing poetry again seriously?

BURGESS

I've seen produced my version of *Cyrano de Bergerac*. This is in rhyme, and it worked well, as I expected it to. But I don't plan volumes of verse — too naked, too personal. I plan further stage translations — *Peer Gynt*, Tchekhov's *Chaika* — and I'm working on a musical of *Ulysses*. I'm much more likely to return to music. I've been asked to write a clarinet concerto, and my music to *Cyrano* has gone down well enough.

INTERVIEWER

Do you ever use musical forms in designing your novels?

BURGESS

Ah yes, one can learn a lot from musical forms. I'm planning a novel in the style of a classical symphony — minuet and all. The motivations will be purely formal, so that a development section in which sexual fantasies are enacted can follow a realistic exposition with neither explanation nor transitional device, returning to it (now as recapitulation) with a similar lack of psychological justification or formal trickery.

INTERVIEWER

Composers traffic heavily in transitions. Isn't this particular instance of literary composition by musical analogy an example of "formal trickery," best understood by the reader who is at least an amateur musician?

BURGESS

I think that music does teach practitioners in other arts useful formal devices, but the reader doesn't have to know their provenance. Here's an example. A composer modulates from one key to another by the use of the "punning" chord, the augmented sixth (punning because it is also a dominant seventh). You can change, in a novel, from one scene to another by using a phrase or statement common to both—this is quite common. If the phrase or statement means different things in the different contexts, so much the more musical.

INTERVIEWER

One notices that the form of *A Vision of Battlements* is meant to be similar to that of Ennis' passacaglia, but can any but the most tenuously analogous relation be established between literature and music generally?

BURGESS

I agree that the musico-literary analogies can be pretty tenuous, but in the widest possible formal sense—sonata form, opera and so on—we've hardly begun to explore the possibilities. The Napoleon novel I'm writing apes the *Eroica* formally—irritable, quick, swiftly transitional in the first movement (up to Napoleon's coronation); slow, very leisurely, with a binding beat suggesting a funeral march for the second. This isn't pure fancy: it's an attempt to unify a mass of historical material in the comparatively brief space of about 150,000 words. As for the reader having to know about music—it doesn't really matter much. In one novel I wrote, "The orchestra lunged into a loud chord of twelve notes, all of them different." Musicians hear the discord, non-musicians don't, but there's nothing there to baffle them and prevent them reading on. I don't understand baseball terms, but I can still enjoy Malamud's *The Natural*. I don't play bridge, but I find the bridge game in Fleming's *Moonraker* absorbing—it's the emotions conveyed that matter, not what the players are doing with their hands.

INTERVIEWER

What about film technique as an influence on your writing?

BURGESS

I've been much more influenced by the stage than by the film. I write in scenes too long for unbroken cinematic representation. But I like to run a scene through in my mind before writing it down, seeing everything happen, hearing some of the dialogue. I've written for both television and cinema, but not very successfully. Too literary, or something. I get called in by makers of historical films to revise the dialogue, which they then restore to its original form.

INTERVIEWER

What happened to the proposed film versions of *Enderby* and *Nothing Like the Sun?*

BURGESS

The filming of *Enderby* fell through because the producer dropped dead at the Cannes film festival. The Shakespeare project came almost when Warner Brothers was being sold, and all existing enterprises were scrapped when the new regime started. It may, however, yet be fulfilled. Film people are very conservative about dialogue: they honestly believe that the immediate grasp of lexical meaning is more important than the impact of rhythm and emotionally charged sound. It's regarded as cleverer to pretend that the people of the past would have spoken like us if they'd been lucky enough to know how to do so, delighted with the opportunity to view themselves and their times from our angle. *The Lion in Winter* is thought to be a triumphant solution of the mediaeval dialogue problem, but of course it's just cheap.

INTERVIEWER

Does your novel in progress pose any special linguistic problems that may create obstacles for Stanley Kubrick as well?

BURGESS

The Napoleon novel is difficult from the dialogue angle, but my instinct tells me to use rhythms and vocabulary not much different from our own. After all, Byron's *Don Juan* could almost have been written today. I imagine the soldiers speaking as today's soldiers speak.

They're speaking in French anyway. As for the Napoleon film, Kubrick must go his own way and he'll find it a difficult way.

INTERVIEWER

Do you expect to write any more historical novels?

BURGESS

I'm working on a novel intended to express the feel of England in Edward III's time, using Dos Passos' devices. I believe there's great scope in the historical novel, so long as it isn't by Mary Renault or Georgette Heyer. The fourteenth century of my novel will be mainly evoked in terms of smell and visceral feelings, and it will carry an undertone of general disgust rather than hey-nonny nostalgia.

INTERVIEWER

Which of Dos Passos' techniques will you use?

BURGESS

The novel I have in mind, and for which I've done a ninety-page plan, is about the Black Prince. I thought it might be amusing blatantly to steal the Camera Eye and the Newsreel devices from Dos Passos just to see how they might work, especially with the Black Death and Crécy and the

Spanish campaign. The effect might be of the fourteenth century going on in another galaxy where language and literature had somehow got themselves into the twentieth century. The technique might make the historical characters look remote and rather comic — which is what I want.

Are Mary Renault's retellings of Greek myths as bad as all that?

Oh, they're not unsatisfactory, far from it. Rattling good reads if you like the sort of thing. They just don't excite me, that's all. It's undoubtedly my fault.

Do you expect to write another novel of the future, like *A Clockwork Orange* or *The Wanting Seed*?

I don't plan a novel about the future, except for a mad novella in which England has become a mere showplace run by America.

Is England going to become simply an over-sized tourist boutique — or the fifty-first state?

I used to think that England might become just a place that liked to be visited — like that island in J. M. Barrie's *Mary Rose* — but now I see that so many of the things worth seeing — old things — are disappearing so that England can become a huge Los Angeles, all motorways, getting about more important than actually getting anywhere. England is now going into Europe, not — as I had once expected and even hoped — America, and I think it will now have Europe's faults without its virtues. The decimal coinage is a monstrosity, and soon there'll be liters of beer, as in *Nineteen Eighty-Four*, and no cheap wine or caporal tobacco. Absorption, anyway, since England either has to absorb or be absorbed. Napoleon has won.

You mentioned that *A Clockwork Orange* has a concluding chapter in the British edition that isn't available in the American ones. Does this bother you?

Yes, I hate having two different versions of the same book. The U.S. edition has a chapter short, and hence the arithmological plan is messed up. Also, the implied view of juvenile violence as something to go through and then grow out of is missing in the American edition; and this reduces the book to a mere parable, whereas it was intended to be a novel.

What happens in the twenty-first chapter?

In Chapter 21 Alex grows up and realizes that ultra-violence is a bit of a bore and it's time he had a wife and a malenky googoogooing malchickiwick to call him dadada. This was meant to be a mature conclusion but nobody in America has ever liked the idea.

Did Stanley Kubrick consider filming the Heinemann version?

Kubrick discovered the existence of this final chapter when he was halfway through the film, but it was too late to think of altering the concept. Anyway, he too, an American, thought it too milk-and-watery. I don't know what to think now. After all, it's twelve years since I wrote the thing.

Did you attempt to get the complete novel published here?

Yes — well, I was very dubious about the book itself. When I wrote the book my agent was not willing to present it to a publisher, which is rather unusual; and the sort of publishers in England were very dubious about the book. So when the American publisher made this objection to the final chapter, I didn't feel myself to be in a very strong position. I was a little hesitant to judge the book; I was a little too close to it. I thought: "Well, they may be right." Because authors do tend to be (especially after the completion of a book) very uncertain about the value of the book; and perhaps I gave in a little too weakly, but my concern was partly a financial one. I wanted it to be published in America, and I wanted some money out of it. So I said, "Yes." Whether I'd say "Yes" now I don't know; but I've been persuaded by so many critics that the book is better in its American form that I say, "All right, they know best."

Would it be possible for an American press to put out a limited, hardbound edition which includes the excluded chapter as a sort of appendix?

BURGESS

I think this should be possible. The best way of doing it is to bring out an annotated edition of the book with this final chapter — an idea which is being resisted by my publishers for some reason, I don't know why. I would be very interested in the comments of the average, say, American student on the differences between the two versions. Because I'm not able to judge myself very clearly now, as to whether I was right or wrong. What is *your* opinion, what do you feel about that?

INTERVIEWER

I find the last chapter problematical in that while it creates an entirely different context for the work, it seems anticlimactic after the neat resurrection of the old Alex, in the twentieth chapter.

BURGESS

Yes.

INTERVIEWER

Still it should remain, because your meaning is altered by the cutting off of the context.

BURGESS

Well, the worst example I know of unjustified translation is to be found in Ford Madox Ford's *Parade's End*, where in the British edition under the imprint of Bodley Head, Graham Greene has taken upon himself to present *Parade's End* as a trilogy, saying he doesn't think the final novel, *The Last Post*, works and he feels perhaps Ford would have agreed with him; and therefore he has taken the liberty of getting rid of the final book. I think Greene is wrong; I think that whatever Ford said, the work is a tetralogy, and the thing is severely maimed with the loss of his final book. An author is not to be trusted in his judgment of this sort of thing. Authors very frequently try to be indifferent to their books. Certainly they are so sick of their books that they don't want to make any serious judgment on them. The problem comes up, you see, when one reads Evelyn Waugh's *A Handful of Dust*, because this frightful ending (where Tony Last spends all his time reading Dickens to this half-breed in the jungle), appeared previously as a short story; and knowing the short story one has a strange attitude to the book. Which makes us feel that here is a deliberate pasting together, where this giant figure at the end that turns up does not spring automatically out of the book but is just taken arbitrarily from another work. Perhaps one shouldn't know too much about these things. Of course one can't avoid it. These two versions of Samuel Butler's *Way of All Flesh* — this raises the problem. Which version would we like better, which is the right version? It's better to know only one thing, to be fairly ignorant of what was going on. You know, behind the version we know.

INTERVIEWER

Isn't this an argument against publishing a complete *A Clockwork Orange*, since a twenty-chapter version is embedded in everyone's mind?

BURGESS

I don't know; they're both relevant. They seem to me to express in a sense the difference between the British approach to life and the American approach to life. There may be something very profound to say about this difference in these different presentations of the novel. I don't know; I'm not able to judge.

INTERVIEWER

In *A Clockwork Orange* and *Enderby* especially there's a persistent strain of mockery toward youth culture and its music. Is there anything good about them?

BURGESS

I despise whatever is obviously ephemeral and yet is shown as possessing some kind of ultimate value. The Beatles, for instance. Most youth culture, especially music, is based on so little knowledge of tradition, and it often elevates ignorance into a virtue. Think of the musically illiterate who set themselves up as "arrangers." And youth is so conformist, so little concerned with maverick values, so proud of being rather than making, so bloody sure that it and it alone *knows*.

INTERVIEWER

You used to play in a jazz band. Is there any hope that their interest in rock music may lead youth to jazz—or even to classical music?

BURGESS

I still play jazz, chiefly on a four-octave electric organ, and I prefer this to listening to it. I don't think jazz is for listening but for playing. I'd like to write a novel about a jazz pianist, or, better, about a pub pianist— which I once was, like my father before me. I don't think rock leads on to a liking for jazz. The kids are depressingly static in their tastes. They do so want *words*, and jazz gets along very nicely without words.

INTERVIEWER

In two of your novels the wordsmiths Shakespeare and Enderby are inspired by the Muse. But you've said as well that you like to regard your books as "works of craftsmanship for sale."

BURGESS

The Muse in *Nothing Like the Sun* was not a real muse—only syphilis. The girl in *Enderby* is really sex, which, like syphilis, has something to do with the creative process. I mean, you can't be a genius and sexually impotent. I still think that inspiration comes out of the act of making an artifact, a work of craft.

INTERVIEWER
Are works of art the products of strong libido?

BURGESS
Yes, I think art is sublimated libido. You can't be a eunuch priest and you can't be a eunuch artist. I became interested in syphilis when I worked for a time at a mental hospital full of GPI cases. I discovered there was a correlation between the spirochete and mad talent. The tubercle also produces a lyrical drive. Keats had both.

INTERVIEWER
Has your interest in Mann's *Doctor Faustus* influenced the use of syphilis and other diseases in your own work?

BURGESS
I've been much influenced by the thesis of Mann's *Doctor Faustus*, but I wouldn't want to have syphilis myself in order to be Wagner or Shakespeare or Henry VIII. Some prices are too high to pay. Oh, you'll want examples of these GPI talents. There was one man who'd turned himself into a kind of Scriabin, another who could give you the day of the week for any date in history, another who wrote poems like Christopher Smart. Many patients were orators or grandiose liars. It was like being imprisoned in a history of European art. Politics as well.

INTERVIEWER
Have you used in your novels any of the GPI cases that you encountered?

BURGESS
I did have the intention at one time of writing a long novel—a kind of *Magic Mountain*, I suppose—about life in a mental hospital; and perhaps I may yet get down to it. Of course, the trouble is it would take on a kind of political significance. People might think of works like *Cancer Ward*; it might be thought as presenting a clearly marked division between the patients and the hospital staff. One would be trading in a sort of political allegory; it's so easy to do that. Yet what interests me about a mental hospital that specializes in General Paralysis of the Insane is this relationship between disease and talent. Some of the tremendous skills that these patients show—these tremendous mad abilities—all stem out of the spirochete. I have pursued this in a couple of novels (or at least in one novel), but to do it on a larger scale would require a kind of rationale

which I haven't yet worked out. I don't think it should be done purely as a documentary novel, as a naturalistic presentation of what life is like in such hospitals; but it does suggest to me that it's tied up with symbols of some kind—tied up with an interior, deeper meaning. Of course one never knows what this meaning will be, but *The Magic Mountain* has its deeper meanings beneath the naturalistic surface. I wouldn't want to imitate that. One has to wait, I'm afraid—a long time sometimes—for the experience one's had to present itself in workable form, as a form that can be shaped into something like a work of art.

INTERVIEWER

Do you see any contradiction in choosing a craftsman like Joyce as one of your literary models while classifying yourself as a "Grub Street writer" at the same time?

BURGESS

Why contradiction? But I've never really regarded Joyce as a literary model. Joyce can't be imitated and there's no imitation Joyce in my work. All you can learn from Joyce is the exact use of language. "Grub Street writer" means Dr. Johnson as well as our wretched columnists, and Johnson was an exact user of language.

INTERVIEWER

You've certainly studied Joyce very thoroughly. Does knowing what he has done open more doors than it closes?

BURGESS

Joyce opened doors only to his own narrow world; his experiments were for himself only. But all novels are experimental, and *Finnegans Wake* is no more spectacular an experiment that, say, *Prancing Nigger* or *His Monkey Wife*. It looks spectacular because of the language. *MF*, believe it or not, is a completely original experiment.

INTERVIEWER

Isn't Joyce's attempt to devote virtually an entire novel to the Unconscious more than a purely linguistic experiment?

BURGESS

Yes, of course. The wakeworld is only narrow in that it's asleep, fixed on one set of impulses only, has too few characters.

INTERVIEWER

Can't contemporary writers uses Joyce's techniques without being mere imitators?

BURGESS

You can't use Joyce's techniques without being Joyce. Technique and material are one. You can't write like Beethoven without writing Beethoven, unless you're Beethoven.

INTERVIEWER

Has Nabokov influenced your work at all? You've praised *Lolita* highly.

BURGESS

Reading *Lolita* meant that I enjoyed using lists of things in *The Right to an Answer*. I've not been much influenced by Nabokov, nor do I intend to be. I was writing the way I write before I knew he existed. But I've not been impressed so much by another writer in the last decade or so.

INTERVIEWER

Yet you've been called an "English Nabokov," probably because of the cosmopolitan strain and verbal ingenuity in your writing.

BURGESS

No influence. He's a Russian, I'm English. I meet him halfway in certain temperamental endowments. He's very artificial, though.

INTERVIEWER

In what way?

BURGESS

Nabokov is a natural dandy on the grand international scale. I'm still a provincial boy scared of being too nattily dressed. All writing is artificial and Nabokov's artifacts are only contrived in the *récit* part. His dialogue is always natural and masterly (when he wants it to be). *Pale Fire* is only termed a novel because there's no other term for it. It's a masterly literary artifact which is poem, commentary, casebook, allegory, sheer structure. But I note that most people go back to reading the poem, not what surrounds the poem. It's a fine poem, of course. Where Nabokov goes wrong, I think, is in sometimes *sounding* old-fashioned—a matter of rhythm, as though Huysmans is to him a sound and modern writer whose tradition is worthy to be worked in. John Updike sounds old-fashioned sometimes in the same way—glorious vocabulary and imagery but a lack of muscle in the rhythm.

INTERVIEWER

Does Nabokov rank at the top with Joyce?

BURGESS

He won't go down in history as one of the greatest names. He's unworthy to unlatch Joyce's shoe.

INTERVIEWER

Have any new writers appeared of late that you think are destined for greatness?

BURGESS

I can't think of any in England. The trouble with American writers is that they die before becoming great—Nathanael West, Scott Fitzgerald, etc. Mailer will become a great autobiographer. Ellison will be great if only he'll write more. Too many *homines unius libri* like Heller.

INTERVIEWER

American writers certainly tend to burn themselves out early, at least. Do you think it takes more than one book for a writer to earn the label "great"?

BURGESS

A man can write one book that can be great, but this doesn't make him a great writer—just the writer of a great book. Samuel Butler's *Way of All Flesh* is a great novel but nobody calls Butler a great novelist. I think a writer has to extend very widely, as well as plunge very deep, to be a great novelist.

INTERVIEWER

Did Fitzgerald write a great novel?

BURGESS

I don't think Fitzgerald's books great—style too derivatively romantic, far less of that curious freshness of vision than you find in Hemingway—Hemingway is a great novelist, I think, but he never wrote a great novel (a great novella, yes). I think America likes its artists to die young, in atonement for materialist America's sins. The English leave the dying young to Celts like Dylan Thomas and Behan. But I can't understand the American literary block—as in Ellison or Salinger—unless it means that the blocked man isn't forced economically to write (as the English writer, lacking campuses and grants, usually is) and hence can afford the luxury of fearing the critics' pounce on a new work not as good as the last (or the first). American writers drink a lot when they're "blocked" and drunkenness—being a kind of substitute for art—makes the block worse. I've found it best, especially since my first wife, who drank less than I, died of cirrhosis, to drink little. But I smoke much, and that's probably worse than five martinis a day.

INTERVIEWER

You've spoken highly of Defoe as a novelist and practical journalist, and you also admire Sterne as a writer. What special appeal do these 18th-century writers have for you?

I admire Defoe because he worked hard. I admire Sterne because he did everything the French are trying so unhandily to do now. Eighteenth-century prose has a tremendous vitality and scope. Not Fielding, though. Sentimental, too much given to contrivances. Sterne and Swift (who, Joyce said, should have exchanged names) are men one can learn technically from all the time.

INTERVIEWER
Speaking of the French — your playful novels of ideas tend to be more in the French literary tradition, perhaps, than any other. Has this kept them from becoming better known in England and America?

BURGESS
The novels I've written are really mediaeval Catholic in their thinking, and people don't want that today. God forbid they should be "French." If they're not read it's because the vocabulary is too big and people don't like using dictionaries when they're reading mere novels. I don't give a damn, anyway.

INTERVIEWER
This Catholic emphasis accounts in part for the frequent comparisons made between your novels and Evelyn Waugh's, and yet you've said you don't find Waugh's aristocratic idea of Catholicism attractive. What do you like about his work?

BURGESS
Waugh is funny, Waugh is elegant, Waugh is economical. His Catholicism, which I despise as all cradle Catholics despise converts, is the thing in him which means least to me. Indeed, it injures his *Sword of Honour*.

INTERVIEWER
This charge has often been made — along with that of sentimentality — against *Brideshead Revisited*, but *Sword of Honour* is often called the best novel in English about World War II. How does Waugh's (or Guy Crouchback's) Catholicism weaken it?

BURGESS
Crouchback's Catholicism weakens *Sword of Honour* in the sense that it sectarianizes the book — I mean, we have Crouchback's moral view of the war and this is not enough: we need something that lies beneath religion. In our age it's a weakness to make Catholic theology the basis of a novel, since it means everything's cut and dried and the author doesn't have to re-think things out. The weakness of Greene's *Heart of the Matter* is derived from its author's fascination with theology: the sufferings of the hero are

theological sufferings, invalid outside the narrow field of Catholicism. When I taught Waugh and Greene to Muslim students in Malaya they used to laugh. Why can't this man have two wives if he wants them, they would say. What's wrong with eating the bit of bread the priest gives you when you've been sleeping with a woman not your wife, and so on. They never laughed at the tragic heroes of the Greeks and Elizabethans.

INTERVIEWER

Does the difference between cradle and convert Catholicism influence an author's work in such an essential way that you tend to prefer a novelist like François Mauriac to Graham Greene?

BURGESS

English converts to Catholicism tend to be bemused by its glamour and even look for more glamour in it than is actually there—like Waugh, dreaming of an old English Catholic aristocracy, or Greene, fascinated by sin in a very cold-blooded way. I wished I liked Mauriac more as a writer. The fact is that I prefer the converted Catholics because they happen to be better novelists. I do try to forget that Greene is a Catholic when I read him. He too is now, I think, trying to forget. *The Comedians* was a kind of philosophical turning point. *Travels With My Aunt* is deliciously free of morality of any kind, except a very delightful kind of inverted morality.

INTERVIEWER

In an essay on Waugh you mentioned "the Puritan that lurks in every English Catholic." Do you see this residue of Puritanism lurking in your own writing at all?

BURGESS

Of course it's in me. We English take our Catholicism seriously, which the Italians and French don't, and that makes us earnest and obsessed about sin. We really absorbed hell—perhaps a very Nordic notion—and think about it when committing adultery. I'm so Puritanical that I can't describe a kiss without blushing.

INTERVIEWER

Are there any limits that you think an author should observe in the language he uses to present controversial subject matter?

BURGESS

My aversion to describing amorous details in my work is probably that I treasure physical love so highly I don't want to let strangers in on it. For, after all, when we describe copulation we're describing our own experiences. I like privacy. I think that other writers should do what they can do, and if they can spend—as one of my American girl students did—ten pages on the act of fellatio without embarrassing themselves, very good luck to them. But I think there's more artistic pleasure to be gained from the ingenious circumvention of a taboo than from what is called total permissiveness. When I wrote my first Enderby novel I had to make my hero say "For cough," since "Fuck off" was not then acceptable. With the second book the climate had changed and Enderby was at liberty to say "Fuck off." I wasn't happy. It was too easy. He still said "'For cough" while others responded with "Fuck off." A compromise. Literature, however, thrives on taboos, just as all art thrives on technical difficulties.

INTERVIEWER

Several years ago you wrote, "I believe the wrong God is temporarily ruling the world and that the true God has gone under," and added that the novelist's vocation predisposes him to this Manichean view. Do you still believe this?

BURGESS

I still hold this belief.

INTERVIEWER

Why do you think the novelist is predisposed to regard the world in terms of "essential opposition"? Unlike the Manicheans you seem to maintain a traditional Christian belief in original sin.

BURGESS

Novels are about conflicts. The novelist's world is one of essential oppositions of character, aspiration and so on. I'm only a Manichee in the widest sense of believing that duality is the ultimate reality; the original sin bit is not really a contradiction, though it does lead one to depressingly French heresies, like Graham Greene's own Jansenism, as well as Albigensianism (Joan of Arc's religion), Catharism, and so on. I'm entitled to an eclectic theology as a novelist, if not as a human being.

INTERVIEWER

In planning your novels have you ever considered separating them, as Simenon does, into "commercial" and "uncommercial" works, or, like Greene, into "novels" and "entertainments"?

BURGESS

All my novels belong to the one category — intended to be, as it were, serious entertainment, no moral aim, no solemnity. I want to please.

INTERVIEWER

Aren't you divorcing morality from aesthetics? This view is certainly consistent with your dismissal in *Shakespeare* of the Anglo-Saxon notion that a great artist must have a great moral sensibility.

BURGESS

I don't divorce morals and aesthetics. I merely believe that a man's literary greatness is no index of his personal ethics. I don't, true, think that the job of literature is to teach us how to behave, but I think it can make clearer the whole business of moral choice by showing what the nature of life's problems is. It's after truth, which is not goodness.

INTERVIEWER

You've said that the novel gets an implied set of values derived from religion but that other arts, such as music and architecture, are, unlike fiction, "neutral." Does this make them more or less attractive at this point?

BURGESS

I enjoy writing music precisely because one is divorced from "human" considerations like belief, conduct. Pure form, nothing more. But then I tend to despise music just because it is so *mindless*. I've been writing a string quartet based on a musical theme that Shakespeare throws at us, in sol-fa notation, in *Love's Labour's Lost* (the theme is CDGAEF), and it's been pure bliss. I've been thoroughly absorbed by it, on planes, in hotel bedrooms, anywhere where I had nothing else to do and there was no bloody musak playing. (Don't the musak purveyors ever think of the people who actually have to write music?) Now I'm a little ashamed that the music engages nothing but purely formal problems. So I oscillate between a hankering after pure form and a realization that literature is probably valuable because it *says things*.

INTERVIEWER

How does political neutrality figure in all this? In your novels the neutrals, such as Mr. Theodorescu in *Tremor of Intent*, are usually villains.

BURGESS

If art should be neutral, if it can, life should be committed, if it can. There's no connection between political and religious neutrality and that blessed *achieved* neutrality of, say, music. Art is, so to speak, the church triumphant, but the rest of life is in the church militant. I believe that good and evil exist, though they have nothing to do with art, and that evil has to be resisted. There's no inconsistency in holding an aesthetic so different from such an ethic.

INTERVIEWER

Several of your recent novels have exotic foreign settings, even though you remarked a few years ago that the artist should exhaust the resources of the "here and now" as a true test of his art. Have you changed your mind?

BURGESS

Yes, I changed my mind. I'm limited by temperament, I now discover, to being moved or excited by any place in the world so long as it's not England. This means that all my settings must be "exotic."

INTERVIEWER

Why do you consider England so dull a subject?

BURGESS

Dull for me if not for others. I like societies where there's a dynamism of conflict. In other words, I think novels should be about the whole of a society — by implication if nothing else — and not just a little pocket inside. English fiction tends to be about these pockets — love affairs in Hampstead, Powell's bohemian aristocracy, Snow's men of power. Dickens gave you the lot, like Balzac. Much modern American fiction gives you the lot. You could reconstruct the whole of modern America from even a little mad fantasy like Phil Roth's *The Breast*. But I may have a personal thing about England — a sense of exclusion and so on. It may even be so simple a matter as liking extreme climates, fights in bars, exotic waterfronts, fish soup, a lot of garlic. I find it easier to imagine a surrealistic version of New Jersey than of old England, though I could see some American genius making a whole strange world of Mr. Heath's inheritance. Probably (as Thomas Pynchon never went to Valletta or Kafka to America) it's best to imagine your own foreign country. I wrote a very good account of Paris before I ever went there. Better than the real thing.

INTERVIEWER

Was this in *The Worm and the Ring*?

BURGESS

Yes. Paris was a town I always tried to avoid; but I've been more and more in it recently and find that the account of Paris I wrote (although it smells of maps and tourist guides) is not unlike the reality. This is true also with Joyce's Gibraltar, in *Ulysses*; one has no need to visit the country to write about the country.

INTERVIEWER

And yet you draw a good picture of Leningrad in *Honey for the Bears*.

BURGESS

Oh, I knew Leningrad. Yes, that's right. But not too well; for if one gets to know a town too well, then the sharpness of the impression is blunted and one is not interested in writing about it. Anyway, the interesting point is that one first meets a town through its smells; this is especially true in Europe. Leningrad has a peculiar smell of its own, and you become habituated to these smells in time and you forget what they are; and you're not able to approach it in those highly sensuous terms when writing about it if you know a place too well. If you're in a town for about a month somewhere, you can't retain a sensuous impression. As with Paris, you smell the Gauloise when you arrive; but you cease to smell the Gauloise in time. You get so used to it.

You've said that Leningrad resembles Manchester. How are they alike?

I think it was just the sense of the architecture, the rather broken-down architecture of Leningrad, the sense of large numbers of the working class, rather shabbily dressed. And I suppose in some ways the *smell* of Manchester — I always associated Manchester with the smell of tanneries, very pungent smells, as you know. I got this same smell out of Leningrad. It's a small thing, but these small things have a curious habit of becoming important. You try to fix a place in your mind. I don't know what the smell of Milwaukee is, I don't think the American cities have any smell. That's probably why they are rather unmemorable. Smell is most elusive of the senses. To a novelist it is somehow the most important of the senses.

You've also said that the serious novelist should be prepared to stay in one place and really get to know it. Do you hope to do this with Italy now?

Again, I seem to have changed my mind. I think I shall want to invent places more than merely reproduce them, and don't please put this down to the influence of *Ada*. The next four novels will be set, respectively in mediaeval England, modern New Jersey, Italy in the last fifty years, Jane Austen's England.

Have your travels given you a special sense of the variety of human types, such as Forster's Prof. Godbole?

Fundamentally people are all the same, and I've lived among enough different races long enough to be dogmatic about this. Godbole in *A Passage to India* is an eccentric mystic of the type that any culture can throw up.

At this point do you regard yourself as an expatriate Englishman or as an exile?

BURGESS

A verbal quibble. I've voluntarily exiled myself, but not forever. Nevertheless, I can't think of any good reason for going back to England except on a holiday. But one is, as Simone Weil said, faithful to the cuisine one was brought up on, and that probably constitutes patriotism. I am sometimes mentally and physically ill for Lancashire food—hot pot, lobscowse and so on—and I have to have these things. I'm loyal to Lancashire, I suppose, but not strongly enough to wish to go back and live there.

INTERVIEWER

What are "hot pot" and "lobscowse"?

BURGESS

Hot pot, or Lancashire hot pot, is made in this way. An earthenware dish, a layer of trimmed lamb chops, a layer of sliced onions, a layer of sliced potatoes, then continue the layers till you reach the top. Add seasoned stock. On top put mushrooms or more potato slices to brown. Add oysters or kidneys as well if you wish. Bake in a moderate oven for a long time. Eat with pickled cabbage. Lobscowse is a sailor's dish from Liverpool (Liverpudlians are called "scousers" or "scowsers") and is very simple. Dice potatoes and onions and cook in a pan of seasoned water. When they're nearly done get rid of excess liquid and add a can or two of cubed (or diced) corned beef. Heat gently. Eat with mixed pickles. I love cooking these dishes and, once known, everybody loves them. They're honest and simple. Lancashire has a great cuisine, including a notable shop cuisine—meaning you can buy great delicacies in shops. Lancashire women traditionally work in the cotton mills and cook dinner only at weekends. Hence the things you can get in cooked food-shops—fish and chips, Bury puddings, Eccles cakes, tripe, cowheel, meat pies (hot, with gravy poured into a hole from a jug), and so on. Fish and chips is now, I think, internationally accepted. Meat and potato pie is perhaps the greatest of the Lancashire dishes—a "drier" hot pot with a fine flaky crust.

INTERVIEWER

I'm tempted to visit Manchester. Lawrence Durrell, another expatriate English writer, has said that since America and Russia are going to determine our future, one is obliged to stop traveling and start thinking when one is in either country. It's different, he says, from going to Italy—a pure pleasure. Do you agree?

BURGESS

Durrell has never yet said anything I could agree with. He reminds me of that TV show woman in America, Virginia Graham. I just don't know what the hell he can mean by that. In America and Russia I meet people, get drunk, eat, just as I do in Italy. I see no signs of purely metaphysical import. Those are left to governments, and governments are what I try to ignore. All governments are evil, including that of Italy.

INTERVIEWER

That sounds vaguely anarchic, or at least un-American. Did you have an undergraduate Marxist period, like Victor Crabbe in *The Long Day Wanes?*

BURGESS

I was never a Marxist, though I was always, even as an undergraduate, ready to play the Marxist game — analyzing Shakespeare in Marxist terms and so on. I always loved dialectical materialism. But it was a structuralist love from the start. To take socialism seriously, as opposed to minimal socialization (what America needs so desperately) is ridiculous.

INTERVIEWER

Doesn't "minimal socialization" require an increase in the size and power of central government? Only the American federal government can fund the equivalent of the English or Scandinavian health plans; the need for inexpensive medical treatment is acute here.

BURGESS

I loathe the State but concede that socialized medicine is a priority in any civilized country today. In England it saved me from bankruptcy during my wife's final illness (though perhaps a private insurance policy might have taken care of it. You can't opt out of the state scheme, however). Socialized medicine — which in England was a Liberal idea anyway — doesn't have to mean out and out socialism with everything nationalized. If America gets it, it will be only the doctors and dentists who will try not to make it work, but, as in England, there's no reason why a private practice shouldn't coexist with a national health one. You go to a dentist in England and he says "Private or National Health?" The difference in treatment is hardly noticeable, but the State materials (tooth-fillings, spectacles, and so on) are inferior to what you buy as a private patient.

INTERVIEWER

Do these views make you a political conservative, then? You've said you would reluctantly vote Conservative in England.

BURGESS

I think that I'm a Jacobite, meaning that I'm traditionally Catholic, support the Stuart monarchy and want to see it restored, and distrust imposed change even when it seems to be for the better. I honestly believe that America should become monarchist (preferably Stuart) because with a limited monarchy you have no president, and a president is one more corruptible element in government. I hate all republics. I suppose my conservatism, since the ideal of a Catholic Jacobite imperial monarch isn't practicable, is really a kind of anarchism.

INTERVIEWER

Many Americans believe their presidency has evolved into a form of monarchy, with unhappy results. Do you see an anarchy as a viable political alternative?

BURGESS

The U.S. presidency is a Tudor monarchy plus telephones. Your alternative is either a return to the limited monarchy of the British Commonwealth — a constitutional monarch is at least out of politics and can't get dirty or corrupt — or devolution into unfederated states with a loose cooperative framework for large development schemes. Anarchy is a man's own thing, and I think it's too late in the day to think of it as a viable system or non-system in a country as large as America. It was all right for Blake or for Thoreau, both of whom I admire immensely, but we'll never get it so full-blooded again. All we can do is keep pricking our government all the time, disobeying all we dare (after all, we have livings to earn), asking why, maintaining a habit of distrust.

INTERVIEWER

You've urged fellow artists to seek depth by "digging for the mythical." Are you more interested in creating new myths or in re-examining old ones, as you did with the *Aeneid* in *A Vision of Battlements*?

BURGESS

At present I'm interested in what structuralism can teach us about myth. I don't think I can invent my own myths, and I still think there's a great deal of fictional revivification possible with regard to such myths as the Jason / Golden Fleece one (on which I plan a novel, incidentally). Existing myths carry useful depth, a profundity of meaning which saves the novelist a lot of inventive trouble.

INTERVIEWER

How does Jason's pursuit of the Golden Fleece apply to our time?

BURGESS

My Jason novel, if I ever write it, will just use the Argonaut story as a framework for picaresque adventures. No deeper significance.

INTERVIEWER

Have you ever considered basing a novel on myths associated with Oriental religions, as Mann did in *The Transposed Heads*?

BURGESS

Strangely, I've been contemplating making a musical play out of Mann's *The Transposed Heads* — very charming, but only a game despite the claims of psychological profundity sometimes made for it. I've six years in the East but am not greatly drawn to Eastern myths, except that of the endless Javanese shadow-play, which is like *Finnegans Wake* anyway. But I've thought of a novel based on Munshi Abdullah's *Hikayat*. That German hunger for the East — Hesse as well as Mann — is very curious. They might not have seen it as so romantic if they'd been colonial officers. Perhaps that's what they really wanted to be.

INTERVIEWER

Structuralism plays a big part in *MF*. How important is it to you as a novelist of ideas?

BURGESS

Structuralism is the scientific confirmation of a certain theological conviction — that life is binary, that this is a duoverse and so on. What I mean is that the notion of essential opposition — not God / Devil but just x / y — is the fundamental one, and this is a kind of purely structuralist view. We end up with form as more important than content, with speech and art as phatic processes, with the big moral imponderables as mere hot air. Marshall McLuhan has been limping along this track independently of Lévi-Strauss. How marvelous that the essential bifurcation which is man is expressed in trousers that carry Lévi-Strauss' name.

INTERVIEWER

Along with establishing a firm connection between language and myth, you've also indicated about the future of the novel that "only through the exploration of language can the personality be coaxed into yielding a few more of its secrets." Would you expand on that?

BURGESS

By extension of vocabulary, by careful distortion of syntax, by exploitation of various prosodic devices traditionally monopolised by poetry, surely certain indefinite or complex areas of the mind can more competently be rendered than in the style of, say, Irving Stone or Wallace.

INTERVIEWER

Are you ever tempted to lavish complex prose on a simple protagonist, as Flaubert did in *A Simple Heart*?

BURGESS

Try and make your language fit your concept of the subject more than the subject itself. "Here's this stupid man who's written a most highly wrought work about a housemaid called Félicité." But Flaubert was concerned, surely, with the nobility of that heart and lavished his prose riches upon it. Style is less a preoccupation than a perennial problem. Finding the right style for the subject, I mean. This must mean that the subject comes first and the style after.

INTERVIEWER

You've referred to yourself as a "serious novelist who is attempting to extend the range of subject-matter available to fiction." How have you tried to do this?

BURGESS

I've written about the dying British empire, lavatories, structuralism and so on, but I don't really think that that kind of subject matter is what I had in mind when I made that statement. I meant the modification of the sensibility of the British novel, which I may have achieved a little, a very little. The new areas are more technical than thematic.

INTERVIEWER

In *The Novel Now* you said that the novel is the only important literary form we have left. Why do you think this is true?

BURGESS

Yes, the novel is the only *big* literary form we have left. It is capable of enclosing the other, lesser, literary forms, from the play to the lyric poem. Poets are doing well enough, especially in America, but they can't achieve the architectonic skill which once lay behind the epic (for which the novel is now a substitute). The short sharp burst — in music as well as poetry — is not enough. The novel has the monopoly of *form* today.

INTERVIEWER

Granted this limited primacy of the novel, it's disturbing that novel sales in general are declining and that public attention is focused more on non-fiction. Are you tempted to turn more to biography, for example, in the future?

BURGESS

I shall carry on with novelizing and hope for some little reward on the side. Biography is very hard work, no room for invention. But if I were a young man now I wouldn't dream of trying to become a professional novelist. But some day, perhaps soon, the old realization will come back —

that reading about imaginary characters and their adventures is the greatest pleasure in the world. Or the second greatest.

What is the first?

That depends upon your own tastes.

Why do you regret becoming a professional novelist?

I think that the mental strain, the worry, you know, the self-doubt, are hardly worth the candle; the agonies of creation and the sense of responsibility to one's muse — all these various things become more than one can live with.

Are the odds much longer today against anyone's sustaining himself by quality fiction writing?

I don't know. I know that the older I get the more I want to live and the less opportunity I have. I don't think I wanted to become chained to an art form, establishing one's identity through an art form; one is a kind of Frankenstein creating a monster, so to speak. I wish I could live easier; I wish I didn't have the sense of responsibility to the arts. More than anything I wish I didn't have the prospect of having to write certain novels, which must be written because nobody else will write them. I wish I were freer, I like freedom; and I think I would have been much happier living as a colonial officer writing the odd novel in my spare time. Then I would have been happier than as a sort of professional man of letters, making a living out of words.

Do film versions help or hinder novels?

Films help the novels they're based on, which I both resent and am grateful for. My *Clockwork Orange* paperback has sold over a million in America, thanks to dear Stanley. But I don't like being beholden to a mere film maker. I want to prevail through pure literature. Impossible, of course.

You've referred to *A Vision of Battlements*, your first novel, "like all my stories since, as a slow and cruel stripping-off of illusion," yet you are often called a comic writer. Is comedy by nature so cruel, or do you consider yourself more a satirist?

Comedy is concerned with truth quite as much as tragedy; and the two, as Plato recognized, have something fundamental in common. They're both stripping processes; they both tear off externals and show man as a poor forked animal. Satire is a *particular* kind of comedy, limiting itself to particular areas of behavior, not to the general human condition. I don't think I'm a satirist.

Are you a black humorist as well—or are all these categories too confining?

I think I'm a comic writer, *malgré moi*. My Napoleon is turning out comic, and I certainly didn't intend that. I don't think I know what black humor is. Satirist? Satire is a difficult medium, ephemeral unless there's tremendous vitality in the form itself—like *Absalom and Achitophel, Tale of a Tub, Animal Farm*: I mean, the work has to subsist as story or poetry even when the objects of the satire are forgotten. Satire is now an element in some other form, not a form in itself. I like to be called just a novelist.

About ten years ago you wrote that you considered yourself a pessimist but believed that "the world has much solace to offer—love, food, music, the immense variety of race and language, literature, the pleasure of artistic creation." Would you make up the same list of saving graces today?

Yes, no change.

Georges Simenon, another professional, has said that "writing is not a profession but a vocation of unhappiness. I don't think an artist can ever be happy." Do you think this is true?

Yes, Simenon's right. My eight-year-old son said the other day: "Dad, why don't you write for *fun*?" Even he divined that the process as I practice it is prone to irritability and despair. I suppose, apart from my marriage, I was happiest when I was doing a teaching job and had nothing much to think about in the vacations. The anxiety involved is intolerable. And—I differ here from Simenon—the financial rewards just don't make up for the expenditure of energy, the damage to health caused by stimulants and narcotics, the fear that one's work isn't good enough. I think, if I had enough money, I'd give up writing tomorrow.

The Novels of Anthony Burgess   William H. Pritchard*

> Let the strict Life of graver Mortals be
> A long, exact, and serious Comedy,
> In ev'ry Scene some Moral let it teach,
> And, if it can, at once both Please and Preach:
> —Pope

Anthony Burgess published his first novel in 1956, his most recent one in the present year, a fact which becomes of interest only when it is added that in the intervening period, he published fourteen additional novels.[1] No doubt the figure is already dated for there are no signs of slowing down; in a recent apologetic valedictory to reviewing theater for *The Spectator* he confessed ruefully to not having written a novel in six months or more. One raises an eyebrow at all this plenty, yet only one of the novels marks itself off as a casual, slight creation, nor does the astonishing rate of production signal slapdash composition. The five novels selected for consideration here represent a judgment of his best "early" and "later" work; no doubt any admirer will have his particular favorite to add to the list. Burgess is a comic writer, a term broad and common enough to cover supposed refinements of it such as satire, grotesque, or farce. None of the labels substantially promotes understanding of his work, nor does the knowledge that he, like all British comic novelists, is "the funniest . . . since Evelyn Waugh." If comparisons are desired, one would begin with the guess that the contemporary novelist Burgess most admires is Nabokov; beyond that one goes to Joyce, to Dickens, ultimately to Shakespeare as the literary examples most insistently behind his work. In *Nothing Like the Sun*, his novel about Shakespeare, the hero sees himself as a "word man," and his author is not likely to quarrel with the term as a description of himself. But then, like Nabokov or Joyce or Dickens or Shakespeare, he is more than just a word man: the brilliant exploration of a verbal surface will lead to the discovery of truths about life, of inward revelation. Or will it, does it in fact lead to such truths in the unfolding of Burgess' best work? The question is an interesting one to entertain, though only after we have

*From the *Massachusetts Review* 7 (1966):525–39. © 1966 by The Massachusetts Review, Inc. Reprinted by permission.

first been moved and delighted by the books themselves and the continuing presence of their author.

I

Burgess is at his most direct and perhaps most simply appealing in his early novels about life in Malaya just before independence; published last year as a trilogy, *The Long Day Wanes*, the books are given continuity through the presence of Victor Crabbe, an embattled liberal school-master for whom things get progressively worse. Crabbe is one of us: reasonable, guilt-ridden, alternately shabby and decent in his relations with others. In a word, colorless, though he looks colorless only when put next to the characters that surround him, grotesques such as Nabby Adams, an enormous police-official whose life is devoted to the insuring each day of his proximity to about two-dozen bottles of Tiger beer (*Time for a Tiger* is the first volume of the trilogy). Or, emerging from the words themselves, Crabbe's boss Talbot, married to a young and adulterous wife, but truly wedded to his stomach:

> "My dear fellow, you ought to eat. That's the trouble with my wife. Thin as a rake, because she won't bother to order anything. She says she's not hungry. I'm always hungry. The climate has different effects on different people. I always have my lunch out. There's a little Chinese place where they give you a really tasty and filling soup, packed with chicken and abalone and vegetables, with plenty of toast and butter, and then I always have a couple of baked crabs."
> "Yes," said Crabbe.
> "With rice and chili sauce. And then a pancake or so, rather soggy, but I don't dislike them that way, with jam and a kind of whipped cream they serve in a tea-cup. Anne, what is there to eat?"

Crabbe's mild "Yes" is a typical Fred Allen-response to the antics per-formed by assorted characters throughout the trilogy. But we are asked to take Crabbe, unlike Fred Allen, seriously as a person. He is presented as a recognizably psychological figure, available for easy identification with on the part of any ordinary reader; his death terminates the trilogy and should evoke some feelings on our part. But the feelings do not appear. We accept Crabbe's fate, whatever it is, without much interest, because we are being so royally entertained elsewhere.

Robert Garis has demonstrated brilliantly how the art of entertain-ment, as it appears in Dickens' novels, is typically a "loud and distinct" one, apprehended firmly and easily by the reader.[2] In what Garis terms Dickens' "theatrical" art, the reader is happy to watch the artist-showman at his performance, and does not expect to receive complex insights into characters who have to be "taken seriously" as we take Anna Karenina or Dorothea Brooke seriously. The satisfied reader of Dickens delights in the showman's ability energetically to command a large and various number of acts by an inexhaustibly creative language. Burgess' comedy, particularly in his early novels, if not as loud and distinct (or expansive and assured) as Dickens', is as purely verbal in its workings; for example, all we need or want to know of the glutton Talbot is that he is gluttonous and that his poems are filled with highly nutritious images: we are satisfied to watch the pancakes and whipped-cream roll by. Or to delight with Nabby Adams in his acquiring, without payment, eight large unopened bottles of Tiger beer, and in his anticipation of "The hymeneal gouging-off of the bottle-top, the kiss of the brown bitter yeasty flow, the euphoria far beyond the release of detumescence." The novel-reader's desire to find out what happens next does not assert itself, for the narrator is in no hurry to press on toward exciting revelations. He contemplates instead, with the satisfaction of Nabby Adams viewing the bottles of Tiger, his own agile high-humored creations

One of the most original and satisfying elements of Burgess' theatricality is a persistent literary allusiveness that teases us to make something out of it and then mocks our efforts. *The Long Day Wanes* invokes Tennyson's "Ulysses," but is Victor Crabbe an "idle king" who eventually drowns in the "deep [that] moans round with many voices"? Only a solemn explicator would be interested in displaying that connection, for the theatrical novelist is less interested in creating symbolic expressions of a complex truth about man than in making play with the words of writers who have expressed such truths. Although the trilogy is filled with allusions to "The Waste Land," their interest does not lie in suggesting that Victor Crabbe fears death by water (he does), but in the purely amusing way they are woven into the narrative and made to seem at once absurdly confected and perfectly natural: "This music crept by Syed Omar in Police Headquarters, sitting puzzled while others were going out to lunch." As Crabbe's wife reads "The Waste Land" to Nabby Adams and his Malayan sidekick, Nabby remarks

> "He's got that wrong about the pack of cards, Mrs. Crabbe. There isn't no card called The Man With Three Staves. That card what he means is just an ordinary three, like as it may be the three of clubs."
> And when they came to the dark thunder-speaking finale of the poem, Alladad Khan had nodded gravely.

> *"Datta, Dayadhvam. Damyata.*
> *Shantih. Shantih. Shantih."*

> "He says he understands that bit, Mrs. Crabbe. He says that's what the thunder says."

This "contributes" nothing to the novel except as one more of the witty satisfactions which occur throughout the trilogy. The long day has indeed waned, and the play made with Eliot or Joyce shows us just how late in the game we are, how far from the epic worlds of our modern legendary authors. Far enough it seems so that we can be entertained by a contemporary's familiar use of them.

These isolated examples of entertainment have little to do with the presentation of the hero, Crabbe, who is brought eventually (like all Burgess' heroes) to some sort of reckoning. Typically, the reckoning involves a sexual humiliation; in this novel, Crabbe learns a shocking fact about his first love, then slips into the water while trying to board a launch. We view this event through the impassive gaze of a Malayan doctor who lets him drown, deciding that "Human lives were not his professional concern." There is no other significant comment on the scene. Although it is perfectly well to say that Crabbe is essentially a device for holding together loosely-related characters and episodes, he is also allowed an inner life we must take seriously — his psychological anxieties are given full expression. When it comes to ending the trilogy, the author doesn't seem to know how seriously he wants to take that life, so it is easier to show up the Malayan doctor's sophistry (if it is that), than to assign significance, however minor, to Crabbe's end. It may seem pedantic to accuse Burgess of trying to have it both ways, since *The Long Day Wanes* is a comedy of humours in which, with the exception of Crabbe's story, the narration is external and detached. But the problem is there, and it becomes more complicated when the theatrical novelist does his tricks through a first-person narrator.

This narrator appears as J. W. Denham in what is surely Burgess' most engaging novel, *The Right to an Answer* (1960). A civil servant in the Far East home on holiday in England for much of the book, Denham is over forty, has bad teeth and a cushy job, and can smell the TV-corruption of England in the late fifties. England is a mess because people have too much freedom, and Denham claims to have learned from Hobbes that you can't have both freedom and stability. By the end of the novel he does not pronounce on matters with the arrogant certainty of the opening pages, but it would be wrong to conclude, therefore, that Burgess has written a moral novel with a dramatic change of view. How much, really, can a narrator learn who early in the book talks this way about Sunday dinner at his sister's:

> There was a smell of old dog in the hall, an earthy rebuke at least to the blurry misty pictures of dream-dogs on the walls. The honest black telephone shone coyly from behind flowery curtains — Beryl's homemade booth for long comfy talkie-talkies with women friends, if she had any. I noticed a poker-work poem of slack form and uplifting content: "In a world of froth and bubble two things stand like stone: kindness in another's trouble, courage in your own." Beryl's unimpaired high-school humour was indicated by a framed macaronic paradigm: "Je me larf, tu te grin, il se giggle; nous nous crackons, vouv vous splittez, ils se bustent." Beryl herself could be heard singing in the kitchen at the end of the hall — an emasculated version of "Green-

sleeves" — and the fumes of heavy greens gushed out under the noise of the masher.

And on and on. Crackling with wordy Nabokovian irritation, the writing individuates Beryl so firmly that there is no temptation to see her as a representative of England's corruption. If this is satire, it is satire which, as Eliot would say, creates the object that it contemplates. Beryl's house is as unforgettably there as the love-nest Lolita's mother designs for Humbert. In neither case are we interested in using the descriptions to censure the ladies in some moral way; by the same token, any claims the narrator makes about his own moral progress will have to compete with his continuous and self-contained verbal brilliance.

At one point in the novel, Denham, playing the inept narrator, apologizes for the lack of action in his tale: ". . . you have had merely J. W. Denham on leave, eating, drinking, unjustifiably censorious, meeting people, especially Mr. Raj, recounting, at the tail of the eye, almost out of earshot, the adultery of small uninteresting people." Mr. Raj is an eager sociologist from Colombo who comes to Denham's home town to investigate the manners and to court an English woman. His most notable capabilities, however, are pugilistic and culinary: in Ted Arden's Shakespearean pub, Mr. Raj disposes of a vocal racist, and Ted muses as follows: "Queer bugger that is. It Jack Brownlow, quick as a flash, right in the goolies. . . . I didn't let on when e did it so quick like. E did it real gentleman like." Eventually Mr. Raj moves in with Denham and his father, to cook Sunday afternoon curries that are too rich and deep for tears: "We fell to. My father spooned in curry and panted. He frequently tried to stagger to the kitchen for fresh glasses of cold water, but Mr. Raj said, 'No, no. I will get. This is my privilege, Mr. Denhams both.' To my father all this was a new world; he ate with Renaissance child's eyes of wonder. 'I'd no idea,' he gasped. 'Never thought.' He was like a youth having his first sexual experience." But all these pleasant events are shattered abruptly as Denham resumes his job in the East and leaves his father in the hands of Mr. Raj, who proceeds to kill him with the kindness of curry. This is one of a series of violent acts, including assault, rape, murder, and the suicide of Mr. Raj, which cause Denham to reexamine his earlier superiority to "the mess." Although after Mr. Raj's suicide Denham moralizes that these are "just silly vulgar people uncovering the high explosive that lies hidden underneath stability" he is allowed a meditation in the concluding chapter which places him in a different relation to these people. Denham disgustedly contemplates his body in the mirror, then moves to his equally unsatisfactory spirit:

> It was the eyes I didn't like, the unloving mouth, and the holier-than-thou set of the nostrils. . . . The mess was there, the instability, but I wondered now if that sin against stability was really the big sin. What I did realize quite clearly was the little I'd helped, the blundering or

not-wishing-to-be-involved plump moneyed man of leave inveighing against sins he wasn't in the position even to begin to commit. For surely that sneered-at suburban life was more stable than this shadow life of buying and selling in a country where no involvement was possible, the television evening, with the family round, better than the sordid dalliance that soothed me after work? . . . If poor bloody innocent little Winterbottom had died, and striving Mr. Raj . . . surely it was something that they invoked the word Love? Even the word was better than this emptiness, this standing on the periphery and sneering.

This seems to offer us a secure vantage-point from which to review the events with understanding. But are we convinced by it? What indeed would it mean to be "convinced" by it? Doesn't the analysis unjustly simplify Denham's earlier behavior, since that behavior has been presented to us through a style which delights? How can we accept "sneering" or "standing on the periphery" as adequate labels for the description of Beryl's house quoted earlier? Or, from the same chapter, is the following menu a sneer at the English Sunday meal? "The meal was pretentious — a kind of beetroot soup with greasy *croûtons*; pork underdone with loud vulgar cabbage, potato croquettes, tinned peas in tiny jam-tart cases, watery gooseberry sauce; trifle made with a resinous wine, so jammy that all my teeth lit up at once — a ghastly discord on two organ manuals." One quickly grows fond of those encased peas, that loud cabbage; the food, through these words, becomes not just awful but fascinatingly awful. Here, as in general, the imaginative vitality of Denham-Burgess' prose elbows aside the moralist who later repents of his hypercritical satiric self.

Denham's relationship to "the mess, the instability" represents a novelistic questioning of the satirist's relationship to life, to the materials of fiction. *The Right to an Answer* is unique in Burgess' work for the way it shows an aggressively comic and satiric intelligence taking us in through a casual first-person style of reporting. At the same time, or perhaps as a result of such aggressive dealing, the "I" repents of it, apologizes to us for putting himself outside the reek of the human. I am really no better than they are, probably not as good, he winningly admits. But if the apology is an engaging gesture of humility, it has things both ways only through a noticeable straining in the very prose of the book. When the narrator refers harshly, in the above passage, to "the sordid dalliance that soothed me after work," just how seriously can we take something which is referred to by a demonstrably witty intelligence as "sordid dalliance"? And does Burgess himself know how seriously he wants to take it? The attempt by a marvelous entertainer to discover a truth about life, to engage in moral reappraisal of himself, results in an uncomfortable sleight-of-hand effect that isn't quite quick enough to escape our notice. And the question remains: how much can the dark comedian afford to enlighten, with sincere reflection, the chaotic scene he has so wittily imagined?

II

This question, asked by the critic, is of course one the artist is under no obligation to answer. Burgess goes on to publish three novels *(Devil of a State, The Worm and the Ring, The Doctor Is Sick)* which in their individually interesting ways avoid the issue and which, for all their excellent goings-on, are not as solidly entertaining as *The Long Day Wanes*, or as humanly ambitious as *The Right to an Answer*. It is the three novels that appear in 1962–63 which present a truly experimental attempt to unite brilliance of entertainment with a seriousness toward human beings — more accurately, toward humanity. *A Clockwork Orange, The Wanting Seed*, and *Honey for the Bears* are (at least the first and last) Burgess' most popular books and they ask to be considered together. All of them concern the individual and the modern state; all of them are felt to have a connection with the quality of life in the 1960's, but they approach life obliquely by creating fantasies or fables which appeal to us in odd and disturbing ways. As always with Burgess' work, and now to a splendidly bizarre degree, the creativity is a matter of style, of words combined in strange new shapes. Through the admiration these shapes raise, rather than through communication of specifiable political, philosophical or religious ideas about man or the state, is to be found the distinction of these novels; for this reason it is of limited use to invoke names like Huxley or Orwell as other novelists of imagined futurist societies.

A Clockwork Orange, most patently experimental of the novels, is written in a language created by combining Russian words with teenage *argot* into a hip croon that sounds both ecstatic and vaguely obscene. The hero, Alex, a teen-age thug, takes his breakfast and morning paper this way:

> And there was a bolshy big article on Modern Youth (meaning me, so I gave the old bow, grinning like bezoomny) by some very clever bald chelloveck. I read this with care, my brothers, slurping away at the old chai, cup after tass after chasha, crunching my lomticks of black toast dipped in jammiwam and eggiweg. This learned veck said the usual veshches, about no parental discipline, as he called it, and the shortage of real horrorshow teachers who would lambast bloody beggary out of their innocent poops and make them go boohoohoo for mercy. All this was gloopy and made me smeck, but it was nice to go on knowing one was making the news all the time, O my brothers.

Although the American paperback edition provides a glossary, one doesn't need it to get along very well after the first few pages. In fact such translation is a mistake for it short-circuits the unmistakable rhythms of speech by which the sentences almost insensibly assume meaning. Moreover, though the book is filled with the most awful violence — what in our glossary or newspaper would be called murder, assault, rape, perversion —

it comes to us through an idiom that, while it does not deny the connection between what happens in the second chapter and what the newspaper calls a "brutal rape," nevertheless makes what happens an object of aesthetic interest in a way no rape can or should be. Life — a dreadful life to be sure — is insistently and joyously deflected into the rhythms of a personal style within which one eats lomticks, not pieces, of toast.

The novel is short and sharply plotted: Alex is betrayed by his fellow "droogs," imprisoned for murder, then by a lobotomizing technique is cured of his urges to violence; whereas music, Beethoven in particular, had inspired him to heights of blood-lusts, he now just feels sick. Caught between the rival parties for state power he tries suicide, but lives to recover his original identity, as listening to the scherzo of the Beethoven Ninth he sees himself "carving the whole litso of the creeching world with my cut-throat britva." The book concludes on this happy note, for oddly enough it *is* a happy note; we share the hero's sense of high relief and possibility, quite a trick for the novelist to have brought off. And without questioning it we have acceded to the book's "message," as radical and intransigent as the style through which it is expressed: "More, badness is of the self, the one, the you or me on our oddy knockies, and that self is made by old Bog or God and is his great pride and radosty. But the not-self cannot have the bad, meaning they of the government and the judges and the schools cannot allow the bad because they cannot allow the self. And is not our modern history, my brothers, the story of brave malenky selves fighting these big machines. I am serious with you, brothers, over this. But what I do I do because I like to do." Doing what you do because you like to do it is what the Burgess hero — Crabbe, Denham, others — has done and has been punished for doing by his creator. But the hero of *A Clockwork Orange* is rewarded and endorsed in a way more recognizably human characters in a more "realistic" atmosphere could not possibly be. In the world of creative fantasy we can admire hero and event as they are shaped by language; our response is akin to the old-fashioned "admiration" proper to the heroic poem. By the same token the defense of self, no matter how twisted it may be, and the condemnation of the state, no matter how benevolent it pretends to be, is absolute. Such a simple and radical meaning is not morally complex, but it must be taken as a serious aspect of fantasy. Within its odd but carefully observed limits the book is entirely consistent, successful and even pleasing, Burgess' most eye and ear-catching performance.

Published a few months later, *The Wanting Seed* pleased critics a good deal less, the general feeling being that Burgess had overreached himself and produced a hodge-podge book. It is true that nothing is alien to its virtuoso atmosphere: elemental poetry, broad jokes, science fiction and political philosophy consort together, couched throughout in a highly pedantic and jawbreaking vocabulary ("corniculate," "vexillae," "fritinancy," "parachronic"). But in this most Joycean of Burgess' novels, that virtuoso atmosphere is precisely what appeals. The novel takes the population explosion as fictional opportunity and imagines a society presided over by a Ministry of Infertility which encourages homosexuality ("It's Sapiens to be Homo," is their motto) and forbids any woman to bear more than one child. As in *A Clockwork Orange* the lawless individual is at odds with a "benevolent" state; the heroine, Beatrice-Joanna, married to Tristram Foxe, a history teacher, is having an affair with Tristram's brother, a government official. Beatrice-Joanna's rebellion consists of her refusal to accept the death of her son and her rejection of the doctor's sensible advice: "Think of this in national terms, in global terms. One mouth less to feed. One more half-kilo of phosphorus pentoxide to nourish the earth. In a sense, you know, Mrs. Foxe, you'll be getting your son back again." Emerging from the clinic, she walks down the great London street (once Brighton but now a part of Greater London) to the sea and perceives it with a special poetry granted her:

> If only, she felt crazily, poor Roger's body could have been thrown into these tigrine waters, swept out to be gnawed by fish, rather than changed coldly to chemicals and silently fed to the earth. She had a mad intuitive notion that the earth was dying, that the sea would soon be the final repository of life. 'Vast sea gifted with delirium, panther skin and mantle pierced with thousands of idols of the sun—'. She had read that somewhere, a translation from one of the auxiliary languages of Europe. The sea drunk with its own blue flesh, a hydra, biting its tail.

Then looking up at the Government Building she sees the figure of a bearded man: "A cynosure to ships, man of the sea, Pelagius. But Beatrice-Joanna could remember a time when he had been Augustine. And, so it was said, he had been at other times the King, the Prime Minister, a popular bearded guitarist, Eliot (a long-dead singer of infertility), the Minister of Pisciculture, captain of the Hertfordshire Men's Sacred Game eleven, and most often and satisfactorily—the great unknown, the magical Anonymous." A hodge-podge of style perhaps, but no more so than *Ulysses*: at one moment the scientific knowingness of a Buck Mulligan, then the moody broodings of Stephen Dedalus, followed by an inventive Bloomlike list. What holds the various styles together is a linguistic virtuoso who moves his characters up and down the map of England: to complain as one reviewer did that the hero and heroine were mechanical contrivances is not to the point, since more "character," more recognizably human dimension, would destroy the fable.

For proof of this, consider the block of chapters describing Tristram's attempt to join his wife in the North of England (he has just escaped from jail and she, pregnant, has fled to her brother-in-law, an old-fashioned Roman Catholic, to have what turns out to be twins). As the state moves from a Pelagian phase to an Augustinian one, a great famine impels man toward cannibalism, fertility rites, the genesis of drama, and from homo-to-heterosexual love. Tristram observes these effects as he moves from

Brighton to Wigan, but we have heard reports of them already, courtesy of Anthony Burgess the announcer:

> . . . In Stoke-on-Trent the carcass of a woman(later identified as Marie Bennett, spinster, aged twenty-eight) grinned up suddenly — several good clean cuttings off her — from under a bank of snow. In Gillingham, Kent, Greater London, a shady back-street eating-shop opened, grilling nightly, and members of both police forces seemed to patronize it. In certain unregenerate places on the Suffolk coast there were rumours of big crackling Christmas dinners. . . . The New Year commenced with stories of timid anthropophagy. . . . Then the metropolis flashed its own sudden canines: a man called Amis suffered savage amputation of an arm off Kingsway; S. R. Coke, journalist was boiled in an old copper near Shepherd's Bush; Miss Joan Waine, a teacher, was fried in segments.

Some might consider this (especially the references to imagined fates of Angries) a debilitating cleverness, fatal to Burgess' art; to me it seems admirably indigenous to his ruthlessly literary sensibility. But in any case, it must be agreed that an attempt to give a hero traveling through such a scene much "dimension" would result in an awkward and uncertain book. *The Wanting Seed* is neither: its inventiveness is large enough that we are content to follow the fortunes of heroine and hero without desiring some further "inward" reach of understanding. What is to be understood — taken in — is put before us in the theatrical manner spoken of earlier. Even the closing paragraphs of the book, coming as they do after the longest of journeys and bringing together the Tristram Foxes and their twins, united on the promenade at Brighton, even these paragraphs are less a moving tribute to a particular man or woman than they are a general and now mythicized embodiment of love, of possibility: "She clung to him, the huge air, the life-giving sea, man's future history in the depths, the present towered town, the bearded man at the pinnacle, all shut out from the warmth of his presence, the closeness of his embrace. He became sea, sun, tower. The twins gurgled. There were still no words." And as if to formalize and make shimmery this closing atmosphere, the narrator dons prophetic robes and plays a late Shakespearean sage or Joycean lyricist, in language stolen from Valéry: "The wind rises . . . we must try to live. The immense air opens and closes my book. The wave, pulverized, dares to gush and spatter from the rocks. Fly away, dazzled, blinded pages. Break, waves. Break with joyful waters. . . ." This looks more vulnerable in quotation than it feels in the act of finishing the novel, although one understands how such writing might give rise to distrust or scepticism about its narrative poise. Burgess knows the extravagant overreaching that attaches to grand incantations, and as a rule his fictions do not make them. But *The Wanting Seed*, like *A Clockwork Orange*, has its affinities with the heroic poem: "faring forward" is saluted by the Bard when he ends his tale with an imitative gesture meant just as seriously as the cannibalistic jokes inspected earlier. In creative fantasy or fable, no suggestion that its figures are merely human is in order: Alex prepares to resume his career as a hoodlum; Beatrice-Joanna and Tristram prepare for — what? The fact is we are not interested in these "characters," only the action in which they have figured. A reader of *The Wanting Seed* must vouch to the extent that, like it or not, it is very much a linguistic action.

By contrast, *Honey for the Bears* would seem to be a return to the real world — The Soviet Union in 1963 — where Paul Hussey, an English antique dealer, and his American wife Belinda are engaged in smuggling in and selling twenty-dozen drilon dresses, the loot for which will be turned over to the widow of a dead friend. A mysterious rash sends Belinda to the hospital where she falls under the influence of a female Dr. Lazurkina who analyzes Paul as a homosexual ("gomosexual" without the "h" in Russian) and spirits Belinda off to the Crimea for what promises to be a long talk. Paul makes his own liaison with a bearded young Russian struggling to be hip and properly disenchanted about the modern state: "Russia or America," said Alexei Prutkov, "what's the difference? It's all the State. There's only one State. What we have to do is get together in these little groups and start to live." But after an unsuccessful attempt by Paul to seduce Alexei's mistress, and a drunken party where Paul suggests the guests strip "stark ballock naked," he is thrown out of Alexei's group with the accusation "What you like, dig, is your own sex, and that's what's so filthy and disgusting." Other humiliations and confusions follow (teeth knocked out, thrown into prison) until Paul leaves Russia, this time smuggling out (as his wife) the son of a Russian composer in disgrace named Opiskin, whose works Paul's dead friend Robert had loved.

It makes little difference whether we call this "plot" (inadequately summarized here) brilliant or absurd, so long as the detailing of it removes all suspicion that Burgess has abandoned us to Real Life in the Soviet Union today. *Honey for the Bears* is just as fantastic or fabulous as its two predecessors; characters (possibly excepting the hero) are viewed externally as ever, and their dimensions (and our sympathies) are thus severely limited. Stylistically the book moves at whirlwind pace with events and thoughts rapidly telescoped through Paul Hussey's mind; for example, on the first page we have this response to an unknown aged master in a wheelchair: "The face was trenched and riven, as by a killing life of metaphysical debauchery. That was it, decided Paul: a head that philosophy had unsexed, some final Shavian achievement. He had seen a head like it on television newsreels; an old proud eagle squatting in Whitehall among students, Banning the Bomb. But these oyster-coloured eyes surveyed with disdain the scruffy redbrick layabouts who nearly filled the Cultural Saloon, the nose twitched at them." Paul's own "unsexing" is to come, when by the end of the book he admits that he no longer knows what he is, sexually. And so the novel invites us, as did the earlier *Right to an Answer*, to relate the satiric intelligence accorded Paul in the passage above, to something he learns in Russia; more generally, to feel a unifying of the style of entertainment with the content of truth.

In the best single piece of writing about Burgess ("The Epicene," *New Statesman*, April 15, 1963) Christopher Ricks argues that this can be done, insofar as the book makes an analogy between sexual and political behavior. Politically the book presents America and Russia as equally monolithic and insufficient states, and opts instead for what Ricks calls a "Third Force." So, by analogy, homo and heterosexuality need not be exclusive choices; without singing hymns to bisexuality it can at least be entertained and admitted to be perhaps more fun, more attractive to the individual who would be free. Ricks points out correctly that this is a subversive message, but that it is transmitted in an "inventive and gay" manner that takes the fear out of it. And he goes on to claim that the book is more humane and "says more" than Burgess' earlier minglings of black violence with comic lightness. It would be pleasant to take *Honey for the Bears* as evidence of this kind of novelistic breakthrough, especially since at the moment it is the most recent full-fledged novel Burgess has given us. But it is much more problematic than Ricks suggests whether the "message" about sex and about politics is convincingly worked into the texture of the novel. There are difficulties in knowing just how to take Paul's sexual humiliations with his wife and Alexei's mistress—they are indeed fiascos, but do not recommend themselves to us as, in book-jacket language, "outrageously funny" or "wildly comic." They are no more comic than Paul's difficulty in keeping his false teeth in place. On the other hand the narrator makes no attempt to extend Paul sympathetic understanding. We are free, if we choose, to connect heterosexual failure with Paul's memories of "poor, dead Robert," though these memories are sentimental moonings we assume the narrator doesn't fully share. But even this is an assumption. Burgess treats Paul any way the spirit moves him: now harshly, now pathetically, now as a witty, perceptive satirical eye—all depending on the exigencies of a moment. When we try to say what these moments add up to the trouble begins. What they claim to add up to is concentrated in two passages late in the novel: in the first of these, Paul relates a dream to his cell-mates about how there was a little man who lived between two greatly opposing tsardoms. They bully the little man by giving him a wife who accuses him of not being a real man, an adequate protector. Like Belinda, the wife walks out. The second passage makes the Paul-as-England identification explicit: "I'm going back to an antique-shop, but somebody's got to conserve the good of the past, before your Americanism and America's Russianism make plastic of the world. . . . You'll learn about freedom from us yet." Even as he says it he feels a "doubt," as does surely the reader. For England (Rick's political "Third Force"?) is simply not *there* in the novel, any more than is Paul Hussey's inner life which, we are told, has undergone some sort of change. Once more, the imagination of comic disorder proves stronger than the fable's attempt to make thoughtful sense out of it.

This is not cause for alarm, nor a gloomy note on which to conclude. When Ricks says, in the essay mentioned above, that Burgess has yet to write a really "first-rate comic novel" we may feel the standards are high indeed after reading through a group of novels distinguished by their abundant qualities of imaginative energy, creative invention, complicated wit, and verbal delight. Since *Honey for the Bears* Anthony Burgess has given us a number of books somewhat off-the-center of his literary vision: juvenalia, a fascinating novelistic sport about Shakespeare, books on language and on Joyce. In a recent TLS article titled "The Manicheans" he mused aloud on why the novel has not made more use of religious experience, and he specified further: "I do not mean the tribulations of priests among the poor, or deanery gossip, or pre-ordination doubts; I mean rather the imaginative analysis of themes like sainthood, sin, the eschatological sanctions of behaviour, even that dangerous beatific vision." One of the best ways to analyze sin is to become a comic novelist; there is every reason to suspect that the remaining themes will occupy Burgess in the novels to come. At any rate we can be grateful for the books we have. After Nabokov there is no other, but that is because, in part, Nabokov sees the world through imaginatively obsessed narrator-madmen who impose their strange shapes on reality. Burgess, despite the variety of narrators and situations in his fiction, speaks to us as one of us: a fallen man with the usual amount of ambition, irritation, guilt, decency and common sense. Given such ordinary qualities or modest sins, how can things go as wrong as they do for the heroes of these painful books? That they go not just wrong, but marvelously wrong, is the result of the one quality Burgess does not share with the rest of us or with his heroes — the art of the novelist.

Notes

1. Depending on how you count. His first three published novels, counted here individually, form a trilogy. Aside from titles mentioned in this essay there is a youthful attempt, recently published, called *A Vision of Battlements*, another early, slight fable, *The Eve of St. Venus*, and two novels published under the pseudonym Joseph Kell. Titled *One Hand Clapping* and *Inside Mr. Enderby*, the latter have been just republished under Burgess' name. A new novel, *Tremor of Intent*, is scheduled for June.

2. Robert Garis, *The Dickens Theatre* (Oxford: Clarendon Press, 1965). Part I — "The Dickens Problem" — is filled with valuable observation about particular artistic styles and about literature in general.

The *Malayan Trilogy*: The Futility of History

Robert K. Morris*

Future historians will need no tomes to chart the choke, sob, and death rattle of the British Empire in the twentieth century. A few verses of Kipling, one or two pieces by Conrad, Waugh, and Forster, an essay by Orwell indicate the intellectual and ideological rift between pukka sahib and native, and lead us into those pockets of cultural confusion that have become the cul-de-sacs of imperialism. To read—if not to believe—Spengler or Toynbee is to know that whether empire wends its way eastward or westward, going in one direction long enough must bring it back to the beginning. A flourishing culture is incipiently a perishing one, the cycle of history being ineluctable, the seeds of imperialism begetting the roots of its own destruction.

About this, English writers have generally proved sanguine Cassandras, loathe to view the setting of Britain's sun apocalyptically. Instead they write nostalgically, ironically, dispassionately (or only intermittently passionately) of the end of colonialism, because, one imagines, the empire has been going out with a whimper and not a bang, and because the real holocausts and catastrophes of our century have outweighed the relatively minor frustrations accruing from British absentee landlordism.

Still, these accounts are monuments to the decline and fall of a once-great power. If they have anything like a major theme in common it is the social, political, and mental attrition of the ruler, who, through iron-fisted tactics or humanitarian impulses that have proved equally effete, must at last buckle to the gigantic, hard, irresistible will of the ruled. In the colonial realms of diminishing returns, attrition is no more geopolitical phenomenon; it is a psychological and spiritual one, as the author of "Shooting an Elephnat," the Kurtz of *Heart of Darkness*, the Mrs. Moore of *A Passage to India* discover. Attrition has been naturally easier to understand post facto than in its stages. And what gradually erodes the foundations of empire, what gradually contributes to its decay, has proved the more complex and valuable confrontation between the writer and his subject.

One of the most contemporary pictures of Britain's nagging *Götterdammerung* is the Malayan trilogy of Anthony Burgess, called in the American edition *The Long Day Wanes*. In theme and action these three novels—running together to a little over five hundred pages—set about to show the twilight of British rule in Malaya and the dawn of freedom for the Malayan states. Burgess's fidelity in treating the problems of a nation

*From *Continuance and Change: The Contemporary British Novel Sequence* (Carbondale: Southern Illinois University Press, 1972), 71–91. © 1972 by Southern Illinois University Press. Reprinted by permission of Southern Illinois University Press.

that has often seemed about as fathomable as a gibber of apes at a conference table opens new doors of perception on unpublicized reaches of empire and on the failed British mission. Less interested in exploring the hypersensitivity of Forster's "good" Indians and "bad" Englishmen (or vice versa), the metaphysics of evil of Conrad's, or the grotesque parodies of institutions and people of Waugh's darker continents, Burgess, a writer of wit and incredible verbal control, digs in to the nitty-gritty of the political, religious, and cultural mess in the Far East.

What he comes up with is a tragi-comic view of imperialism and an anatomy of the heart of Malaya. In technique Burgess is close to Waugh, but in sensibility he is closer to Orwell. Both understand the tempers of peoples pitted against the Western brand of progress, self-consciously and nationalistically dedicated to their emergence. But unlike Orwell, who views Burma as a force of homogeneous wills (and consequently *one* will) bent upon undermining and overturning the white man's power, Burgess sees Malaya in all its heterogeneity; sees its timeless conflicts arising as much from indigenous human nature as from abstractions like "brutality and jingoism" (to quote Orwell on Kipling) of imperialism; sees its people given to the same vices, vanities, frustrations, desires, and excesses, be they black, white, or yellow, English, Chinese, Eurasian, Malaysian, or Indian, Christian, Moslem, Buddhist, or Hindu.

Tough-minded, at bottom an ironist and comedian rather than a satirist, Burgess keeps the proper artistic distance from problems that obviously speak for themselves. Yet he is anything but cautious and tentative. The opening line of the trilogy — "East? They wouldn't know the bloody East if they saw it" — is a headlong plunge into Burgess's central theme: distrust, both intellectually and humanistically, of the historic process, a process made more futile than risky owing to pretense, turpitude, and, most often, simple ignorance. Soft-pedaling the philosophic or emotional implications, Burgess sets out to prove that only empirically must the setting of one sun necessarily mean the rising of another; to prove (as Robert Penn Warren has written of *Nostromo*) that the "moral regeneration of society depends not upon shifts in mechanisms, but upon the moral regeneration of men."[1]

History is chapter and verse of the trilogy, and Victor Crabbe, quondam teacher of history its hero. Crabbe, liberal, sensual, dry, superior in intellect, conscience, and guilt, displays a comically bungling dexterity in the sure-footed descent that marks his own literal death and the symbolic death of the British Empire in Malaysia. Somehow boosted higher and higher up the tottering ladder of administrative school posts, but nevertheless grown more ineffectual in his ability to strike a rapport all around, Crabbe suffers corresponding personal defeats, deteriorating in his physical and social habits, withdrawing into a shell of cynicism, scuttling randomly — as befits his name — over the flotsam and jetsam of his life, a life of failures without successes, nadirs without climaxes, battles without victor-ease. Crabbe's move from disillusionment and disaffection to alienation, from dissipation to revulsion, from sordidness and impotence to an absurd death, counterpoints the rise of Malaysia and contrasts ironically the sudden agony of individual change with the impersonal, maddeningly leisurely forward march of events.

Throughout the trilogy, history and hero interpenetrate. Both are extremely viable, history being for Burgess not memory but the living pattern that Crabbe (agent, reflector, commentator, pawn) experiences. By living in the present, Crabbe hopes to escape, or at least blot out a past that he dreads. ("Memory had no significance . . . dreams were not memory," he muses before his shaving mirror. The gulf between *The Long Day Wanes* and *The Time of Time*, or the *Alexandria Quartet*, or, to a lesser degree, *Strangers and Brothers* is, over so singular a theme as memory and the past, immense.) Crabbe's psyche, however, is but part of Burgess's historic perspective and his novelistic method. Underplaying the sense of the past which in the timeless East doesn't exist anyway, or at most exists uniformly—"Malaya . . . warm, slummy comfort as permanent as the surrounding mountain-jungle"—and focusing on what is immediate and palpable, Burgess paints continuous pictures of English and Malaysian "history," and impels into the cycle the dead past, the fluctuating present, the unpredictable, but certain, future.

Via James Joyce—Burgess is a Joycean scholar as well as a practicing disciple—has come, undoubtedly, a concern with Vico and cyclical theories of history. Burgess is less attracted by Vico's general laws of growth, decay, and regrowth through which all civilizations must pass, than by his analogy of civilizations evolving parallel to children developing—acquiring knowledge, that is, through growing experience. Thus with Crabbe and thus with Malaya. As freedom dawns for the new nation, in the jungle is written the ironic coda to his own education. Journeying upriver to investigate the murder of a colonial—a journey that invites comparison with Marlowe's in *Heart of Darkness* and Tony Last's in *A Handful of Dust*—Crabbe meets the rubber-planter George Costard, symbol of British Toryism and the foundering empire.

> I'm in this game to keep something alive that's very, very beautiful. The feudal tradition, the enlightened patriarchal principle. You people have been throwing it all away, educating them to revolt against us. They won't be happy, any of them. It's only on the estates now that the old ideas can be preserved. I'm the father of these people. They can look up to me, bring me their troubles and let me participate in their joys. Don't you think that's good and beautiful? They're my children, all of them. I correct them, I cherish them, I show them the way they should go.[2]

In this slightly irregular Viconian mirror, Crabbe sees reflected the distorted shapes of his own education. The past, now almost totally suppressed, rises before him when he inadvertently discovers that Costard was the lover of his first wife, now dead, drowned when a car Crabbe was driving skidded on an English country road and plunged into an icy river. Illuminated, disillusioned, limping from a scorpion bite — one of Burgess's many "touches" — Crabbe slips as he is boarding the temporarily deserted launch that took him up river and himself drowns.

Hegelian thought, too, sifts through *The Long Day Wanes*. The interpreter of Vico for the post-Renaissance world, the intellectual ante- cedent of Spengler and Toynbee, Hegel placed the keystone, if not the foundation, of the arch through which all modern students of history must pass. Cold, precise, deterministic in its metaphysics, the Hegelian dialectic is both logical and phenomenological, but ultimately antihumanistic and ethically deplorable to anyone who sees the historical process continually renewing itself at the expense of human beings, to anyone who views as hopeless and nihilistic a process by which ends not only justify means, but are sacrificed to them. Thesis, antithesis, synthesis; the unholy trinity of materialism! And the synthesis that becomes a new thesis in this eternal genesis of organization and reorganization may be stronger, though not necessarily better, as Burgess suggests at the opening of the trilogy's final volume, *Beds in the East*. "Dawn of freedom for yet another nation, freedom and all the rest of the abstractions. Dawn, dawn, dawn, and people waking up with various kinds of mouths and carried-forwards of the night or day before. Dawn, anyway."[3]

One other appendage of the Hegelian doctrine is sportively twisted by Burgess: the belief that great men are those whose personal aims coincide with the aims of history. For Burgess, there are no such men; or, with Joyce's Bloom or Earwicker, one man becomes "allmen," great and small. Crabbe runs the gamut of historic personages, metamorphosed in thought into Hamlet, Aeneas, Theseus, Don Quixote, Ulysses (the title of the trilogy is a line from the Tennyson poem), and Caesar. The coda to the sequence — a liberation-day party at which Crabbe's secretary is seen crying in her crab mousse — is, in fact, a memento mori on his historical effectiveness. "Poor, Victor . . . poor, poor Victor," she sobs. "He came, he saw, he conquered," responds a young subaltern. "Victor ludorum."[4] Victor of the games! The allusion and bilingual pun ironically formulate Crabbe: a tragi-comic Caesar, failed in apparently the simplest of mis- sions, the least meaningful of intrigues, the most rudimentary of relation- ships.

Antihero Victor Crabbe (Victoria Cross for inconspicuous bravery?) is also an anti-Hegelian who has lost his cool as well as his dialectic. He is, though part of the historical flux, at odds with it, undermined by his romanticism and hopelessly clashing with the impenetrable will, the immovable spirit, the inscrutable mind of the East. Like yet another Joycean hero — the Stephen Dedalus of *Ulysses* — Crabbe teaches history, and he, too, is trying to awake from its nightmarish provisos — not the "cry in the streets" of "dear, dirty, Dublin," but the slow-motion antics of

Malaysian life that too easily draw one into forgetfulness. Images of sleep, beds, drunkenness sift through the trilogy, beginning with the titles of individual books. The first, *Time for a Tiger*, alludes to the brand name of a potent, stupefying beer; the second, *The Enemy in the Blanket*, to potential surrender to expatriation and Eastern sensuousness; the last, *Beds in the East* — a quotation from *Antony and Cleopatra* — to relaxation of all responsibility and, ironically, loveless total abandonment.

These irresistible forces must finally get the better of Crabbe. We first meet him fitfully sleeping next to his wife, Fenella; and, morning after morning, he wakes to neglect her, to seek out sordid liaisons, to twit his superiors, to alienate his colleagues and friends, to fall prey to enemies — potentially every native is the white man's enemy — lurking in the blanket. Even for Westerners "the patterns of the East are few." But Crabbe's life of plod and monotony reflects less an actual resistance to change than a flouting of Establishment codes. It is ideologism, not apathy, nor egoism, nor even idealism that carries him over the ruts. His vulnerability, erosion, death are forged by the desire to dissipate a particular vision of human life and culture cherished for hundreds of years by the anomaly known as British colonial: one who through an infectious romanticism has preserved enchantment (albeit superficial) with the dreamy poetry and retard of the East, and (worse) a patronizing charity toward its natives.

> The romantic dream . . . was no longer appropriate to an age in which sleep was impossible. The whole East was awake, building dams and canals, powerhouses and car factories, forming committees, drawing up constitutions, having selected from the West the few tricks it could understand and use. . . . Liberalism, itself a romantic dream had long gone under . . . and there was no longer any room for the individual, there was nothing now that any one man could build. . . . It was time he cleared the romantic jungle in which he wanted to lurk, acknowledged that life was striving not dreaming, and planted the seeds of a viable relationship.[5]

Thus autistically, and by soft lies, we bridge the way things were and the way things are, and, like Crabbe, become the dupe of our best intentions and failed resolutions. The intention to shrug off this somnolence so sanely and keenly inveighed against is perfectly countered by the desire not to. "Good, too, Logic, of course; in itself, but not in fine weather" runs an epigraph to the sequence. Ambivalence, not speciousness, gnaws at Crabbe. Inching forward with Malaysia and loosing it for independence, or retreating and devouring the lotus of indolence; these are choices that neither entirely exclude nor entirely complement each other. Malaysia, the East are of themselves ambivalent. On the surface, the daily comedy of quarrels, flurries, peccadilloes, laíssez faire, innocent trespasses on ingrained but passé taboos; below, the whirring, demonic dynamo. The East, as Burgess sees it, is both active and passive, containing the principles of yin and yang, humming at both poles of the dialectic at once: a phenomenon alien to the West, which, nurtured on Hegelian propositions, submits to the certainty of either cyclical or linear progression.

Change and no change, history and no history are the paradoxes Crabbe wrestles with and cannot master, just as the East itself is seemingly unable to master its master paradox, everywhere displayed but nowhere decipherable: starved and naked Communist guerrillas in the jungle, luxury and decadence in the cities; the deadly logic of revolution confronting the politics of conservatism; gracious, civil protocol facing "ambushers, eviscerations, beheadings"; the thrust for freedom vis-à-vis complacency; primitive magic against rationalism, polygamy against prostitution, life cult against death cult.

It is not difficult to understand Crabbe's obsession with history throughout *The Long Day Wanes*. History-less forces, built up over thousands of years, are suddenly pushing him onto the threshold of discovery, and, as inert as he is, impelling him over the detritus of the lives of the Westerners who have escaped from timelessness into the mainstream of history: Nabby Adams, Fenella Crabbe, Rupert Hardman. All, despite their weaknesses, were fighting the lure of the East, refusing to remain cloddish or to become, in the final sense, absorbed.

"Absorbed" is a motif that begins metaphorically and ends in earnest literalness. The word evokes and controls contexts of thought, as much Burgess's as Crabbe's. Little ambiguity remains after the extended interplay of definitions. In every sense Crabbe *is* absorbed into the East, into the "head-reeling collocation of cultures," into the emotion, if not the actual rationale of history. The East abstracts, engrosses, engulfs him, only as the pulsation of a timeless body existing as a timeless pattern could.

His colleague, Raj, lightly prophesies early in the trilogy, "The country will absorb you and you will cease to be Victor Crabbe. . . . You will lose function and identity . . . You will be swallowed up."[6] This trifling badinage of the smoking room later becomes a kind of intuitive warning. Crabbe's immediate, sensuous impressions of changeless Kenching (fictitious capital of the fictitious state, Dahaga) surrender to the disturbing realization that the "future would be like the past," that those British who remain in Malaya might also, like the dozens of migrants and conquerors before them, be absorbed. And shortly before his separation from Fenella (more sinned against than sinning), Crabbe takes refuge in the comfort of a cliché, both defensible and admissable, yet nevertheless implying acquiescence to the overwhelming principle. It is the cracking of his carapace, the point of no return. "We've got to be absorbed into these customs. We're still too tough to be ingested quickly, but we've got to try and soften ourselves to a bolus, we've got to yield."[7] Raj's earlier words, flashing through Crabbe's mind during the fatal journey into the interior, now become converted into an ironic anti-prophecy as he rejects the idea of "his never going home, his complete assimilation to the country . . . [his] leaving his bones up river . . . the grave quickly becoming a native shrine to be loaded with supplicatory bananas and flowers."[8] What indeed happens so absurdly to Scobie in the *Alexandria Quartet* happens grotesquely to Crabbe. History is past master at distorting, at giving the lie. "History [Crabbe comments vehemently on the launch] . . . the best thing is to put all that in the books and forget about it. . . . We've got to throw up the past otherwise we can't live in the present. The past has got to be killed."[9] Crabbe, of course, who is the past for the East *is* killed, while the Indian veterinarian Vythilingham, professionally and ideologically removed from that great abstraction "humanity" for which Crabbe so ungainly sacrifices himself, looks dispassionately on. Crabbe struggles and subsides, his body absorbed into the river, his spirit into "jungle, river and sky," his class and empire into a Malaysia that foreshadows an absorption, as ironic as his own, into the past and history.

Like Tony Last's or Jay Gatsby's death, Victor Crabbe's symbolizes the dissipation of an illusion, the end of an era, and consequently is charged socially and morally. But his remains a psychological disaster. For Burgess is at hard core a realist who believes in character and in creating believable characters. Crabbe's psychological rout is predictable, though nonetheless eloquent. Once he begins growing in awareness — and it isn't long into the novel before he does — perceptions multiply so rapidly that he barely has time to take stock of them; their diversity and intensity, as well as his own sensitivity, undermine him. Burgess calls Crabbe into life not only amidst a confusion of cultures but amidst a profusion of "things." We know Crabbe as much from his sensations as from his revelations; not least of all the attraction for, the total immersion in, the sensuousness and movement of a Malaysia teeming with "mosques and . . . muezzins," fishmongers and magic, "shadow-plays about mythical heroes, bull-fights and cock-fights . . . axeing, love-potions, coconuts, rice, the eternal rule of the Abang."[10]

We know Crabbe, too, from the other characters who, at times, so dominate that he becomes a weaker, partially a subordinate, figure. The technique, an old one, is in the great tradition of the English comic novel, which, from Fielding on, has basically been the novel of memorable minor types. It is this peripheral world of *The Long Day Wanes* that is in many ways more remarkable and less remote than the central one of Crabbe's consciousness. It is the periphery of Durrell's Alexandria, of Powell's London, of Mrs. Manning's Bucharest and Athens; a periphery that evokes the fullness of Darley or Jenkins or Guy and Harriet Pringle; that energizes the sequence and prevents its falling (as too often the case with Snow or Mrs. Lessing) into unrelieved intellectual patterns.

These sometimes tragic, generally comic, foils to Crabbe are individually set in each section. Nabby ("Abel") Adams, the beer-swilling sergeant of police, boondoggler par excellence and perhaps Burgess's best single creation in the trilogy, hulks through *Time for a Tiger* with Rabelaisian appetite and lustiness — a warm, natural, giant of a man, exaggerating through expansiveness and instinct Crabbe's constriction and inertia. Adams is a kind of idle Hercules, nonintellectually absorbing the East, while Crabbe, the misguided, beset Atlas, labors under it, shouldering its burdens, crushed by it in the end.

And so, almost, is Rupert Hardman, lawyer, who occupies most of the second book. Hardman, a practicing expatriate riddled with *Weltschmerz*, seeks to revitalize himself, mend his finances, and "become" the East through his marriage to Che Normah — a sort of "bathycolpic" Wife of Bath — which entails surrender of identity through change of name and conversion to the Moslem faith. Hardman is a step beyond Nabby and one before Crabbe, for he wishes, at first, to play no role, to match — at its simplest level — the thing for the fact. But if Nabby can absorb, and Crabbe be absorbed, Hardman can do neither. Nor can he convince himself that a cycle of Cathay is better than fifty years of Europe, and so defects for England, deserting his pregnant, though still inordinately nympholeptic wife on a voyage to the Holy Land.

In part three are the separate stories of Rosemary Michael and Robert Loo. Rosemary, "black but comely," evoking delights of "houris, harems, and beds scented with Biblical spices," is a naïve, pliant sex-pot, obsessed with the idea of marrying a European, and through most of the novel hoping that Joe, current in her formidable list of white lovers ("she could not stand the touch of brown fingers"), will call her to England and to the finest society. Robert is a musically precocious and sexually repressed young Chinese, who, in his father's restaurant, amidst the babble of voices and blare of the jukebox, against the "cyclorama of tins of mild and corned beef," composes symphonies. Rosemary and Robert, one in comic pretentiousness, the other in pathetic earnest, are also heirs of two cultures. Both are in the rudimentary stages of sophistication; without having fully abdicated their birthright as children of the East, they display, unwittingly, the inverse yearning of East for West. Both, too, in their frustrations and desires, express the birth pangs and confusion of the coming Malaysia; and both are "pursued" by the West: she by a farcically lecherous stage Turk ("a Muslim . . . who looked like a European"); he, in quite another way, by Crabbe, who dreams of his (Loo's) becoming free Malaysia's first serious composer.

Nabby Adams, Rupert Hardman, Rosemary Michael, and Robert Loo represent two faces, East and West, and are set apart from Crabbe; or rather, being of another breed, he is excluded from their ken. He functions differently. Though they are introspective, though they live under the zodiac of individualized obsessions — snobbery of caste, religion, position or race, desire for power, wealth, women or motor cars, dedication to drinking, lusting, or fornicating — their *idée fixe* is not, like Crabbe's, universal. Like most who rarely intellectualize the condition of life, they accept it or do not accept it; but at all events know what they want. As extraordinary and eccentric as Burgess's characters may be, their concern is with realities, not abstractions. Burgess, in his comic wisdom, has seen how we are all tragically self-centered. Even while a nation vibrates with new consciousness and hope as it stands ready to leap into freedom, its people are concerned with their petty, immediate, (to them) significant lives, with, in short, palpable truth, not any sort of enduring one. They opt for "human lives . . . not humanity." Crabbe easily becomes the outsider. Hagridden by ideals and the idea of humanity with which he can inspire no one, he drives against self-interest and the ethos — randomly, moodily, finally morbidly questing after an impossible dream.

Thus, while others seem to shift or balance, Crabbe is the only one who properly changes, moving as he does vertically as well as horizontally. The drama within is played all the while against the externalities — against those who remain or depart, against Malaysia, against class and country — and against the crucial constant, time itself, by which, through which, he is supported and undermined. Time marks his psychical and cyclical risings and fallings, time marks the incurrent awareness that his powers are waning along with the long day, and time seemingly marks, its own inherent paradox: the Western concept of time, that is, being at odds with and useless in an East where time is beyond conventional construction. Crabbe's change often seems violent, as any change would seem violent in a world where time is standing still; and the process of change here, too, is an inverted one, marked by the regularity of a negative time.

This is much less a paradox than it appears, though the effect is curious. Through a rain of Eastern languages (snatches of seven, all told), through precise, idiomatic dialogue, and through a rhetoric that can do somersaults, in places even shoot off rockets, Burgess captures the flowing immediacy of the present. Yet running side by side, from beginning to end, is a feeling countering the present, a feeling of opaqueness and sameness. There are scenes of soliloquy and stream-of-consciousness — the most controlled techniques for rendering time slowly — and the iteration of motifs (especially words like "timelessness," "changelessness," "unchanging") that have a dying fall, impinging upon our senses as much as upon Crabbe's, and slowing down action to a standstill.

Metaphorically Crabbe is lured by the life around him into the endless sea of time. Yet being an occidental he fights against its breakers. Not so the oriental, who knows that time is timeless, that inaction is the way of the East and the great Lao-tse, and that, logically, inaction is therefore timeless. It's useless to understand, pinpoint, analyze it with such extrusive philosophies that Europeans like Vico, Hegel, Bergson, or Einstein propound. Asia contemplates time, does not resist it, bathes, and becomes awash in it. This is the hardest lesson for Crabbe, and he learns it only by giving up trying to understand it and abdicating all occidental sensibilities, but learns it much too late.

Time, impinging in the East with the force of timelessness, charts Crabbe's change, not rigorously but through loose stages, outlined objectively as well as subjectively. Burgess's point in using the ominiscient narrator is to sift the psyche of the East almost simultaneously with that of Crabbe, imparting a realistic or naturalistic flavor to the novel, and keeping it always on the pitch of discovery in true *Bildungsroman* fashion.

Perspectives shift in time — it is yet another of the ways in which we watch Crabbe change — but time itself, the immovable blackcloth, scarcely shifts at all. The idea, simple as it is cosmic, logical as it is persistent, burgeons out of the East, rooted as much in providence as in passivity or "mere impossibility." A word, a concept, a way of life controls the idea. It is *Tida' apa*. " '*Tida' apa*' meant so much more than 'It doesn't matter' or 'Who cares?' There was something indefinable and satisfying about it, implying that the universe would carry on, the sun shine, the durians fall."[11] To the mind of the East *Tida' apa* is psychologically and temporally the reflex action of inaction, implying that all change, being the same, is therefore useless and unnecessary; an oriental *Weltanschauung* that even today — the trilogy dates from 1956 — has not completely been dissipated, despite Japan's leap from isolation to world conquest, despite the dramatic rise of communism in China, Korea, Vietnam, or Malaysia itself. For many, *Tida' apa* — apart from its stoic or quasi-religious connotations — bespeaks a certain optimism for the East, whereas for the West inevitability or fatality is viewed pessimistically. And to the Western mind, decadent in its glut of progress, *Tida' apa* seems sheer nihilism, somewhat more frightening, in fact, for being nihilistic and positive together.

The phrase causes at first mild rebellion in Crabbe, intent on shoring up the ruins of his own past by building anew a future for the Malaysians.

> The process of which . . . he was a part was an ineluctable process. His being here, in a brown country, sweltering in an alien classroom, was prefigured and ordained by history. For the end of the Western pattern was the conquest of time and space. But out of time and space came point-instants, and out of point-instants came a universe. So it was right that he stood here now, teaching the East about the Industrial revolution, [about how to] judge Shakespeare by the Aristotelian yardstick, hear five-part counterpoint and find it intelligible."[12]

But it is not right, neither for them nor for Crabbe. Here can be seen the first moment of a dissolving dialectic, as Crabbe rationalizes from inevitability, justifies the wrenching of segments from history to fit the case. It is, like his indiscretions of the ego and libido, born of an infatuation for what is novel in the Orient. Crabbe courts the Orient as a lover, still hidebound by his wife, courts a mistress. His real wife, Fenella, comes to fully realize what his laxity prevents him from ever realizing, that Western values cannot easily be subsumed in novelty for very long, that there must always be atavistic clashes between East and West. Fenella, a hypersensitive woman, and a painstaking, if not terribly good poet, writes a poem about Malaysia, describing it as a land where time has no movement, where the hours "set like ice-cubes," where people live "in sight of that constant eye" of the sun, where the "beasts" live in "day's denomination." Fenella sees how impossible it is for the Westerner to live in the timeless, monolithic present that blots out or buries the past: to scrap, that is, the time and space continuum of history for the "point-instants" of the universe of *Tida' apa*.

Fenella's poem does momentarily spur Crabbe's longing for England. It comes at a pivotal point in the novel, a point about which he can spin back and recover some of his past, a point after which he cannot. Crabbe remains committed, fearing that relaxation of hope will cut him off even further from human intercourse; fearing, too, the botch he knows the Malaysians will make of their first months of independence without some steady hand, a fear both truistically and altruistically founded.

The assistant headmaster, Jaganathan, an ugly, pompous, jealous sort, hopeful of taking over upon independence, unwittingly helps sever further Crabbe's ties with the West. Blackmailing Crabbe about his various revolutionary activities and writings as an undergraduate in England with the intention of bullying and bending him, has precisely the opposite effect. For while Jaganathan's naïveté and buffoonery in matters of Establishment college-Communists (though the paranoia over communism in Malaysia is still neither simple nor comic), infuriates Crabbe, it also churns up a stony nostalgia for an idealism spawned in the now-dead world of his salad days. It confirms his ties with the East, revives him, alerts him once again to the viability of continuance and change.

Crabbe really feels that he can be instrumental in building the new Malaysia. As the novel moves toward its denouement and peripeteia, Crabbe, the raw ideals of youth transformed at last into middle-aged thoughts of purpose, moves toward the timeless dream of history. Despite general antagonisms, despite many troublesome persons like Jaganathan, despite anxiety over irrevocable choices, despite having cut himself off from his wife, despite all self-castigations, he regains, with something of the earlier intensity, this vitalizing idealism.

> Crabbe looked at himself [in the mirror]: hair now riding back from his forehead, the beginning of a jowl. He looked down at his paunch, pulled it in, flinched at the effort, let it out again. He thought it was perhaps better to be middle-aged, less trouble. That growing old was a matter of volition was a discovery he had only recently made, and it pleased him. It was infantile, of course, like the pleasure of controlling excretion, but transitional periods in history had always appealed him most—Silver

Ages, Hamlet phases, when past and future were equally palpable, and opposing, could produce current.[13]

This is not the voice of a Prufrock—though in a kind of Eliotesque extension Crabbe does find the "objective correlative" for his own middle-aged transition in the transition of Malaysia—but of a Leopold Bloom. Life, and it is significant that it *is* life, is affirmed, placed (however ironically things may turn out) in the framework of renewed discovery. Nor is it Crabbe's fault entirely that such affirmation casts a long, fatal, negative shadow. Given the fickle premises of history and the argument of change, the conclusion is inevitable. For Malaysia, the past must become one thing; for Crabbe, another—the bridge to his death. This all-important bridge—somewhat shakily constructed at the eleventh hour by Burgess, considering the weight it must carry—leads from logic to metaphysics. With the recognition that the past, England, "the mandarin world" is dead—a recognition reached by travels over the rough roads of Fenella's melancholia, Hardman's eloquence, Costard's slightly hysterical jeremiads—Crabbe immerses himself in the timeless dream most completely. This is Burgess's *coup de théâtre* in *The Long Day Wanes*. Crabbe drowns.

But the *Malayan Trilogy* is not just a composite of rhetorical fripperies, wit, puns, flirtations with language, and love affairs with technique. It is not merely a comedy of misplaced idealism, alienation, despair, impotence, or transparent ideologies—though it is, of course, all these as well. It is foremost a continuing drama of change: how one man encounters and experiences it, founders upon and succumbs to it. It is a novel of one man borne by one current while beating against another, of one hard-shelled but vulnerable, of one aloof but involved, of one not deep, but sensitive and sincere. It is a novel of one better than so many, yet, in the end, not quite sufficient.

Though Crabbe does battle with the snobbism and mediocrity of his own class and with the indolence and insouciance of Malaysia, he is, when all is tallied, perhaps a crusty vestige of that Western liberalism and humanitarianism that has historically proved so ineffectual. As the "timeless dream"—a motif not only insistent but impossible to escape—history is futile. Yet one goes on in spite of it, does not surrender because of it. For the sense of the present for the East is ever omnipresent, blotting out the past, ordaining the future. Crabbe's own early musings on the finality of the past, the fiction of history (" a kind of story" is how he defines it for his class) anticipates the conclusion to the novel as well as provides precise commentary on history's futility:

> It was unnatural to give life to the dead [i.e., through memory]. The dead are fractured, atomized, dust in the sunlight, dregs in the beer. Yet the fact of love remains and to love the dead is, in the nature of things, impossible. One must love the living, the living fractured and atomized

into individual bodies and minds that can never be close, never be important. For if one were to mean more than the others, then we should be back again, identifying and, with sudden shocks, contrasting, and bringing the dead back to life. The dead are dead.[14]

Throughout the trilogy, Crabbe, for all his major failings, abides by this philosophy, is filled with this sort of love. He is all too human — one who, like most, revels in great victories but most often welters in little failures. He worships the living and the promise of living, but for him, as for England, the day has waned. The present, which was once the future for the past, will now become the past for the future. And Crabbe, a victor-come-lately, like the very stork of the night who comes last (as a second epigraph to the novel has it) and is "torn to pieces" while the others "get them gone," has been sacrificed to this irresistible historic principle, symbolized so often in the sequence by the eternal sun — the image of timelessness itself — that has set before, will set again, on countless, weary empires.

Black and Ugly: Toward the West   A. A. DeVitis[*]

I The Right to an Answer

In his *Malayan Trilogy*, Anthony Burgess is successful in describing the influx of the West into the Malayan world partly because of the characterization of Victor Crabbe, the protagonist. As Crabbe becomes more and more involved with the East and as the reader begins to understand the claims of politics, religion, and race upon a polyglot nation emerging into the machine menace of the twentieth century, a certain rapport is established between author and audience. Romantic, bewildered, visionary, Crabbe moves into the arenas of politics, religion, and race and develops, primarily through his reactions to people caught in bewildering situations, a rich, comic appreciation of a world that is content with insanity and determined on destruction. Crabbe lives and acts "as if" there were some ultimate purpose behind existence, but he is fully aware of life's ironic absurdities.

As a result of the characterization, the reader discovers quite soon that the real problems underlying communication and understanding between East and West are not so much ideological as theological: that the relationship of man to God and thence to man forms a religious complex that needs not so much explanation as appreciation. No scene in Burgess's

*From *Anthony Burgess* (New York: Twayne, 1972), 69–79. Reprinted with the permission of Twayne Publishers, a division of G. K. Hall & Co.

trilogy better illustrates this point than the comic "bridge" party, the device by which Crabbe intends to plant the seeds of pride in an indigenous art among the disparate groups of Malaya. The themes, then, that inform the action of the *Malayan Trilogy* are religious: commitment and responsibility, guilt and personal redemption. The jargon of present-day Existential thought can be employed in this regard to explain and justify: Existentialism can even be used to assess the heroism of the protagonist, and Crabbe does come perilously close to achieving heroic stature in the course of the novel.

But Crabbe, preoccupied as he is with guilt, reflects a religious more than a philosophical concern. Indeed, in Burgess's world it soon becomes apparent that all actions ultimately reflect a concern with man as a creature capable of performing good and evil actions. Sometimes this theological preoccupation is symbolically implied; sometimes it is belligerently portrayed; but more often than not, it is disguised in comic dress. Nevertheless, the final consideration remains religious. Crabbe's death in the *Malayan Trilogy*, enigmatic, poignant, symbolically and artistically appropriate, implies but does not insist upon a theological comment, as does Scobie's final action in Graham Greene's *The Heart of the Matter*. Whether Crabbe stumbles accidentally, his cane unable to support him, or whether he falls into the river's waters intentionally, is assuredly a problem of theological purport; but Burgess wisely does not insist, and it is unnecessary for him to do so. The symbolism of death by water portrays tellingly enough the religious aspects of the scene. If the reader feels forced to make a judgment, he does so at his own risk.

In *The Right to an Answer* (1960),[1] the concern with the nature of responsibility is extended and achieves a new comic ambiance through the sybaritic narrator, J. W. Denham. And again the reader is introduced to a world that is at once real and allegorical. Like the *Malayan Trilogy*, *The Right to an Answer* is an extremely witty book. Like the trilogy, its parts, which at first appear disparate, nevertheless cohere, primarily because of the originality of the characters, the ingeniousness of the comic devices, and the "black humor" that both horrifies and delights.

Richly textured, *The Right to an Answer* is "a study of provincial England, as seen by a man on leave from the East, with special emphasis on the decay of traditional values in an affluent society."[2] The influence of Vladimir Nabokov is apparent on Burgess's art in the emphasis that Burgess places on language as he forces it to enlarge character and add dimension to his religious theme. In a review of Andrew Field's *Nabokov: His Art in Life* (1967), Burgess comments on Nabokov's method and throws light on his own in devising a novel. Speaking of Quilty, the antagonist of *Lolita*, Burgess observes: "The enemy Quilty (*Qu'il t'y mène*—let him take you there) opens up a surrealistic world where identities are unsure, the enemy is the *alter ego*, action is dream. Each new reading of the book . . . invites warier treading."[3] And he then observes that Nabokov, in reacting to the plain style—Hemingway's and Maugham's—reminds the reader that plainness engenders emasculation of language; Nabokov "shows that pedantry can be a kind of dandyism, and that ecstasy and rich humor are not really strange bedfellows" (*The New York Times Book Review*, July 2, 1967, p. 20).

The use of the alter ego, of action as dream, and of language as enlarging upon and as leading into ritual, each underscored by hilarity and grotesque comedy, are, indeed, devices borrowed from Nabokov; but again, as in Burgess's earlier books, the demands of the theme determine the originality of the book. The subterranean life of the novel is what distinguishes it: a seeming slip, "communionism" for "communism"; a pattern of drinking and eating, suggesting the Roman Catholic mass; gestures of benediction; and a gangster-God justifying an anti-heroic protagonist.

In his Malayan trilogy, Burgess introduced a Westerner into the East; in *The Right to an Answer*, he introduces a Ceylonese into the English suburban world of wife-swapping, pub-drinking, "telly" viewing, and film-star worshiping. The world that Mr. Raj enters is the world of English suburbia, a world dominated by television but a world still capable of provoking tragedy.

The narration of the *Malayan Trilogy* is in the third person, but the action is chiefly portrayed through Crabbe's romantic eyes; history and change are his preoccupations. The narration of *The Right to an Answer* is first person; and it becomes important to understand the protagonist if any assessment of the novel's theme is to be arrived at: "I'm telling this story mainly for my own benefit. I want to clarify in my own mind the nature of the mess that so many people seem to be in nowadays," writes J. W. Denham on the first page. "I lack the mental equipment and the training and the terminology to say whether the mess is social or religious or moral . . ." (7). The social, religious, or moral mess that is England is what Burgess confronts the reader with in the course of the novel's activities; and he places his fine focus on adultery and responsibility.

On leave from his well-paying job in Japan, Denham, the narrator, finds himself in the suburbs of a large midland city visiting his father, a retired printer. Early in the account of his visit to his father, Denham observes that the church spire interferes with television reception; but his father does not mind, especially since his sight is failing. Denham also observes that the life of the community centers on either the "telly" or the pub; and, of the two, the pub is preferable because the people there, even though they come from the sterile suburb, do drink Babycham and bitter, and do go through the motions of living. The Black Swan or Mucky Duck, presided over by Ted Arden, whose resemblance to Shakespeare is explained by his descent from Shakespeare's mother's family, stands "in a pocket of village"; it is "the dirty speck round which the pearly suburb had

woven itself," "a tiny reservation for aborigines" (12). The setting of the
novel is terrifying, surreal.

After watching the "telly," whose images produce doppelgangers
"that seem to stand a step behind," Denham and his father make their way
to the pub. There Denham observes a version of musical chairs called
"wife-swapping." He meets Winter the printer, whose name he immediately divines as Winterbottom (Cold Arse). Then he meets Winter's wife,
Alice, who is in the company of Charlie Whittier, Jack Brownlow, and
Brownlow's wife; Denham recognizes this group as a Saturday-night
foursome. Ted Arden, the Mucky Duck's host, occasions a reverie concerning the nature of British social and communal life. Denham knows that he
himself is rich enough to stock his father's house with all the drinks of Ted
Arden's pub, to install a small bar if he wants to: "But it is recognized in
England that home drinking is no real pleasure. We pray in a church and
booze in a pub: profoundly sacerdotal at heart, we need a host in both
places to preside over us. In Catholic churches as in continental bars the
host is there all the time. But the Church of England kicked out the Real
Presence and the licensing laws give the landlord a terrible sacramental
power" (21–22).

When Ted Arden asks Denham to stay behind after the others have
left, Denham feels that Ted is giving him grace, holding back death, and
making him a lordly gift of extra life. In the presence of Hieronymus
Bosch-like grotesques – Selwyn, an imbecile with the gift of prophecy;
Cedric, the barboy; Arden himself and his wife, Veronica; and a gruff
boxer – Ted Arden invites Denham to pay for a bottle of mysterious liquor
whose Cyrillic label indicates that it might be Russian vodka. "I reckon the
Russians is as good as what we are," growls the boxer. "What is this
Communionism? It's everybody doing their best for everyone else, the way
I see it" (23). The liquor is ceremonially dispensed amid talk of "R.C.'s"
and "C. of E.'s" and "Primitive Methodists." What the drinking scene
amounts to is a black mass. The Mucky Duck speaks obliquely of the Holy
Ghost. Drunk on the liquor, Denham borrows Arden's sacerdotal office
and delivers a sermon on adultery. He and Winterbottom leave the pub
together to seek out the adulterous Alice so that she can give her husband
the house key. Another key is thrown to the brawlers from a bedroom, but
it is not Winterbottom's. Wife-swapping appears to be a way of life in the
suburbs. Denham, however, has given a name to Alice's activities and by
doing so has set in motion events of tragic consequence.

At his sister Beryl's house, Denham meets Everett, a one-time
Georgian poet, a friend of Harold Munro, and writer once for the *Blast*
and *Adelphi* but presently on the literary page of the local *Hermes*. Beryl,
a Dickensian caricature, plans for Denham to give Everett several hundred
pounds so that he can have a volume of his collected poems privately
printed. Denham is not averse to the idea, especially after he has met

Imogen, Everett's daughter, who is a marvel of comic obscenity: "Damn it all, the least you can do is spend a couple of hundred quid on my father. It's the job of the rich to help the poor men of genius, isn't it?" she says (54).

When a business involvement forces Denham to leave England temporarily, he meets in Ceylon a gangster in the heroin racket and also the incomparable Mr. Raj. To the gangster, Len, Denham tells the story of his evening in London before flying to Colombo. He had been approached by a girl and had gone to a hotel with her; she had asked him to pay her in advance, then had bilked him of five pounds by leaving through the bathroom and the adjacent empty bedroom. Len, who listens with fascination, professes not to believe in violence, only in punishment; and the concept of the gangster-God, broached in *A Vision of Battlements*, is expressed through him: "[V]iolence is a different thing from punishment. You mustn't be too easy on people. It only encourages them to carry on with the same lark. Give them a good sharp punishment, something that'll last. It's only for the good of humanity, when all's said and done. And for their own good too" (68). To this statement, Denham remarks that Len ought to be God. Len agrees that, if he were God, he would do things differently; and he raises his fingers in a parody of benediction as he speaks.

Mr. Raj introduces himself to Denham, claims the kinship of the British Commonwealth, and makes Denham responsible for introducing him into the society that Denham is returning to, that of the Midland town where, coincidentally, Mr. Raj is to pursue his studies in the university. "Apollo in frozen milk chocolate, though the eyes melted and burned," his body scooped and passionate, like Charlie Whittier's, Mr. Raj, dressed in a superb sharkskin tuxedo, tells Denham with a "wide fanatic smile" that he is going to the university to write a thesis to be called "Popular Conceptions of Racial Differentiation" (70–71). He asks Denham to help him penetrate into the folds and recesses of the better English society. "I doubt not," he says, "that with your help I shall soon be *persona grata*" (71).

Through a series of comic involvements, Mr. Raj is introduced to the clientele of the Black Swan and to the adulterous quartet. Soon he is living with Denham's father and occupying Denham's room; the doppelganger finds himself in possession of the white man's father, whom he tends and cares for as though he were his own; but, feeding him rich curries that both enchant and intoxicate the elderly man, he finally brings about his death. At the Black Swan, Raj is forced to defend himself against Brownlow, whom he knocks down expertly several times. And, while Ted Arden is showing off a collection of weapons and old books, Raj manages to steal a small gun, which he promises Denham that he will use only to intimidate those who attempt to bother him on the streets at night.

Raj confesses bewilderment concerning English ways and surprise at the amount of blood that is involved in Christianity; for blood is something to wash off, not to be washed in. "I come here to study ineffable and imponderable problems of race relationships," he says to the Denhams. "So far I have had mixed career. Fights and insults, complete lack of sexual sustenance—most necessary to men in prime of life—and inability to find accommodation commensurate with social position and academic attainments" (125). During his first evening in the Denhams' home, Mr. Raj is moved by the moment; and he makes a toast to Love: "Love, yes, that is the answer. We not fear, ever, if only we have in our hearts, if only we give and, in reciprocity, receive, this greatest of all human treasures" (133). Believing himself in love with Alice Winterbottom, Mr. Raj is confused by English women who, promising everything and giving nothing, keep men panting.

When Denham returns from Colombo to England in Mr. Raj's company, he discovers that Everett's daughter Imogen has run off to London with Winterbottom; and he wonders what Imogen can see in the sulky little printer. When Imogen proposes to be Denham's mistress, he pretends to be shocked by her proposition, although he does acknowledge her attraction for him. "Allright, I shan't make you another offer. You've had it now. But you'll be to blame if I start doing anything worse," Imogen says (90). And Denham answers characteristically, "I accept no blame for anything. You ought to spend a nice quiet evening sorting out your own moral position. . . . You can leave me out of it" (90–91). Denham does, however, lend the errant lovers seventy-five pounds, accepting responsibility only for their physical well-being. Money for Denham is a means of avoiding involvement. "There are no free gifts nowadays: everything has to be paid for. And time, which costs nothing, costs the most," he observes early in the book (21).

To Denham, who returns to Japan by ship, Raj sends messages and letters begging for clarification of English ways, asking advice about the possibility of platonic relationships. Denham delays answering, primarily because he does not want to acknowledge responsibility for Raj's difficulties, until he can do so no longer. He finally sends a cryptic cablegram, which Raj interprets to mean that such relationships are not possible among men and women of normal passions. But Alice continues to lead him on, and Raj continues to care for Denham's father. It does occur to Denham that he receives no real news of his father—even a line or two in Raj's letters would be some indication of the old man's health; but again, not wishing to be overly involved, he neglects to inquire about the old man.

In Singapore, on Bugis Street, Denham again encounters the gangster Len. After proclaiming an admiration for Graham Greene's novels, Len continues the explanation, begun in Ceylon, of his moral code: "you could only get close to God if you really got down to the real dirt, so to speak" (147). The "real thing," Len believes, is justice, and he demonstrates himself to be a perverted Manichaean with a God complex: "[I]t seems to me that you can't have a pair of scales with one pan in this world and the other in the next. That's where I part company with God. . . . [P]eople have got to be taught here and now. That way every one of us is a little bit of God. That's what God is, perhaps, just all of us" (148).

Denham learns that Len and several of his cohorts had followed while in London a girl who had skipped out on her client through an adjoining bedroom without having given service for the five pounds that she had requested in advance. The girl, Imogen, had been beaten up by Len and his gangster friends: "A couple of teeth is as good a punishment as any" (151). Furious at Len's "trying to be God," Denham threatens to knock out several of the gangster's teeth. "It isn't as if I've done anything wrong," argues Len; "I just put the balance right, that's all. If you did that to me I'd have to do something of the same sort to you. And so it would have to go on. You'd have to learn about justice too" (151). Denham is made uncomfortably aware of the fact that a harm done to one is done to all, and that to deny this fact is to deny life itself.

Summoned back to London by Ted Arden to attend his father's funeral, Denham confronts Mr. Raj, who tells Denham that he loved his father. But Denham blames him for the old man's death, implying as he does so that he does not consider the black man the equal of the white. When Raj challenges him, Denham replies that, although the men of the East use the words "love," "equality," and "brotherhood," they interpret the words irresponsibly. "I have failed to make contact . . . failed, failed, failed," says Mr. Raj (190).

Mr. Raj goes to Alice and finds her with Winterbottom who, taking Denham's advice, has a returned to her. Raj kills Winterbottom, using the gun he had borrowed from Ted Arden. Unable to tear her neighbors away from their "telly" during peak viewing hours to witness the real death taking place next door, Alice comes to Denham. When Denham finds Raj, Raj kills himself in front of Denham, and he winks as he does so. To Raj, a Hindu who believes in the oneness of life, death is perhaps a joke.

The novel's theme is expressed by the poet Everett who comments obliquely on the passionate activities that make up the plot. With Imogen returned to him, Everett plans to begin writing a new kind of poetry, "A poetry which says that none of us really has a right to an answer" (181). Everett explains that the question that demands an answer is ultimately one question and that, although everyone knows what that question is, it is still not easy to define. The reader remembers that earlier in the novel Mr. Raj had spoken of love and understanding.

Denham, aware of himself and of his unwillingness to participate in the activities of life, reminds the reader uncomfortably of Conrad's Axel Heyst, but he lacks Heyst's true gallantry. Denham knows himself to be a pretender: "Thank God I have never been committed, as a salesman in Africa or Asia, to any philosophy of ultimate identification through closer and closer and deeper and deeper contact, over which to grow, at length, grey with frustration. . . . There was just this man, J. W. Denham, buying and selling, alone and content to be so, except in work, play, bed, his shadow moving over exotic backcloths . . ." (193). Considering himself above and apart from the world of "telly" viewers, the zombies and the madmen, Denham has learned to pretend contact, to listen and to acquiesce to what he does not care to understand. The world of the picture tube reveals flat characters, wobbling shadows; yet he himself is no more substantial than those images that he despises.

After his father's funeral, Denham returns to his work in Japan. His mistress has left him, perhaps frightened into life by the real world that accosted her one dark night in the disguise of street hoodlums. He is soon visited by Ted Arden and his wife who are making a trip on the money that Everett has gotten for them by selling the early *Hamlet* quarto that he and Denham had discovered among Arden's family relics on the night of Denham's father's funeral. The section of the play to which Denham had turned to judge the value of the quarto had been, aptly, the "To be or not to be" speech.

After taking leave of Ted Arden and Veronica, Denham looks at himself seriously in the mirror. There is no doppelganger to confuse the picture, as there had been on his father's television set. What he sees is a self-indulgent, disgustingly hirsute, balding man. The unloving eyes and the hard mouth displease him. As he thinks back over the events of the previous several months, he concludes that his life of "not-wishing-to-be-involved," though comfortable, is empty. And he concludes that the life that Mr. Raj, who had come too soon "for the blending," had contended with — "the troubled ocean" in the *Hamlet* quarto — is at least a means of measuring a man's moral being.

The *Malayan Trilogy* deals with commitment, and dedication to the Malayans inspires in Victor Crabbe an all-but-accomplished heroism; *The Right to an Answer* deals with the theme of noninvolvement and loneliness. Both novels are, however, concerned with guilt and responsibility. The question that deserves to be answered is asked by Mr. Raj; and, at the novel's end, when Denham turns to Mr. Raj's unfinished manuscript about the problems of race relationships, he becomes aware of the answer: *"Trust is love, credit is a form of love, reliance on the police force or army of a state is also a form of love. . . . Love seems inevitable, necessary, as normal and as easy a process as respiration, but unfortunately"* (218). The manuscript ends with the word "unfortunately," without punctuation.

The Right to an Answer, more straightforward in manner than the *Malayan Trilogy*, manages, by means of juxtaposing comic scenes with scenes of social and religious purport, to suggest the necessity of formulating an answer for the question posed by the Ceylonese Raj. The expression which Mr. Raj hears as "bitter fun" instead of as "a bit of fun," is used several times in the course of the novel to define the peculiar effect produced by Raj on the people who meet him; the expression also defines the tone and feeling that the novel formulates. From Raj's first comic appearance, in his superbly cut tuxedo made of sharkskin material, he delights and enchants the reader. His function as alter ego involves him much more intimately in the ways of British life than an objective observer should be involved. That he has come too soon for "blending," as Burgess calls integration, is the point that lends the novel both its comic and its tragic value. That Burgess should risk the theme to a comic vehicle is not so remarkable when his indebtedness to Nabokov is appreciated.

What is remarkable is that Burgess succeeds as well as he does. The pub as the center of human activity is symbolically appropriate, especially when Burgess describes those who linger on its outskirts: the imbeciles who leer down at weed patches, the cocks that crow all day, the little girls in pinafores who "schnockle" over half-eaten apples, and the boys who all seem to have cleft palates. The workmen in the pub, Selwyn and Cedric, an imbecile and a near-imbecile, also enhance the surrealistic quality that informs the symbolism; and the fact that Selwyn was born with a caul and has the gift of prophecy intensifies the feeling of religious obliquity touched upon when Denham remarks that the church spire interferes with television reception. The wobbling shadows of the television sets form phosphorescent contrasts to the passionate activities of Denham's alter ego, Mr. Raj. Yet all the activity is related by a hollow man. Black and white dominate in the novel; there is very little color; and the sun figures not at all.

What disturbs the reader, however, is Burgess's means of establishing the values of a previous age—through the character of grasping Ted Arden, a descendant of the Ardens of Shakespeare biography. The gratuitous discovery of the *Hamlet* quarto is a device necessary to bring the Ardens into Japan, where Denham is at home; and this visit is necessary to acquaint the reader fully with Denham's failure. When Denham says that, upon retirement, he will return to England and marry Imogen, the reader knows that Denham has not learned what Heyst had learned: that a habit long lived cannot be broken. Imogen is a dream out of Shakespeare, but Denham is a wobbling shadow. Perhaps if he had knocked out the gangster's teeth, as he threatened to do when he was told about Imogen's beating, he might have discovered his humanity, just as Heyst had discovered his when he had obeyed Lena's command to save her from Schomberg's evil.

Notes

1. Anthony Burgess, *The Right to an Answer* (New York, 1966). References are to the paperback edition. Fuller bibliographical information is included in the Bibliography.

2. Anthony Burgess, *The Novel Now*. Subsequent references will be included in the text.

3. Anthony Burgess, "Pronounced Vla-DEEM-ear Nah-BOAK-off," *The New York Times Book Review*, July 2, 1967, p. 20. Subsequent references to this review will be included in the text.

Nothing Like the Sun: The Faces in Bella Cohen's Mirror

John J. Stinson*

That Anthony Burgess owes a large literary debt to James Joyce is a fact freely admitted by Burgess and easily recognized by those who have read several of his novels.[1] Striking similarities of several different types to Joyce's work appear in Burgess' fiction not only because of conscious or semi-conscious emulation of his master, but also because of strong natural affinities between the two men: Burgess is a linguist and has a fascination for and love of words, he is a musician and composer and structures his novels at times by musical analogy, he effectively uses cinematographic forms, he employs heavily mixtures of mode and interplays of style, he is a lapsed Roman Catholic. To what degree certain elements of Burgess' fiction are ascribable to the direct example of Joyce cannot, of course, be determined with any degree of exactitude, but various emanations of Joyce's style, language, and vocabulary (including some neologisms, portmanteau words, and multilingual puns) do appear significantly enough in Burgess' fiction. The most interesting example of Joyce's influence upon Burgess occurs in *Nothing Like the Sun*, a novel which, in fact, provides one of the most intriguing examples of direct literary filiation in all of modern literature. A small lesson in an important aspect of Burgess' fictional technique generally and a more thorough understanding of *Nothing Like the Sun* can be had when it is first recognized that this novel had its genesis in the Scylla and Charybdis episode of *Ulysses*.

Nothing Like the Sun (1964), a fictionalized life of Shakespeare turned out for the quartercentenary of the Bard's birth, has quite properly been regarded by most critics as largely a *tour de force*. What makes it even more of a *tour de force* than anyone seems to have realized, however, is the extent to which the novel grows out of Stephen Dedalus' Shakespeare theory as that posturing and pedantic young man presented it in the library scene in *Ulysses*. It is only, however, by beginning with such a recognition that we can discern that the artificiality of *Nothing Like the Sun* (about which several of these same reviewers complained) is fully purposeful, that it is an important (although perhaps not fully integral) part of the novel's form, and that it abets its meaning.

Burgess himself mentions Stephen Dedalus in connection with *Noth-*

*From *Journal of Modern Literature* 5 (1976): 131–47. © 1976 by *Journal of Modern Literature*. Reprinted with permission.

ing Like the Sun, although the attribution falls far short of what might more reasonably have been acknowledged. In an essay that provides a sort of craftsman's journal on *Nothing Like the Sun,* "Genesis and Headache," Burgess cites Stephen as the source for the important plot element of Shakespeare's being cuckolded by his own younger brother, Richard.[2] But in an interview, in reply to the question of whether "the idea for *Nothing Like the Sun* [was] influenced by the discussion of *Hamlet* in the library scene in *Ulysses,*" Burgess responded, "Oh, totally."[3] His next sentence, did, however, heavily qualify that perhaps slightly off-guard admission: "Well the notion of Ann's adultery with the brother is very close to what Stephen gives us."[4] The initial blanket admission seems illuminating nevertheless; Burgess is certainly astute enough to recognize that authorial explanation beyond the casual-sounding hint is frequently both self-defeating and demeaning. Neither Burgess nor the interviewer explores the relationship between the two works any further.[5]

Examination does soon bear out, however, the fact that each and every one of the major elements in Stephen Dedalus' Shakespeare theory is incorporated in some way in *Nothing Like the Sun.* So as not to be thought to prejudice the issue by lending false emphasis or by manipulation, let us attend for a moment to what William Schutte says in his thoroughly sound study *Joyce and Shakespeare:* "He [Stephen] has taken the dubious step of assuming that Shakespeare's works directly reflect events in his personal life. Most of the essential points in his theory—the infidelity of Ann, the identification of Hamlet with Hamnet, the treachery of Richard and Edmund, the psychological undoing of Shakespeare as a result of his home situation, the betrayal of Shakespeare by his "dearmylove," and the reconciliation at the end—are the result either of Stephen's making inferences from established facts or of his giving a biographical significance to events in the plays or poems."[6] In *Nothing Like the Sun* Stephen's basic operating premise (that the man Shakespeare can be known through the poems and plays) becomes the basis for the whole fiction but, more tellingly, all the chief elements of Stephen's theory appear importantly with the single exception that Richard alone (rather than he and Gilbert both) is made the partner in the incestuous adultery with Anne. Admittedly, not too much is done in Burgess' book to make the Hamlet-Hamnet identification, and this is natural since the main narrative of the story proper ends just as WS (as Shakespeare is referred to throughout this novel) is moving into the dark period of his life, the period of the great tragedies. (It is only in the epilogue that we skip ahead to find him lying on his deathbed back in Stratford.) But, though brief, the Hamlet-Hamnet identification is indeed made and is more noteworthy by the fact that Burgess goes somewhat out of his way to make it. On one of his extremely rare visits back to Stratford, WS has this demand made of him by the nine year old Hamnet:

"Tell me a story and let me be in the story." WS smiled. "Well, once there was a king and he had a son and the son's name was Hamnet. . . . And the king's father died but his ghost came back to tell the prince that he had not truly died but had been murdered. And the man that had murdered him was his own brother, the uncle of Hamnet."
"Which uncle—Uncle Dickon [Richard] or Uncle Gilbert or Uncle Edmund?"
"This is a story only. The uncle wished to marry the queen and become the ruler of all the land."
"Oh, it would be Uncle Dickon then."
"Why Uncle Dickon?"
"Oh, he says he is King Richard now that William the Conqueror is away in London."[7]

Stephen's reductive theory about the effect that Anne had on Shakespeare's life is shared by Burgess and made a main fiber of the novel's plot. Inferring much from the known historical fact that Anne was eight years older than Shakespeare, and seeing "Venus and Adonis" as in part an autobiographical note reflective of both its author's situation and his troubled state of mind at the time of its composition, Stephen sees Anne as a conniving woman "who tumbles in a cornfield a lover younger than herself" (*Ulysses*, 191). Stephen also thinks her "hot in the blood" (202); though, too, her sexual aggression must be thought of as the product of both craft and lust. Stephen sees in her victory the psychological debilitation of the man Shakespeare:

He was overborne in a cornfield first (ryefield, I should say) and he will never be a victor in his own eyes after nor play victoriously the game of laugh and lie down. Assumed dongiovannism will not save him. No later undoing will undo the first undoing. The tusk of the boar has wounded him there where love lies ableeding. If the shrew is worsted yet there remains to her woman's invisible weapon. There is, I feel in the words, some goad of the flesh driving him into a new passion, a darker shadow of the first, darkening even his own understanding of himself. A life fate awaits him and the two rages commingle in a whirlpool.

They list. And in the porches of their ears I pour.

—The soul has been before stricken mortally, a poison poured in the porch of a sleeping ear. But those who are done to death in sleep. . . . (196)

This passage from *Ulysses* goes a long way toward explaining what would otherwise be one of the strangest scenes (in terms of the style, mode, and tone as well as the event described) in *Nothing Like the Sun*, WS's fateful seduction by the practiced hand of Anne Hathaway. It is not put there in the way that it is, it seems, simply because Burgess has strong propensities for the comic-grotesque (what D. J. Enright, writing of this novel, has complained about as the "copulative grandguignolesque"[8]), nor because of the radically dualistic philosophy which Burgess conveniently terms Manicheanism, an outlook which sees all things of the flesh as powerfully and enduringly opposed to the things of the spirit, but because he wishes his own argumentative thrust, embodied in the fiction, to be virtually identical to that of Stephen Dedalus and perhaps even to ring the echo of it in some readers' minds. In *Nothing Like the Sun* there is neither pretense nor attempt at realistic preparation for the scene of WS's seduction by Anne. WS simply wakes the morning after the May games (perhaps Burgess has also read C. L. Barber) from a sick drunk in the wood just off the Shottery tavern green to find himself, with the taste of vomit in his mouth, being all but raped ("stooping to conquer" [*Ulysses*, 191] is Stephen's way of putting it, via Goldsmith) by a woman he has, to his memory, never seen before (33–35). One can almost say that, as Stephen suggests, WS was poisoned in his sleep (thus making, as Stephen does, an equation not only with "Venus and Adonis" but also with *Hamlet*); one can definitely say that the wily and hot-blooded Anne hath both her will and her way (Stephen was not the first to make that pun).

That parallels such as these are due not so much to the employment of common sources by Joyce and Burgess as to Burgess' following Joyce directly is, I think, established not only by the weight of accumulated evidence, but by the striking similarity of some small particulars. We might simply take one example that comes next in the novel's sequence of events. After the forced marriage of WS to Anne, the narrator ruefully philosophizes, "He was in a manner tricked, coney-caught, a court-dor to a cozening cotquean. So are all men, first gulls, later horned gulls, and so will ever be all men, amen. It was easier to believe so, yet the real truth is that all men choose what they will have" (36). This might be laid alongside the passage in *Ulysses* where John Eglinton says that

> The world believes that Shakespeare made a mistake . . . and got out of it as quickly and as best he could.

> —Bosh! Stephen said rudely. A man of genius makes no mistakes. His errors are volitional and are the portals of discovery. (190)

Some major scenes also in Burgess' novel seem to find their initial inspiration in *Ulysses*. But Burgess researches them more fully and thus imparts to them the embroidery suggested by history or tradition. One of the most memorable scenes in *Nothing Like the Sun* is another near-grotesque, the description of the hanging and quartering at Tyburn Common of Dr. Roderigo Lopez and two others for conspiracy and treason. Burgess describes the execution of the trio as a great popular carnival of sadism; the scene is one of grotesque violence, but the context and coloration are meant to convince us that the orgasm of hate for Lopez, the Portuguese Jewish physician, was what really occurred, that it was thoroughly in keeping with debased human nature. As Burgess would have it, Shakespeare was not above exploiting the hatred for Jews that followed upon the notoriety of the Lopez case, with Shylock thus having his origin here. WS gives the people what they want; he says, "That is what the people wish to believe, they wish him [Shylock] to be a kind of Lopez" (178). The Lopez execution is mentioned by Stephen in *Ulysses* in support of his argument that "all events brought grist to his [Shakespeare's] mill" (204). The whole of *Nothing Like the Sun* is, at least on one level, little more than an imaginative working out of that opinion. In Stephen's theory, and in Burgess' novel, art and nature are all but interchangeable. Stephen illustrates his thesis by asserting that "Shylock chimes with the jewbaiting that followed the hanging and quartering of the queen's leech Lopez, his jew's heart being plucked forth while the sheeny was yet alive [this touch duly appears in Burgess]: *Hamlet* and *Macbeth* with the coming to the throne of a Scotch philosophaster with a turn for witch-roasting" (204–205).

At least a few minor elements of Stephen's exposition, itself a *tour de force*, appear in Burgess' novel. Space does not permit their detailing, but two brief examples can be cited. It might be remembered that Stephen rises ingeniously to meet Eglinton's challenge that he prove Shakespeare a Jew (205–206). Burgess, of course, does not literally have his WS a Jew. It can be noted, though, that on two separate occasions other characters in the novel refer to WS as a Jew because of his tight-fistedness with money (96 and 111). And in *Ulysses* Stephen "proves" Shakespeare a Jew by first adducing his greed for material things and the jealous possessiveness of his character generally. It seems, too, that Burgess probably had Joyce in mind when he makes a symbolic identification of WS and Christ. Stephen makes the identification of Shakespeare with Christ when he calls him a "Christfox" (193); twice (205 and 222) Burgess has WS utter a "*consummatum est.*"

Given the relative oddity of Stephen's theory (and it should be credited to Stephen that he has the candor to admit to Eglinton that he really does not believe in it himself [213–214]), it is all the more remarkable that all the major ingredients of that theory should find incorporation in Burgess' novel. The reverse, of course, is not true. Certain parts of the fabric of *Nothing Like the Sun* have no basis of suggestion in Stephen's theory. There is one element which does have its suggestion in *Ulysses* that might easily be overlooked. Burgess imagines a homosexual relationship between W. H. (for whom his candidate is the Earl of Southampton) and WS. Stephen does not concern himself at all with the relationship between the two men, but the suggestion is strong that he perceives a homosexual character to it. "The court wanton spurned him for a lord, his dearmylove,"[9] says Stephen, on the evidence, presumably, of the sonnets. Perhaps the reason that he does not elaborate on the relationship between the two men or its homosexual cast is that he suspects two members of his small audience, Eglinton and Best, to be themselves homosexuals.[10] Thus, even this element finds its basis of suggestion in *Ulysses*.[11] The only two really important ingredients of Burgess' book that seem to have no possible origin in *Ulysses* are those that posit that the Dark Lady was actually non-Caucasian (Burgess seems to have gotten that view from G. B. Harrison) and that WS was a victim of syphilis.

One of the most pressing problems that Burgess quite naturally faced was that of imparting some artistic unity to his book. But ought a biography — even a fictionalized biography — have a theme? Does the selectiveness employed by the biographer in some way falsify reality? As I shall attempt to explain later in this paper, I think that Burgess brings himself to a serious encounter with these and related questions although, characteristically for a writer who shares much of the "new sensibility" in literature, he seems to do so playfully. There is, though, a theme of sorts in the book, the repeated one that runs throughout Burgess' novels, that of the primacy of evil, the irresistibly strong inclination toward evil that man has inherited because of original sin. This recognition comes to WS when, in the throes of his first syphilitic fever, a presence that certainly seems to be the Tragic Muse descends upon him (the year apparently being 1599, a time immediately preceding the creation of the great tragedies), the manner of her descent suggesting that of Anne on that fateful May morning many years before: "She released unbelievable effluvia. It seemed not possible. The hopelessness of man's condition was revealed in odours that came direct, in a kind of Eden freshness, from the prime and original well" (219). One might well feel that Burgess here employs, what is for him, an all-too-predictable and overly rigid thematic overlay. But what should be noted in this conjunction is that Stephen too can be seen to make original sin a central part of his thesis when, close to the conclusion of his exposition, he says, "But it was the original sin that darkened his [Shakespeare's] understanding, weakened his will and left in him a strong inclination to evil" (212). The whole context of Stephen's remarks can, in fact, support Burgess' essentially romantic thesis that Shakespeare's teeming humanity, his superabundant vitality of both flesh and spirit, amounts to both his tragedy and his triumph. Stephen compares Shakespeare with the God of Creation, and one sees what he means: Shakespeare creates a world in his own image — or, more accurately — a world that comes from the full, rich humanity within himself. As Eglinton says, "he is all in all" (212). In both Joyce and Burgess Shakespeare is seen as an archetypal man, and even common readers are meant to see reflections of themselves in him.

But even if all men can find parts of themselves in Shakespeare, Burgess goes a clear step further. By means of an interior identification, Burgess, half playfully, half seriously, clearly sets himself alongside Shakespeare. He does this by hiding his own name in *Nothing Like the Sun* in the way that Stephen, in a rather dubious contention, maintains that Shakespeare does in the plays: "He has hidden his own name, a fair name, William, in the plays, a super here, a clown there, as a painter of old Italy set his face in a dark corner of his canvas" (209). While there is some doubt that Shakespeare does do this, or that any significant meaning should attach to it even if he does, there can be little doubt but that Burgess does do it quite deliberately and that it does have a significant meaning of sorts. Burgess' real name is John Wilson, his full name actually being John Anthony Burgess Wilson. In *Nothing Like the Sun*, not one, but two different Wilsons are mentioned, although each is mentioned only once. The name of one is actually John Wilson; that of the other is simply given as Wilson. Neither one is of the slightest importance in any context other than the symbolic one and that only by virtue of the name itself. Those well read in the Burgess canon will know that he has chosen to employ name symbolism from the very first (Victor Crabbe in the Malayan trilogy, for example), but as a ready and convincing proof that the name Wilson is symbol and not just surface, it might be noted that one of the three epigraphs to Burgess' more recent novel, *MF*, is a direction from *Much Ado About Nothing*: "Enter Prince, Leonato, Claudio, and Jacke Wilson," and that Burgess himself, writing about *Nothing Like the Sun* in the essay "Genesis and Headache," has complained "that the novel's first reviewers failed to notice the author's personal monograms sewn into the fabric of the work" (43). Obviously something is to be made out of the name John Wilson, and it is not difficult to deduce what was intended. It seems reasonably clear that, since Wilson means "Will's son," Burgess is proclaiming himself the son of Shakespeare. Such an identification is cemented by the precise circumstance in which the name Wilson appears for the first time in the novel. Very shortly before he leaves Stratford, WS is working as a law clerk; when his brother Gilbert enters to announce the birth of the twins Hamnet and Judith, WS is blotting the name he has just transcribed, WILSON (73). Will's son, Hamnet, seems thus identified with Burgess, and one recalls the full train of Stephen's associations about Hamnet in relation to Shakespeare. The other Wilson, John Wilson, met later in the novel, is apparently an actor who, with his mildly irreverential attitude for a liturgical formula, reminds one of the stronger, more studied irreverence of Buck Mulligan. As some strong wine is being used to christen the new Globe theatre, Wilson intones "Ego te baptizo, in nomine Kyddi et Marlovii et Shakespearii" (206). If this is lighthearted blasphemy, no doubt some readers will consider Burgess' equation of himself with Shakespeare at least equally blasphemous.

Burgess' identification of himself with Shakespeare is fully consonant with his own and Joyce's practice of creating archetypes that are mock-ironic and serious at both and the same time. Inevitably, too, Stephen's mild caveat comes to mind: "The mocker is never taken seriously when he is most serious" (199). Today, within the dispensation of the "new sensibility," we understand that well; Stephen's caution is unnecessary. Joyce, though at least several things more, was both a definitive explorer and a pioneer of this new sensibility. Joyce succeeds in being a Modernist and Post-Modernist both. Burgess understands this well about Joyce, and his own fiction neatly straddles this artificial literary fence and others as well.

Various echoes and reflections of *Ulysses* other than those already mentioned appear in Burgess' novel. Following the example of *Ulysses* itself in regard to its mode of employment of other works of literature, Burgess includes his echoes and reflections half earnestly, half jokingly. When, in the "Circe" episode of *Ulysses*, Stephen and Bloom together look into Bella Cohen's mirror, there seems to appear the sad-eyed and beardless face of Shakespeare, "crowned by the reflection of the reindeer antlered hatrack in the hall" (567), an ignominious token of his cuckoldry. His beardlessness very possibly suggesting his emasculation at the hands of his wife, this Shakespeare bears close resemblance to Burgess' WS. With *Ulysses* serving *Nothing Like the Sun* something in the way that the *Odyssey* does *Ulysses* (Stephen's theory does provide Burgess' novel its framework[12]), it seems apparent that Burgess wants us to see himself, Bloom, and Stephen returning the gaze of Shakespeare on the other side of that mirror. Expecting, then, that his readers will see his WS refracted in the Joycean mirror, Burgess creates a hall-of-mirrors effect that is, like so much in *Ulysses* itself, either mock-ironic or serious, dependent upon one's precise angle of vision. Burgess quite obviously realized the folly of attempting to capture the real Shakespeare ("nothing like the sun" suggesting, among other things, Burgess' failure to capture, in his own words, the "authentic effulgence"[13]) so that he opted for the good recourse of making his WS (the initials rather than the name *Shakespeare* abetting this) an archetypal man, a man whose story represents permanent patterns of human experience. Burgess makes WS very much a human figure and the universality of his experience emerges clearly enough in its own right, but Burgess underscores it, and imparts to it some sharply spinning ironies, by tying it to *Ulysses* and thereby gaining the added wealth of all those archetypes or temporal recurrences in *Ulysses* suggested by the ideas of "metempsychosis" and the "umbilical telephone line."[14]

A suggestive list (I compress greatly in order to conserve space) of the relationships in the Bloom-Stephen-Burgess-Shakespeare constellation might be established thusly:

Burgess-Shakespeare

1. Along with a more subtle play with form and frame, sometimes thought a distinctively Post-Modernist innovation (although endemic also with Swift, Joyce, and Nabokov, for example, among others), Burgess ironically distances himself from his own creation by the employment of a frame: the novel proper is given as "Mr. Burgess' farewell lecture to his

special students" (7). Feeling freed from the limitations of his own sad flesh by virtue of some rice wine, this Burgess becomes consubstantial with Will the Father; he declares in the epilogue, "This is no impersonation, ladies and gentlemen" (222). Burgess' persona, presumably also a Wil-son, proclaims his descent from Shakespeare. "I am of his blood," he says. "The male line died in the West. It was right it should continue in the East" (223). Readers are meant to be reminded that Fatimah, WS's Dark Lady, promised to send her son back to the East (201), no doubt to the Malaya from which she came and where "Burgess," like the real-life author, seems to give his farewell address as a teacher. But not only Shakespeare's son, Burgess becomes, like Stephen's Hamlet, the ghost of his own father. And in *Nothing Like the Sun* it is WS who muses after Hamnet's death, "The son was the father" (161).

2. Both Burgess and Shakespeare are, like Stephen and Joyce himself, "word-boys."

3. Stephen proffers the idea that Burgess embodies in the novel — that everything was grist for Shakespeare's mill; Burgess proves, as his greatest *tour de force*, that even Stephen's clever-schoolboy[15] theory can be made grist for his own artistic mill.

4. Burgess' WS might appear to be an exploiter and an opportunist: at first glance it would seem that he exploits the rife anti-semitism that followed the Lopez affair by creating Shylock. Burgess might seem to exploit the quartercentenary of Shakespeare's birth by writing a novel subtitled "a story of Shakespeare's love life."

Burgess-Stephen

1. The main lines of the Shakespeare theory of each are virtually identical.

2. "Burgess" becomes progressively more and more tipsy as he recounts the narrative of Shakespeare's life while sipping his students' parting gift of samsu wine; Stephen's discourse on Shakespeare occurs soon after he has stood several rounds at a pub for the practiced drinkers of the *Telegraph* office. And, in "Circe," when Shakespeare's face appears in Bella Cohen's mirror, Stephen is far under the weather. With drink, it seems, the individual consciousness merges into the collective.

3. If Burgess' fictional theorizing is at all convincing, it is because he successfully carries out the instructions Stephen issued himself to put across his own glittering exercise in theory: "Local colour. Work in all you know. Make them accomplices" (188).

4. Both Stephen and Burgess out-theorize the theorizers; that special breed of books about Shakespeare that combine dry, academic pedanticism and fluttery, excited gossip is mocked but at the very same time used to good advantage. (Exactly the same is true of *MF*: it has variously been described as a structuralist novel and as a "send-up" of structuralist theory.

Likewise *Honey for the Bears* and *Tremor of Intent* are spoofs of Ian Fleming's James Bond novels, but at the same time gain real vitality, quite apart from satire, from a close reproduction of the quality of the originals.)

Stephen-WS

1. One might suppose that, aside from the quite unremarkable correspondence one bears to the other as sensitive-young-men types with a fascination for language, no real parallel exists between the two. But even in the language that describes WS, Burgess sounds some fairly definite echoes of the Stephen not only of *Ulysses* but of *A Portrait of the Artist As a Young Man* as well. Take, for instance, this plaintive statement of WS: "Ever since I was a tiny boy I have been gravely told of my duty—to my family, church, country, wife" (191). Another passage describing the state of WS's soul as he wallows in self-pity and a lust made somehow even more delicious by a few deep pangs of attendant guilt is strongly redolent of the opening paragraphs of chapter three of *A Portrait*: "Slap into it, eating fast and beastly, sending out for more, fancying goose-breast richly sauced baked in a fat coffin of brown and flaky paste, herborage, nut-and-honey cake topped with cinnamon cream. Ugh, glutton. Then to thy bed, belching in sloth, to lie there, paper unwritten on save by random sprawling greasy greedy fingers, ale-drop jottings, dust settling on the pile. Aye, lie, conjuring images of lost Her, in postures of abandon before thee, moaning in nasty lust" (*Nothing Like the Sun*, 157).

2. John Shakespeare, WS's father, is made to suffer severe business reverses; like Simon Dedalus, he moves, on the psychological plane, into insecure old age while making constant and somewhat pitiable gestures toward maintaining his dignity.

3. Both Stephen and WS are analogized to Christ.

4. Stephen is betrayed by Cranly, Mulligan, and others; WS is betrayed by Southampton as well as Anne.

WS-Bloom

Fundamentally, Burgess' WS remains, like Bloom, a man of resolutely middle-class values. Anthony DeVitis is totally correct in his judgment that "there is no glamorizing of the subject."[16] This is seen in several ways:

1. WS's chief and constantly pressing motivation is that of economic and social success.[17]

2. WS perceives his playwriting as chiefly a craft; he views his writing career in much the same light as he does his trade as a glover. In his own thrice-repeated analogy he compares the five feet of his pentameter with the skillfully easy turning out of five perfect fingers in a glove.

Bloom's idea of literary art, of course, largely involves turning out a story to illustrate a proverb.[18]

3. Initially made somewhat uneasy in a milieu where adulation was recently reserved for the university wits, WS suggests something of Bloom's defensiveness about his lack of a college education.

4. As Bloom is, by various techniques, both mythologized and then almost cruelly demythologized, so too is WS. But largely he is seen as an eager bourgeois rather than as the idolized Bard and demythologization prevails.

Other similarities besides those of the common middle-class patterns also exist:

1. Somewhat ambivalent in his sexual orientation (as humorously revealed in "Circe"), Bloom is to some degree like WS, a cosmopolitan sort of bisexual who, unlike Bloom, seems utterly untroubled by his sexual impartiality.[19]

2. Burgess retains all the Joycean identifications between the two, most especially that each is cuckolded and that the only son of each has died, WS's at eleven years, Bloom's at eleven days (the universal note here being sounded here in WS's "agonised cry of all bereaved fathers" [161]).

3. WS is twice referred to as a Jew (96 and 111), connecting him with Bloom (both times, however, because of his alleged stinginess with money, a trait not properly attributable to Bloom).

4. In the epilogue, as WS and "Burgess" the narrator very nearly merge (WS dies at the same moment that, apparently, "Burgess" collapses into a drunken stupor), WS announces that "my disease was a modern disease" (220). In an earlier scene, as Southampton took his leave of WS to cast his lot with Essex and, in his own eyes, to become a man of action, thus rising beyond his former self to the exalted company of heroes, the playwright saw that he himself was, conversely, a man ahead of his time, that heroism was not possible for him because (ironically enough for the creator of the great tragedies), he already saw that heroism and tragedy were past their time. He saw beyond them to something far smaller and narrower, something holding out only little possibility of human ennoblement (194). His dilemma was essentially that of Leopold Bloom, the (in part) mock-heroic figure who has justly come to be regarded as a prototypal twentieth-century man.

5. WS is obviously the "sun" of the title. He is, as Eglinton says, "all in all" (212); all energy begins and ends with him. In *Ulysses* Bloom too is symbolically seen as the sun, most notably at the end of "The Cyclops" episode where his "raiment [is] as of the sun" (345). And Bloom can indeed be seen, as one commentator has put it, as a "radiant sun in the Dublin gloom."[20] Then, too, as in seventeenth-century religious poetry (and in much earlier Christian literature and symbology) *sun* also suggests *son*, and Bloom, as well as Stephen and WS, is identified with Christ. Burgess

being Wil-son, there is the possibility here of much quickly accelerating circular symbolism.

6. At the very beginning of the narrative the boy WS has one of his frequent meetings with Jack Hoby, an old and disoriented sailor living out his last days in Stratford (13–15). This ancient mariner recurs to the memory of WS as he lies on his deathbed: "The lands, Hoby, you told me of, the strange birds, the talking fruit, the three-legged men — they all exist; you were no liar" (222). In *Ulysses*, of course, Bloom is seen in archetype as Odysseus, Sinbad the Sailor, Robinson Crusoe, and the Ancient Mariner, among other fabulous voyagers. Appearing strategically at the beginning and end of the novel, Hoby provides another sort of frame for the narrative, expanding, as does the larger frame, the individual into the archetypal.

Anne-Molly

Both represent, as in Joyce, the eternally feminine element;[21] Burgess retains the Joycean parallels but does not extend them, save perhaps for one small but curious parallel. In *Nothing Like the Sun* Anne[22] is driven to a high point of erotic stimulation by witnessing outside her bedroom window the ugly assault of a blood-thirsty crowd upon Madge, the old fortune teller suspected of being a witch; compellingly aroused, Anne calls for WS to perform the sexual act right at the window (76). In *Ulysses*, Molly, we remember, was sexually aroused by the sight from her window of two dogs copulating (89), the stimulus here being not a sadistic one as with Anne, but nevertheless a remarkable enough one in its own small, unromantic way.

The links between *Nothing Like the Sun* and *Ulysses* are a few too many to be conceived of as either coincidental or merely incidental, but what, at base, do they really signify? It need not take a particularly harsh detractor of Burgess to feel that the whole matter of the literary filiation here is but wantonly silly, and wholly purposeless, sport. Still more severe observers might feel that Burgess is essentially just throwing academic critics some bones of literary symbol and allusion to keep them from smelling out the true odor of cheap literary exploitation. And some others might conjecture that the reason was simply pedestrian — that it gave the author a framework and thus provided needed discipline.

Proponents of Burgess' art naturally see things differently. Carefully attuned to the possibilities released by the "new sensibility" (possibilities fructified in the works of Barth, Barthelme, Pynchon, Hawkes, Heller, and even Nabokov, among others),[23] they will identify such elements in Burgess' fiction as blatant artifice, two-dimensional characterization, black comedy, manufactured camp, intentional kitsch, linguistic distortion, mixed modes, and interplays of style as calculated devices by which form becomes meaning (meaning virtually inexpressible in any other way), and by which a reader's consciousness of the strange, pluralistic universe we live in is imaginatively expanded. Burgess begins, rightly, to suggest that these sorts of purposeful playing with form have not been apprehended for what they are by critical commentators on *Nothing Like the Sun*: "it hurts, of course, when one's most carefully contrived artificiality is dismissed as something unlicked and crude."[24] In the light of what seems to be rapidly becoming (if it is not already that) a rich and marvellously varied Burgess *oeuvre*, an *oeuvre* which contains vital and extended elements frequently associated with the American "new novel," *Nothing Like the Sun* can be convincingly seen as a valid and integral artistic work, perfectly consonant with the author's characteristic process of approaching serious themes through light-hearted, but purposeful, indirection.

It is with legitimacy that Burgess has been viewed as a philosophical novelist in that his themes engage problems of ontology, epistemology, linguistics, taxonomies, and theories of history. In *Nothing Like the Sun*, he forces the reader, by the whole frame, form, and content of his novel, to test Stephen Dedalus' theory that art and nature are interchangeable. When it is realized, however, that Burgess' own art proceeds not from nature but from Stephen's "art" and Joyce's art (and even beyond that to the Shakespeare books of Brandes, Lee, and Harris that helped Joyce with Stephen's theory), a whole intriguing layer of crisscrossing ironies is added. To fault *Nothing Like the Sun* for its lack of mimetic realism is to miss almost wholly the point. The basic endeavor of *Nothing Like the Sun* is to bring the reader to a confrontation with the question of just what is meant by biography, fiction, myth, and history. If art and nature are one, so too are fiction and biography very nearly one: the processes of selection employed by the biographer are certainly closely akin to those employed by the fiction writer. In *Nothing Like the Sun* Burgess' probe is both broad and deep. Beyond the level of pure content and as a kind of supra-thematic but nevertheless integral element, some of the most abidingly penetrating questions about art are raised: What is the relation of art to reality? How does language form or alter our perception of reality? What is a "fact"? What is the basis of judgment by which historians or biographers decide which facts are important? Is one man's myth another man's history? *Ulysses* can well be regarded as a source book for the structuralist critic in that it attacks these questions with daring, imagination, and wit. Burgess is doing much the same thing in his fiction, though, in keeping with the tenor of the times, he does so more lightly and more teasingly, preferring, at most, the stinging sally to the direct and extended onslaught not uncommon to Joyce. A proper understanding of the purposeful artificiality in *Nothing Like the Sun* proves it to be, I believe, Burgess' most thoroughgoing but subtle play with fictive form and a strong contribution toward a worthy Post-Modernist literature. It seems, in fact, a distinctively Post-Modernist realization of the type of viable relationship possible between

tradition and the individual talent, something that Burgess most gener-
ously provides also in his latest novel, *Napoleon Symphony*.[25] And if
Burgess completes (as, judging from past experience he almost certainly
will) projected historical fictions on Christopher Marlowe and Jesus,
Nothing Like the Sun will seem far less anomalous in his own canon and
will, perhaps, be regarded as a central book capable of teaching us much
about his fictions generally.

Notes

1. Burgess is the author of *Re Joyce* (W. W. Norton and Company, 1966), a very
capable and enthusiastic introduction to Joyce for the common reader that does, however,
owe more to American Joyce scholars than Burgess allows. He is also the compiler and editor
of *A Shorter Finnegans Wake*. Various smaller connections between Joyce and Burgess
continue to appear: Burgess addressed the 1972 Modern Language Convention on a Joyce
topic; his wife, Liliana, is said to be translating *Finnegans Wake* into Italian; and Burgess
announced as of spring, 1973, that he had just completed a musical based on *Ulysses*. For a
general assessment of the literary relationships between Joyce and Burgess one might consult
Melvin Friedman, "Anthony Burgess and James Joyce: A Literary Confrontation," *Literary
Criterion* (University of Mysore, India), IX (1971), 71–83.

2. Anthony Burgess, "Genesis and Headache," in Thomas McCormack, ed., *After-
words* (Harper and Row, 1968), p. 42.

3. Thomas Churchill, "An Interview with Anthony Burgess," *Malahat Review*, XVII
(1971), 123.

4. Churchill, p. 123. Burgess cites Stephen Dedalus when he uses this theory again in
his coffee-table *Shakespeare* (Alfred A. Knopf, 1970), p. 25.

5. Geoffrey Aggeler, "The Comic Art of Anthony Burgess," *Arizona Quarterly*, XXV
(1969), 234–251, had noted earlier that *Nothing Like the Sun* seemed to have been "at least
partially inspired by Stephen Dedalus' discourse on Shakespeare" (248), but since Aggeler's
was a broad general survey, he had to let the matter pass without much further observation.

6. William M. Schutte, *Joyce and Shakespeare* (Yale University Press, 1957), p. 54.

7. *Nothing Like the Sun* (Ballantine Books, 1965), p. 119. All subsequent references to
the novel will be to this edition and will be incorporated directly in the test. A pun involving
the term "William the Conqueror" in appellation to Shakespeare is also found in *Ulysses*
(Vintage Books, 1961), p. 201, but in this instance the Richard conquered by William is
Richard Burbage, not Richard Shakespeare. All page references to *Ulysses* will be to the
edition cited above and will hereafter appear directly in the text.

8. D. J. Enright, "Mr. W. S.," review of *Nothing Like the Sun*, *The New Statesman*,
April 24, 1964, p. 643.

9. *Ulysses*, p. 202. Although Burgess' WS never calls Southampton "dearmylove," he
does several times address him as "dear my lord."

10. Mulligan seems to think so too. See Stanley Sultan, *The Argument of Ulysses* (Ohio
State University Press, 1964), pp. 159 and 164.

11. In *Re Joyce*, p. 132, Burgess does profess that Stephen's "Shakespearian scholarship
[is] formidable."

12. Burgess had used the *Aeneid* as a framework for his first novel, *A Vision of
Battlements*.

13. Anthony Burgess, *The Novel Now* (W. W. Norton and Company, 1967), p. 138.

14. A specific Burgess reference to Stephen's idea (by way of the theosophists) about the
umbilical telephone line occurs in *The Doctor Is Sick* (Ballantine Books, 1967), p. 115:

"Edwin picked up the telephone, dialed — remembering his James Joyce — EDEnville 0000, and asked for Adam."

15. It is George Russell (A. E.) who is given the not unsensible opinion that "all these questions are purely academic . . . I mean, whether Hamlet is Shakespeare or James I or Essex . . . the speculation of schoolboys for schoolboys" (*Ulysses*, 185).

16. A. A. DeVitis, *Anthony Burgess* (Twayne, 1972), p. 146.

17. Burgess states this idea very clearly in his *Shakespeare* (17) and in *Urgent Copy* where he says that "Shakespeare's main aim, I think, was to make money" (159). Burgess would be ingenuous enough to admit another Shakespeare / Burgess parallel in this regard.

18. See *Ulysses*, p. 69.

19. Christopher Ricks has quite rightly pointed out that several of Burgess' major characters have epicene qualities: "The Epicene," review of *Honey for the Bears*, *The New Statesman*, April 5, 1963, p. 496. And, interestingly enough, most of Burgess' main characters bear relatively marked similarities to Bloom and WS. Geoffrey Aggeler (in an article previously cited) is quite correct in saying that "Victor Crabbe in *The Long Day Wanes*, Paul Hussey in *Honey for the Bears*, Edwin Spindrift in *The Doctor Is Sick*, and Tristram Foxe in *The Wanting Seed* all share a great deal with Leopold Bloom. They are all sensitive, cultured, well-meaning but ineffectual, cuckolded non-heroes involved in non-heroic Odyssean quests which terminate in some sort of return to a mate who has proved herself to be an unfaithful Penelope" (236). Since virtually all of Burgess' non-heroes are possessed of artistic tempera-ments, their epicene quality can perhaps be explained in part by Stephen's theory of the androgynous nature of the artist, also to be found in "Scylla and Charybdis." Richard Ellmann, *Ulysses on the Liffey* (Oxford University Press, 1972), pp. 86–87, offers a good explanation of this aspect of the theory and delineates as well several symbolic correlatives in *Ulysses* by which Joyce makes equations between the sexual and artistic acts. And there is the slightest suggestion that "Burgess," the narrator in *Nothing Like the Sun*, is androgynous as well. Note the sexual suggestions possible in the names of several of the "*special* [Burgess' emphasis] students:" Miss Alabaster, Miss Ishak ("I shack up with?"), Miss Kinipple, and Mr. Limpe (limp wrist?), Mr. Whitelegge, Mr. Lillington (suggesting the trilling voice of the blatant type of homosexual?).

20. Leo M. J. Manglaviti, "Joyce and St. John," *James Joyce Quarterly*, IX (1971), 154. Other critics, using non-Christian mythic overlays, see Bloom as Solar Hero.

21. That Anne of *Nothing Like the Sun* is meant to be identified with all women is perhaps represented by an association established between her and the female students in "Burgess'" class. In the epilogue, as WS lies on his deathbed, Anne is ready with her pennies to hold down his eyelids. The girls in the narrator's class are likewise ready, at the same moment that that point in the narrative is reached (214), with their pennies, presumably the charge for the bathroom facilities. And in *Ulysses*, the detail about the pennies is, in fact, mentioned by Stephen: "She laid pennies on his eyes to keep his eyelids closed when he lay on his deathbed" (190).

22. Burgess spells the name of Shakespeare's wife *Anne;* Joyce *Ann.*

23. There is in these writers, as in Burgess, a treatment of systems which is essentially parodistic, but Burgess (unlike these writers generally) does not incline nearly so much toward Absurdism. If Burgess created, like Barth whom he resembles in several ways, ironic hall-of-mirrors effects, he does not feel himself lost in the funhouse. In this he is more like Joyce who, in Ihab Hassan's words, employs a radical literary imagination "in the interest of essentially conservative feelings" (Ihab Hassan, "Postmodernism: A Paracritical Bibliography, *New Literary History*, III [1971], 15).

24. "Genesis and Headache," p. 44.

25. Present in *Napoleon Symphony*, a novel structured on the form of Beethoven's *Eroica* Symphony, is a type of artificiality somewhat similar to that employed in *Nothing Like the Sun.*

Love's Labor's Lost: Sex and Art in Two Novels by Anthony Burgess

Bruce M. Firestone*

In the epilogue to his wide-ranging collection of literary essays, *Urgent Copy,* Anthony Burgess sketches the circumstances which preceded (and to a great extent precipitated) his belated blossoming as professional novelist and man of letters. "I went to the Gates of Hercules," he writes, "the sundered lips of Europe and Africa, to Deucalion's flood and Noah's. In other words, I was posted to Gibraltar."[1] Here, on a rock colonized by the British but reeking of both its Spanish and Moorish heritage, the Catholic Burgess encountered finally a living reconciliation of the Catholic/Protestant dichotomy which had troubled his own Manchester youth. Protestant Britain, perched precariously on the foundations of two powerful alien cultures, had somehow forged these (and her own) into a diverse and yet oddly harmonious multi-culture — a place where, as Burgess says, Arabs discussed Aristotle on the colonnade of an Iberian University. This strange colony came to serve for Mr. Burgess as a proof, even a model, of the feasibility of "confluence." "In Gibraltar," he writes, "my muse seemed to have found what it was looking for in the way of a subject matter — a conflict that had turned into a confluence."[2]

Mr. Burgess likes to portray the universe as a "duoverse," that is, a cluster of contending opposites which agitate against moderation. "The thing we're most aware of in life," he writes, "is the division, the conflict of opposites — good, evil; black, white; rich, poor — and so on."[3] And since living in the center of this conflict is, to use Mr. Burgess's illustration, like trying to picnic in the middle of a football field, we gravitate naturally (and gratefully) toward any ideology which is able to convince us that this conflict is actually an illusion, that in fact there *is* somewhere an ultimate unity in which all extremes resolve themselves. To this end the Church proffers God; socialism, the classless society; and the artist, his art.

"Art," according to Burgess, "is the organization of base matter into an illusory image of universal order."[4] The artist is an alchemist, drawing on the inherent disorder and dissonance of the human experience and somehow transmuting them into a dazzling display of order and harmony. Contending forces which divide our allegiances in the real world are tamed and reconciled in the artistic creation, or at least seem to be, and the illusion of unity is the final product of this creative process.

Yet though most people, according to Burgess, are possessed by the need to unify, they generally accept solutions rather than work out their own. How many Calvinists are there, after all, for every Calvin; how

*From the *Iowa Review* 8 (1977): 46–52. © 1977 by The Iowa Review. Reprinted with permission.

many Marxists for each Marx? Only the sexual division, the thing that makes a man different and apart from a woman (and vice-versa), is actually resolvable on an individual and thoroughly *active* level. This ritual, *grâce à Dieu*, is the exclusive possession of no one class or profession — there is, one assumes, no sexual aristocracy — and it may serve the artist as well or as poorly as it does anyone else. But it is of particular importance in Burgess's novels about artists because, as another means of achieving confluence, sex is closely allied with the creative act. It is, in fact, consistently used to reflect the condition of the less democratic syntheses which his artist-characters pursue.

Sex and art, then, serve as two separate though related expressions of the same drive, and because Burgess's protagonists in *Nothing Like the Sun* and *A Vision of Battlements* resort frequently to both, the two provide a good perspective on the conflict and confluence theme which figures so prominently in the ever-burgeoning Burgess canon.

A Vision of Battlements is Mr. Burgess's first novel. Although not published until 1965, the book was written some 16 years earlier. "When the Easter vacation of 1949 arrived," Burgess writes in his introduction, "I was empty of music but itching to create. And so I wrote this novel. It filled up the vacation, kept me out of mischief, and also satisfied a vague curiosity I had always had: could I, for good or ill, compose an extended piece of prose without getting bored." A second, more submerged reason for the novel "was to see if I could clear my head of the dead weight of Gibraltar. I had lived with it so long that it still lay in my skull, a chronic migraine: a work of fiction seemed the best way of breaking it up, pulverizing it, sweeping it away."[5]

And indeed "the rock" looms like a threatening deity over the affairs of Sgt. Richard Ennis, Burgess's half-fictional protagonist who finds himself posted in wartime Gibraltar as instructor in the newly formed "Army Vocational and Cultural Corps." The unit is divided into two branches: the forward-looking "Vocational," which goes about training men to build a new world when the war is over; and the backward-looking "Cultural" (Ennis's), which is supposed to inculcate an appreciation for the arts, but languishes instead in the inattention of what C. P. Snow was to call the New Men. Ennis wants to make it in this new world, for his own sake as well as for his wife's (she eventually runs off with an American — the new world personified), but finds himself irresistibly attracted to the old: to his art, to the ancient culture of the Spanish and the Moors, and to his Spanish mistress, Concepción.

Burgess's description of the dilemma is characteristically direct: "Ennis had become a manichee, at home in a world of perpetual war. It did not matter what the flags or badges were; he looked only for the essential opposition — Wet and Dry, Left Hand and Right Hand, Yin and Yang, X and Y. Here was the inevitable impasse, the eternal stalemate"

(*Vision*, pp. 68–9). And down the line the alliances form. Ennis's English wife, Laurel, is cool, refined, aseptic; Concepción is rich, warm, fragrant. While Laurel is the England of the Norse gods and the briny sea, Concepción is Spain, the ancient mingling of Latin and Moorish cultures, the stronghold of the Catholic Church — not the defensive, displaced Catholicism of Ennis's (and Burgess's) Northern England, but the proud, entrenched faith of Mediterranean Europe. And while Ennis is portrayed as sexually impotent with his wife ("Really, you *are* impetuous"), he is seen to enjoy a quite satisfactory relationship with Concepción, the product of which, predictably enough, is conception. Laurel, off in England writing long and nagging letters to Ennis, excites little passion; Concepción, his dark and alluring mistress, *is* passion.

The dichotomy, of course, brings to mind Shakespeare, particularly the Shakespeare of the sonnets, who serves, if somewhat posthumously, as the subject of Burgess's *Nothing Like the Sun*. Fair England and dark Africa once more compete for the allegiance of the artist, and once more, it is the very delicate, refined beauty of the aristocratic North balanced against the rich and passionate allure of a black woman. In *Nothing Like the Sun* Concepción reappears as the dark lady, an East Indian woman of mysterious background whom Will woos and wins for his mistress; and Laurel's place is taken by young Harry (WH), Earl of Southampton, patron and sometime object of Will's hypergamous affections.

The important distinction between the two pairs, however, is not so much that the fair image turns male, but that the hostile/reverent attitude which characterized this relationship in *A Vision* takes on the added aspect of sexual attraction. With Laurel, Ennis is unable to achieve any sexual compatibility; rarely, in fact, does he think of her in sexual terms. But with young Harry, Will manages to express both his hostility and his admiration through the ambivalence of their homosexual relationship. Sex serves as a vengeance as well as a pleasure, and as a result, the role of the fair image in this novel becomes much more complex and much more vital.

Burgess carefully adumbrates the relationship which is to develop between Harry and the poet by inserting early in the narrative a number of passages which establish Will's homosexual leanings. When, as a boy, he fantasizes about life at sea, Will thinks of "spewing among rude and rough rascals made roaring lustful with salt beef and, a mere week at sea, cursing and raging in their fights over the ravaging of the soft white body of a boy, a boy refined and gentled with snippets of Ovid and maxims out of Seneca." And Will's response is "a dark excitement . . . that guilt at once pounced on in a rearing wave to wash away."[6]

Even in the context of his marriage, where Will soon tires of his conjugal prerogatives, Burgess reveals a latent but already strongly developed disposition in the young poet. He tells how, after the birth of a child,

Anne would steal their young son's clothes and, "decked as a pretty page, she would taunt him and simper before him and say: 'Take me, master, in whatever way you have a mind to.' This would fill his whole head with beating blood, so that he was blind and went for her blindly. She was, he saw, hunting out corners of corruption in his soul which he had hardly guessed at before" (*Nothing*, p. 40). The dark goddess continues to dominate his thoughts and his aspirations, but a second current of desire runs along parallel throughout, the attraction to male youth and beauty. "Catch as catch can," a fortune teller advises him, "A black woman or a golden man" (*Nothing*, p. 15).

With the relationship which finally blossoms between Will and his aristocratic patron thus prefigured, it is no surprise when, on first meeting, the poet's eye is immediately drawn to Harry's physical beauty: the red pouting mouth, the fair white skin, the sparse golden beard. "There was something in his eyes that WS did not like—a slyness, an unwillingness to look boldly. But he was beautiful enough, there was no doubt of his beauty" (*Nothing*, p. 91). By the end of the scene, the attraction has become firmly established: "WS looked down bitterly on this Adonis, so languid, so satiated of all his world could give. He saw himself taking him and stripping him of his silk and jewels and then beating him till he cried. I will raise great weals on thy tender delicate skin, puppy" (*Nothing*, p. 94).

Interestingly, homosexuality figures prominently in *A Vision* as well. As early as 1949 Burgess was apparently associating the creative impulse with the homosexual sensibility. Trapped in the artistic wasteland of the Army Vocational and Cultural Corps, Ennis finds himself drawing closer and closer to the epicene coterie of Sgt. Julian Agate, "ballet dancer, one-time Petrouchka praised by Stravinsky and patted by Diaghilev" (*Vision*, p. 18): "The little dinner parties they held were gay with talk, foot-touching under the table, covert hand-holding. As they sat at the snowy table in the Winter Gardens Restaurant, digesting a meal that was as near civilized as one could hope for in the early days of European peace, smoking, chaffing, giggling over coffee, Ennis often felt almost happy. The world of women was far; the cool flutes of the epicene voices were soothing him to a strange peace" (*Vision*, p. 86).

The lustrous Agate embodies the cultural and artistic values which the new world of Major Muir (head of the A.V.C.C.) and his associates threatens to destroy. Agate has all the effeminate mannerisms that the convention demands, and Burgess exploits them for comic relief. But clichés notwithstanding, the role is important because it establishes quite early in the canon of Burgess's work this identification between art and the epicene. When, later in the novel, Ennis finds himself caught in another heterosexual affair—again with an English woman, again unfulfilled—his thoughts turn to Agate: "He wished he were back in a billet with Julian, in the calm epicene atmosphere where lust could be transmuted into creative energy. . . . He felt cloddish, cheap, boorish, just as he had often felt in the presence of Laurel" (*Vision*, p. 148).

In the light of Burgess's concern with artistic synthesis, particularly synthesis as it carries over into sexual activity, homosexuality certainly seems a distortion of the drive to unite the male/female division. In *A Vision*, this is partially explained by the notion of channeling the energy which derives from the tension of conflict out of the natural heterosexual solution into the more demanding but ultimately more satisfying possibilities of art. The greater the sense of division, the more potent (and productive) the drive to unite it. When Ennis talks about transmuting lust into creative energy, it is to this that he is referring. The "calm epicene atmosphere" of Julian and his circle serves to dam the energy which might otherwise dissipate in lesser (i.e., sexual) activities.

But the relationship between the creative and the sexual impulse is much more complex than this simple equation of psychodynamics suggests, primarily because other factors enter into the process. For Ennis, as well as for Will, sexual excitement becomes almost a necessary condition for the creation of art. Time and again these artist / protagonists find themselves composing, often against their own will, at the height of their sexual passions. In the process of making love to a girl he has met, Ennis finds his mind having a mind of its own: "He kissed her again, holding the kiss, indeed waiting for her response. Excitement began to flood his body welling as blood wells from a razorcut. . . . He kissed her bared neck, unable to hold back words. 'I do love you, Lavinia. My darling, I do love you.' At the same time, his aloof brain worked out a passage of double fugue" (*Vision*, pp. 171–2). Sex and music, in fact, become for Ennis mutually productive. Just as passion stimulates the flow of his music, so music can bring on the other thing: "Yet, as he and his room-mate sat together in their billet, Ennis composing, Julian embroidering silk or darning socks, a sudden wave of desire, of a sort of intolerable homesickness for Concepción would come over him. This was especially when the heat of inspiration, by some deep law of sympathy, provoked sexual heat. Excited as a new theme appeared or an old theme began to develop new possibilities, his pulse would start to race, and his nostrils would be suffused with that maddening smell of musk, his ears would tickle with the softness of her loosened hair" (*Vision*, p. 86). The bond between the instincts becomes so close, in fact, that Ennis need only watch two flies copulate on the ceiling and his bountiful muse descends.

In a sense, sexual heat becomes the *muse*, the inspiration to create. This is certainly the case in *Nothing Like the Sun*, where the entire narrative is built up around the conviction that the sonnets Shakespeare wrote stemmed from his bisexual entanglements. WS the poet is torn between a dark lady and a fair youth, and the passion which each excites is the inspiration for the poems which flow from his pen. That the dark lady is a muse figure Burgess makes no bones about. The first line of the book, "It was all a matter of a goddess — dark, hidden, deadly, horribly desirable" (*Nothing*, p. 3), ushers in the magic of her presence. She exists in the poet's imagination — surfacing often in dream-like fantasies — long before, as mistress, she actually appears in the narration. In one dream, the connection between the passion she arouses and the poetry she will inspire emerges forcefully:

> He turned, ready to swoon, unwinking, at the vision. She was naked, gold, glowing, burnished, burning, the sun, all desire of him.
> "I am altogether thine. Do thou take what is thine."
> Oh, his young heart. Oh, the giddiness, the mad beating. He fell before her, fell at her golden feet. She raised him with strong arms of gold. They fell into swansdown, behind curtains of silver silk. And there was the promise that when the moment came, and soon, too soon, it must come, he would be possessed of all time's secrets and his very mouth grow golden and utter speech for which the very gods waited and would be silent to hear (*Nothing*, p. 9).

But neither the homosexual nor the heterosexual relationship endures through the maturing of Shakespeare's own artistic abilities, and by the time he is ready to begin the period of the great tragedies both have virtually expired. Love ceases to be his goddess — fair or dark — and, simultaneously, love ceases to be his muse. The venereal disease which he contracts (Burgess speculating here) represents the product of his love, just as the miscarriage and death of Concepción in *A Vision* represent the end result of Ennis's love. Heterosexual love proves not only unproductive, as is the homosexual, but *destructive*, a force which is capable of inspiring the soul to create, but which in the process exacts a terrible price. The goddess is no longer one of love and sweet verse, as the early comedies certainly suggest, but an embodiment of the evil which shackles the lives of good men in the tragedies. Scabrous and near death, WS perceives that the disease which has come of his love is a metaphor for the evil that dominates all mankind, that ". . . the great white body of the world was set upon by an illness from beyond, gratuitous and incurable. And that even the name Love was, far from being the best invocation against it, often the very conjuration that summoned the mining and ulcerating hordes" (*Nothing*, p. 231). In both novels then the movement is away from this form of inspiration, and toward deeper and more personal wells of creative energy. Sexual love reveals itself to be far more destructive than it is procreative, and the division between man and woman, so alluring in its promise of synthesis, yields only to the confluence of the protagonist's art.

Notes

1. (New York: Norton, 1968), p. 267.
2. *Ibid.*, p. 268.

3. *Ibid.*, p. 265.

4. *Ibid.*

5. *A Vision of Battlements* (New York: Norton, 1965), pp. 7–8.

6. *Nothing Like the Sun* (New York: Norton, 1964), p. 8.

Enderbyan Poetics: The Word in the Fallen World

Michael Rudick*

Let me begin with an episode from *The Clockwork Testament*: O'Donnell in a New York bar offers Enderby a circumstantial account of the homosexual experience that allegedly lay behind Hopkins's poem "The Bugler's First Communion"—how the priest received the actor's maternal grandfather in the presbytry and "gave him, you know, the stick". Enderby shudders. His first response is the intimation of a second heart attack, and his conclusion is, "What a filthy unspeakable world. . . . What defilement, what horror"; but after a moment's reflection and abatement of the initial shock, "What did it matter, anyway? It was the poetry that counted."[1] Here in this episode, then, are the two principal thematic issues Anthony Burgess has proposed to his readers in the Enderby novels: first, this world of Enderby's—London, Rome, Tangiers, New York City—which on occasion asks to be described as unspeakable, not just for its customary obtuseness, but also for its actively demoralizing power, its capacity, almost its providence, for engineering the most poignant human betrayals; and second, the poetry, which does or does not matter, according as one may read it, and as one may read the world.

How it matters, if it matters, in Enderby's world, are questions I wish to address through a discussion of Enderby as a literary critic. He is, of course, no such thing, but a criticism, a kind of poetics, is inferrable, and its description may serve two aims. The first is to try to characterize him as a poet, and that only partially by using his critical stance to judge the products his creator has endowed him with; rather, I wish to concentrate more upon examining the endeavor of poetry as it is to Enderby. My second aim is to comment on what is happening in these novels, what Enderby's story is and what significance Anthony Burgess asks us to find in it.

This necessitates the liberty of looking at the first three Enderby novels as more or less of a piece. *The Clockwork Testament* surely proceeds from an impulse different from and much later than that which produced *Inside Mr. Enderby* and *Enderby Outside*. Nevertheless, a good many of the themes articulated in the earlier Enderby books are picked up again in

*This essay was written specifically for this volume and is published here for the first time by permission of the author.

The Clockwork Testament. We may not be encountering in it quite the same character, but there can be little surprise in finding Burgess to have resurrected Enderby in 1974, and to have charged him with the satiric mission appropriate to that time.[2] The poet-hero, however, carried some of his own imperatives, and my discussion may suggest not only a seriousness for the later novel that transcends mere topicality, but as well its sequential connections with the earlier two works.

There is no claim to be made that Enderby and Anthony Burgess agree with one another on the subjects of poetry and criticism, whatever occasional similarities are to be found between the lives and opinions of the creator and his creature. In published interviews and in his literary journalism, Burgess has often spoken of how he understands the nature and place of poetic art. One may take the further liberty of quoting him in his own voice, at least as choric comment on his protagonist. Enderby has as well connections with other writer-protagonists in Burgess's work (WS, Miles Faber, Toomey are prime examples), novels which explore creativity, propose certain ideals of artistic achievement, and suggest certain conditions under which artists fall short of the ideals. There is enough comparability among these fictionally projected claims to warrant some generalization, but a full and consistent poetic is not forthcoming from them. In a real sense, Enderby is a special case, enjoying a role as the novelist's *factotum* — witness his yet more recent resurrection in a fourth novel, *Enderby's Dark Lady* (1984) — for the burdens of poetry in only one of the contexts in which Burgess explores the endeavor.

One means of *entrée* is to consider the problem of poetry as an anologue of another of Burgess's characteristic preoccupations, the opposition of social meliorism, represented by Pelagianism, to the anthropology of pessimism and the debilitating effects of original sin, represented by Augustinianism. *A Clockwork Orange, The Wanting Seed, Tremor of Intent,* and most recently, *Earthly Powers* are the novels whose stories preeminently articulate this theme, but it is played upon in the Enderby novels as well, where it surfaces most openly in connection with poetry. Enderby's allegorical poem *The Pet Beast* projects it.[3] The plot by Wapenshaw and his associates to eradicate Enderby's lyric impulses is an instance of Pelagian meddling. In *The Clockwork Testament*, Enderby's last poem, abandoned at the end for want of relief from "raw doctrine" (*CT*, 79), is about St. Augustine and Pelagius; and Enderby's talk-show adversary, Man Balaglas (Burgess's more-than-caricature of B.F. Skinner) is the latter-day Pelagius *par excellence.*

In drawing out the ideological lesson merely, we can observe that Anthony Burgess's projections of the Augustine-Pelagius opposition almost always demonstrate the futility or the corruption of extremes.[4] But Burgess is, to be sure, characteristically harsher on the Pelagian optimists and social engineers than on the believers in original sin. Pelagians make better satiric targets because their posturings are so much more ridiculous and

their exploitations entail denying possibilities of individual human value—
as Enderby explains to Ms. Tietjens (*CT*, 37), "If you get rid of evil you get
rid of choice . . . If you don't choose, you're not human any more". Yet in
Enderby's poem, the condition of the mythical populace in thrall to its
guilt—what the pet beast has been made into—hardly evinces an ideal.
The Pet Beast is, like many of the Enderby poems we become acquainted
with, peculiarly prophetic of things that will happen to him. He, too,
finds his Pelagian liberators in the persons, first of Vesta Bainbridge, then
of Wapenshaw; as the monuments of culture in galleries and libraries in
the labyrinth's peripheral corridors collapse upon the beast's martyrdom,
so Enderby's artistic powers collapse upon his being tractably drawn out of
his poetic immurement. *The Pet Beast*, we are told, will make the
labyrinth and its prisoner into a symbol: "a treasury of human achievement; beauty and knowledge built round a core of sin, the human
condition" (*E*, 18).

We can try to draw a correspondence between that and the Enderbyan condition. None of the novels is meant to enforce a dogma, but as
they employ a satiric mode, they project a hierarchy of values. At a
minimum, they project an experiential dialectic. *Enderby*—inside and
outside—is the story of a poet battling for the life requisite both to his
freedom and to his art.[5] *The Clockwork Testament* is the story of a poet
battling for his particular understanding of freedom and art, against a
world that has to have it another way. The battle itself is demanding of
extreme positions, and superficially at least, Enderby's extreme is ill-
equipped to cope. The very placability of the pet beast is paradigmatic for
him; this as much as anything makes Enderby so susceptible a victim,
sliding so easily into an assumption of the world's burdens: to be the butt
of his upstairs neighbors; to take responsibility for the courtship of 'Arry;
to come eventually to terms with Sir George Goodby; and, as it were in
crescendo, to assume the assassinship of Yod Crewsy (". . . if that ghastly
yob were dead he was glad he was dead. He had desire and motive and
opportunity" [*E*, 252]); and, finally, to assume the place, the effects, and
to a degree, the character of the dead Rawcliffe. It is not an exaggeration
to see Enderby as a creature of guilt, and to recognize how helpless he is.

One of the developments in *The Clockwork Testament* is our meeting
an Enderby who seems tolerably freed from these clogs formerly at his
heels. No longer quite the gentle pet, he can give as much as he gets; the
swordstick replaces the toilet seat as his weapon and, we may affirm, his
iconographic attribute. In the end, he is "*Enderbius triumphans, ex-
ultans*" (*CT*, 131).

All this, though, with an exception, and it lies in Enderby's continued
self-immolation on the altar, or on the block, of poetry. An illustration is
the following exchange that takes place in Enderby's creative writing class.
Lloyd Utterage's "litany of anatomic vilification" has been presented;

Enderby objects to the ineptness of metaphoric correspondence between pricks and dog turds. He is accused by Arnold Something of, to put it mildly, missing the point: "Poetry is made out of emotions", says Arnold. Enderby: "Oh very very very much no and no again. Poetry is made out of words."[6] And after more defense, Utterage to Enderby: "You play your little games with yourself. All this shit about words" (*CT*, 65–67).

Utterage utters his own age and is utterly of that age, self-absorbed, impervious to whatever may lie outside his immediate periphery. Enderby's critique may, in the largest sense, qualify as the reaction of one who cannot without disgust hear poetry used to express or promote hate, though even the more limited appeal to traditional canons of poetic language makes too abstract a claim on the moment-bound sensibility of Utterage and his coevals. Mannered and unmannerly as their verses may be, these students nevertheless show an alarming acuteness in interpreting their teacher's criticism. Refusing the metaphoric union of pricks and turds, Enderby opens himself to attack on by-now familiar grounds, his own divorce, whether instinctive or willful, of art from physical functions, which is paid for by his own dysfunctions in sex and digestion. Utterage's final thrust intuits the Enderbyan connection of autoeroticism and the fruits of digestion, and this may be said to hit Enderby where he lives. He has heard things like this before. In one of his more humiliating moments, for example, Vesta tells him, "Surely the trouble with all your work is that it reads as though it's cut off from the current" (*E*, 159). And the mysterious lady who appears in the final pages of *Enderby Outside* accuses him of being a Prufrock; the vision of himself "puffing in his slack whiteness" is enough to call off any notions of his disturbing the universe, and the connection of that with his poetry is made evident (*E*, 399).

We need, then, to turn from Enderby's equivocal achievement as a poet to the idea of poetry that lies behind this achievement. Putting aside his ideologizings on the poet's condition of freedom and the kind of independence necessary to creation, we find Enderby's most characteristic way of talking about poetry—his own and that of others—is through a kind of exegesis. From some illustrative examples in the novels, and from some passages in Anthony Burgess's literary journalism, we can assemble the principles of what I will call Enderbyan exegesis, and from this there emerges something of a theory of poetry. First, an Enderbyan exegete must find fascination in relations among the phenomena of nature: symmetries, oppositions, correspondences, whether synthetic or necessary. These percepts, when put into the right language, are what poetry is made of, and to be valuable poetry, the phenomena articulated must have some endurance; they cannot be altogether arbitrary or tied irrevocably to a single discrete moment, but they should be visible and audible through time, that is, they can or will be perceptible again, at least imaginatively. The articulation of these symmetries, oppositions or correspondences invites a close look at, especially, their physical contours, and these must be reflected in or find their equivalence in the verbal contours that express them.[7]

Let me venture a suggestion of Enderbyan exegesis, trying it out on six lines of the third sonnet in Dylan Thomas's "Altarwise by Owl-Light":

> First there was the lamb on knocking knees
> And three dead seasons on a climbing grave
> That Adam's wether in the flock of horns,
> Butt of the tree-tailed worm that mounted Eve,
> Horned down with skullfoot and the skull of toes
> On thunderous pavements in the garden time . . .[8]

We look first for what Enderby called, in his exegesis of Hamsun's self-styled poem, "the irreducible minimum of meaning". The poem's job is to "hold the complex totality of linguistic meaning within a shape you can isolate from the dirty world" (*CT*, 70–71). Dylan Thomas's lines, after one fashion of translation or paraphrase, refer to the atonement, Christ's triumph over death and original sin. But this is maximal meaning, or historical content, not linguistic meaning. We are to be concerned not with what the lines say, not with their ideological referent, but rather with their perceptual engagement, and so not with the symbols of cross and holocaust and sin and redemption, as a Christian critic would interpret them. To follow that route of exegesis would be to deny language its power to be other than a static and arbitrary reference to concepts. If comparison is helpful, we might observe that Hamsun's poem, such as it is, may record his moment of dalliance with Ms. Tietjens, but its credentials as poetry depend for Enderby on something else. So, in Thomas's lines, the poet's accomplishment is not in his having found words to describe or record the atonement; it is instead in the verbal texture's expression of more immediate percepts, phrases like "knocking knees", "dead seasons", and "skull of toes" in their expression of halting and falling, opposed to, while being incorporated in, rising—the "climbing grave", the worm that mounts the tree and Eve, and in the heighth and depth of death ("skullfoot and the skull of toes / On . . . pavements") and its countermovements ("horned down"). It is not necessary to specify or judge the ultimate intelligibility of each semantic element in these verses. But in them, the "play"—Enderby's word, used *mutatis mutandis*—between life and death, rising and falling, tottering and driving, the coalescence of perceptions in words and phrases like "climbing grave", "horn" and "thunderous", "mounted" and the like—in these the poetry resides, the durable element whose power will not be effaced even should Christianity fold under the weight of Pelagian oppressiveness.

A student of twentieth-century criticism recognizes nothing especially radical in this mode of reading. It has the same kind of concentration upon rhetorical elements, especially tropes, which is common to what is called

New Criticism, although that identification must be held provisional. This exegesis eschews the heresy of paraphrase, and it insists on poetry's autonomy from adventitious historical connection and from authorial intention. It may find richness and delight in verbal face-offs and tensions, but it does so in a restricted way, surely less ambitious than much new critical reading. Enderbyan exegesis is satisfied to identify linguistic play and watch it shape an utterance into something with a resilient skin. It seems not to be interested in profound ironies or in the encapsulation of discords and abstract dichotomies in the tight language of paradox. The principle operates in Enderby's process of composition, as he puts together the "chance elements" (*E*, 239) that make a poem: "And then the fragments of a new poem came with a familiar confidence into Enderby's head. He saw the shape, he heard the words, he felt the rhythm. Three stanzas each beginning with birds. *Prudence, prudence, the pigeons call.* And, of course, that's what they did call, that's the way they'd always called. *Act, act, the ducks give voice.* And that was true, too" (*E*, 29). Perhaps the worst of Enderby's poems, as awful as what it prophesies for him, it well illustrates the principle: if pigeons and ducks do and will sound like that, then there is no perceptual distortion in the language or, presumably, poetic falsity in the birds' advice.

There does exist a fairly specific analogue to this in modern criticism, identifiable in certain efforts by John Crowe Ransom to categorize kinds of poetry according to their contents and their aims. No influence of Ransom on Burgess, not even an indirect one, need be proposed; the similarities in Ransom's analysis are in fact not so useful to this argument as are its drawing out the consequences of Enderby's poetics, something more germane to Enderby's story.

As is well known, Ransom's criticism (like Enderby's) concentrates on images, whose function is indispensable to his theory of poetry. He is one of the New Critics, perhaps the first among them, who insisted that poetry is a special kind of knowledge, opposed to the knowledge of science, which is abstract and has utility and exploitation of nature as its goals. Poetry, in contrast, is the knowledge of nature in its particularity; it depends on an "innocent," non-exploitative apprehension of nature, whereby its objects are conceived of whole and for their own self-existent sakes. Poetry renders "the body of the object" through images, permitting contemplation of the object in its totality and its independence.

Most pertinent to Enderby's endeavors are Ransom's ideas on what he calls Physical Poetry. This is the poetry which "dwells as exclusively as it dares upon physical things", that is, "on things as they are in their rich and contingent materiality". Ransom observes that there are few or no pure instances of this, naming imagism and the "pure poetry" cultivated by George Moore and his circle as modern schools which tried to approach this absolute. But Ransom's most important argument is that "All true poetry is a phase of Physical Poetry." Its medium is the image, which, as the most immediate representation of the natural object, is prior to any idea abstracted from the image; the idea is "the image with its character beaten out of it."[9] Behind this is a nearly nominalistic metaphysic, and the epistemology is very much empiricist. The antithesis of Physical Poetry is Platonic Poetry, which deals in abstract ideas rather than particular images. This, too, is not to be found in a pure form; a poetry without images is, to Ransom, no poetry at all. The evident analogue to Enderbyan poetics is the priority and privilege of poetry that apprehends the particularity of nature through images. Ransom could speak for Enderby when, citing two verses from Ariel's song (*Tempest*, I.ii), he says, "Here it is difficult for anybody . . . to receive any experience except that of a distinct set of images. It has the configuration of image, which consists of being sharp of edges, and the modality of the image, which consists in being given and non-negotiable, and the density, which consists in being full, a plenum of qualities . . . The art of poetry depends more frequently on this faculty than on any other in its repertory; the faculty of presenting images so whole and clean that they resist the catalysis of thought."[10] And Enderby would applaud especially the definitions of configuration, modality, and density, but as well as the image's effect of forestalling ratiocination, the process of abstracting the image into an idea.

The synthesis in Ransom's dialectic of Physical and Platonic Poetries is, of course, Metaphysical Poetry, valued by Ransom for interests close to the literary modernism his poetics sought to defend, but valued also for its importance to the religious agenda scarcely concealed in his criticism. Metaphysical Poetry is that which gratifies a necessary human aesthetic craving; it fills the moment of suspension "between the Platonism in us, which is militant, always sciencing and devouring, and a starved, inhibited aspiration towards innocence which, if it could only be free, would like to respect and know the object as it might of its own accord reveal itself."[11] It is the poetry which unifies the two objects of knowledge, the individual and the abstract. Inferentially close to this is Burgess's own remark on imaginative literature: "It's not made out of concepts; it's made out of percepts . . . Concepts only come to life when they're expressed in things you can see, taste, feel, touch. . . ."[12] The Enderbyan correspondence, however, appears to apply only at the lower reaches of Ransom's dialectic, something that can be made clearer through an excursion into another of Ransom's efforts at a poetic hierarchy.

In a variant expression of the typology above, he names three achievements possible to poetry. First, it may observe nature, "transcribe" it (Ransom is not diffident at using this term), and so serve "as knowledge by images." At a higher level, it "animates nature" through tropes, thus lifting the status of the inanimate or the inferior to the level of human sensibility. At its apogee, poetry, here scarcely distinct from religion, may animate abstractions, that is, reparticularize and dignify what platonic and positivistic impulses have degraded through their utiliarian predatoriness.[13] There is a sense in which Enderby aspires to this last achievement; a poem abandoned because images cannot be found to relieve "raw doctrine" shows him at least recognizing that synthesis of percept and concept is imaginable. But his criticism appears not to recognize it, shows itself unequipped to account for a poetry which is, in Ransom's understanding, Metaphysical. If my Enderbyan exegesis of Dylan Thomas's lines does justice to the method, it still does less than justice to that poem by the standards of a criticism that would approach accounting for its power. Enderby's poetic is a criticism which, in a manner of speaking that reveals something of Enderby's limit, will not allow the word to become the Word. It is adequate to the poetry of Ransom's first and second orders; it values success in representing the natural object as a self-existent entity and success in charging nature with a life of its own, but it stops short of admitting the animation of universals. It cannot, then, come to terms with a poetry that might ultimately recover privilege from its most militant competitors, whether Platonic or Pelagian. These two categories occupy analogous positions in the "systems" of Ransom and Enderby, and both have characteristics in common, most evidently the exploitative imperiousness of both claims to authority over human and natural independence and individuality.

This bears on Enderby's success as a champion of value in the lists against these competitors. We have seen that he is not unarmed, but have also seen that he is persistently on the defensive. The defense is a stance the novels' norms turn into an extreme. The corollaries of this stance — love of poetic tradition, cultivation of form, refusal to glorify the time-bound or idiosyncratic — are almost universally scorned. Yet Burgess sees to it that Enderby's stance is the one a reader must find inevitable, judged in opposition to the legion of barbarians, philistines, and blockheads Burgess creates as antagonists. Faced with the assaults of self-serving vultures, pop culturists, psychiatrists, and poetasters, Enderby can only be heroic, however comically so, in pressing the disinterested claims he does. These are the novels' means of advocacy; they invite a reader's affirmation of Enderby's position, and they are the witness of Burgess's success as a satiric artist.[14]

But there are other confrontations for Enderby in these novels, ones in which the oppositions are not drawn by Burgess with the customary satiric intent. Two of them are important to this discussion: the concluding passage of *Enderby Outside*, the hero's meeting with the figure who might be interpreted as his Muse, and then Enderby's encounter with his own creation, Gervase Whitelady (1559–91), in *The Clockwork Testament*. Both confrontations have Enderby again on the defensive, but neither of them evokes the characteristic independence, resistance, or scorn on Enderby's part evinced, for example, before Vesta in the Papal demesnes or in the splendidly written victory over Wapenshaw (*E*, 223–29). The lovely lady who tutors Enderby in poetry and offers him one thing more is mysterious, but palpable. Gervase Whitelady is impalpable, though less mysterious in his effects. Both incidents confront Enderby with his failures.

Discussing a projected film adaptation of *Enderby*, Burgess said, "In the book . . . he becomes a major poet".[15] This was to take the will for the deed; Burgess was not remembering accurately what he had written. "Minor poet," the nameless lady calls him, "Be thankful for what you've got. Don't ask too much, that's all" (*E*, 399). Her sybilline advice two pages later, telling him not to "try and tame dogs or enter a world of visions and no syntax," may be warning Enderby off joining the dissipated bards busy making it new at the Doggy Wog Bar; however, one of Enderby's difficulties is the lack of courage to face that: "You're frightened of the young and the experimental and the way-out and the black dog" (389). The lady's diagnosis of Enderby is an accurate one. Fear, and the guilt he says he'll have scope for (403), have crippled Enderby, as much in poetry as in sex. He shares in the judgement Posterity delivers at the end on the expatriate artists in Tangiers: "They are nothing" (405).

"He was nothing," Enderby says of Whitelady to his students, "so you can forget about him. One of the unknown poets . . . spurned by the Muse" (*CT*, 56). Here, Enderby must be confronting himself. "Christ, Whitelady has identity. But what he doesn't have and what he never had is the sensation of having sensations. Better and cleverer people than we are can be invented" (57). Is it fanciful to suggest that Enderby has failed at that, the proof of his failure being the inability to create anything other than himself, a Whitelady, another minor poet? This approaches more closely the Enderbyan predicament than does Lloyd Utterage's later accusation, "Closing your eyes to what's going on in the big big world" (67). The metamorphosis of Enderby into a social critic or a social scientist would help him no more than his "religiolesbian" landlady's books "concerned with the *real* issues of life" helped him over the impasse in his Augustine-Pelagius poem (26). Enderby dropped that poem for want of a dramatic or symbolic means to tell the story with. There might have been a solution, but it was quickly displaced by the idea of *The Odontiad*, "a poetic record of dental decay in thirty-two books" (42), returning Enderby to his more comfortable field of concentration, the transcription of natural process, here of course connected with another Enderbyan preoccupation, the digestive process.

The attention Enderby pays to his gut is one of Burgess's devices for insinuating the failure of Enderby's nerve. The play with Gerard Manley Hopkins's language throughout *The Clockwork Testament* is symptomatic of the same kind of inadequacy. Scarcely a page passes without a quotation or at least a tag or reminiscence of Hopkins's poetry laced into Enderby's speech. But this is little more than luxuriance in lavish language. The incident discussed at the beginning of this paper is another symptom. Whatever its plausibility, Enderby appreciates the possibility of a homosexual genesis for "The Bugler's First Communion" — a wordman can be susceptible to what words suggest — but shock and disgust at it is his stubborn resistance to the more disturbing potentials of human experience poems can reveal. Only the poetry matters, the language cut off from the experience behind it. As shot through with Hopkins as the novel is, one waits to hear Enderby, whether in prayer or sacrilege, utter, "Mine, O thou Lord of life, send my roots rain!" But neither that nor relics from other painful Hopkins sonnets occupies a place in the hero's consciousness. The word is not allowed to become the Word. Recognizing this may be the confirmation of the mysterious lady's proposition that "poetry isn't a silly little hobby to be practised in the smallest room of the house" (E, 389–90).

It may be misguided speculation to interpret what Burgess was about doing as he wrote the final episode of The Clockwork Testament, the scene of Enderby's triumph over another mysterious lady, this one from Poughkeepsie (or is it somewhere else?), who has come to humiliate him. But a comparison of endings allows this much to be ventured as a point of departure. Sexual failure at the close of Enderby Outside is associated with poetic failure. Sexual mastery for Enderby in The Clockwork Testament comes too late to affect the poetry; it no longer matters. The dream of the Augustine and Pelagius movie — "at last artistically dealt with" (CT, 136) — may show Enderby's creative powers to have been gathered up into an altogether different medium, just as the nostalgic satisfaction at the genius of his earlier verse (129, 136) has the effect of resigned farewell. Whatever apology for poetry he has had to tender the mad lady from Poughkeepsie is a work of supererogation, so ludicrous has the assault been, and so sublimated is Enderby's character. Anticipation of imminent death has something to do with this, but we have been prepared for an Enderby who will outdo an imagined Luther (129) through the swordstick episode on the subway; even the spectre of Whitelady "looked down amazed" at Enderby's chivalry (111).

The anonymous lady has an identity, or at least a connection with another identity. She seems British and Catholic, she claims to have been deserted by an impotent husband whose corruption — including an addiction to Enderby's verse — she says she caught, and, most curious of all, she recalls four lines of off-color doggerel Enderby had composed on his honeymoon (CT, 123; E, 137). She is, then, a re-embodiment of Vesta Bainbridge, and from Vesta other associations ramify: the stepmother, Miss Boland, perhaps the exasperating Muse, even Wapenshaw — in effect all the figures Enderby quailed before in fifty-six years of timidity, guilt, and defensiveness. The sexual triumph, free from scruple ("there was no question of mumbling of begging now," 131), is Enderby's tardily and symbolically achieved compensation. It is also the satirist's triumph, or his indulgence, or his act of contrition for having so long tried his hero's endurance by suffering him to be preyed on by vulgarity, obtuseness, and small-mindedness. But the triumph is neither one of freedom over social engineering, nor one of poetry over propaganda. Even death is but a qualified surcease from burden: "it is a sort of satisfaction," says Posterity over Enderby's corpse, "for *nunc dimittis* is the sweetest of canticles", but her speech ends by asserting the human condition inescapable (150–51).

Burgess will evidently allow no transcendance. Measured against Ransom's ideal of the poet-liberator who furnishes the human consciousness with better than is imaginable to science or positivism or moralism, in effect a return to prelapsarian innocence, Burgess's claims, to the extent Enderby reflects them, permit at best honorable failure. But no small honor; a benign poetics and a benign character still perform their office. If poetry to Enderby has been "play," if he is guilty as charged of "playing games," he exemplifies a gratuitousness that keeps him, like the poetry he values, "isolate from the dirty world." Burgess has said, "The important things in life are games," and has insisted, as though to belie the importance of games, that art, like play, is the opposite of duty.[16] Loyalty — dutiful loyalty — to this gratuitousness is the virtue Enderby never stops paying for. He is Burgess's picture of postlapsarian innocence.

Notes

1. Anthony Burgess, *The Clockwork Testament, or Enderby's End* (1975; rpt. New York: Bantam, 1976), pp. 82–85. Subsequent citations are in the text, marked *CT*.

2. The principal burden is the author's oblique self-defense for having written *A Clockwork Orange* and having allowed it to be filmed; Burgess still complains of being, in popular opinion, identified too exclusively with that book (see his interview with Samuel Coale, *Modern Fiction Studies*, 27 (1981), 448). But there are other burdens on Enderby's shoulders, and one of the novel's problems, if compared with its predecessors, is Burgess's not altogether controlled mix of satiric antagonists.

3. Anthony Burgess, *Enderby* (1963, 1968; New York: Norton, 1968) pp. 17–19. Subsequent citations are marked *E*.

4. See Geoffrey Aggeler, "Pelagius and Augustine in the Novels of Anthony Burgess", *English Studies*, 55 (1974); 43–55.

5. I am adapting here in general outline the reading of *Enderby* by Robert Morris in *The Consolations of Ambiguity: An Essay on the Novels of Anthony Burgess* (Columbia: Univ. of Missouri Press, 1971), pp. 75–89; I am more concerned, however, with how Enderby's poetic bears on the larger issues.

6. This is an instance of the extremity defensiveness produces. A more balanced Enderbyan statement, perhaps, is his observation about graffiti on public lavatory walls: some may be considered "a kind of art, since they were evidently attempts to purge powerful emotion into stylized forms" (*E*, 231).

7. Enderby's reading of Hamsun's poem (*CT*, 70) is one *locus* for this; another of importance is Burgess's review of translations of Omar Khayyam in "Graves and Omar", *Urgent Copy: Literary Studies* (New York: Norton, 1968), pp. 205–6.

8. Dylan Thomas, *Collected Poems* (New York: New Directions, 1957), p. 81. Burgess has written that "Dylan was the greatest lyric poet of the twentieth century" ("The Writer as Drunk", *Urgent Copy*, p. 89).

9. John Crowe Ransom, "Poetry: A Note on Ontology", *The World's Body* (1938; rpt.

Baton Rouge: Louisiana State Univ. Press, 1968), pp. 114–120.

10. Ransom, *The World's Body*, p. 118.

11. Ransom, *The World's Body*, p. 130.

12. Interview with Geoffrey Aggeler (1971), *Anthony Burgess: the Artist as Novelist* (University: University of Alabama, 1979), 27. Compare the statement of WS: "There is the flesh and the flesh makes all. Literature is an epiphenomenon of the action of the flesh" (*Nothing Like the Sun* [Harmondsworth: Penguin, 1966], p. 234).

13. John Crowe Ransom, "A Psychologist Looks at Poetry", *The World's Body*, pp. 158–61.

14. Let this mark one difference between the art of Enderby and the art of Burgess in these novels. Burgess comments on the difference between literary works and didactic works in what is Pornography?" (*Urgent Copy*, p. 255). According to the distinction suggested, Enderby's poems would never move a reader to action (though the written-to-order Thelma and 'Arry sequence might be the exception); Burgess's satire, however, treads the line between active and aesthetic response.

15. Interview with Thomas Churchill, *Malahat Review*, 17 (1971), 111.

16. Interview with Coale, p. 441. Compare Ransom: poetry is "distinct as a form of knowledge . . . It at a minimum views the world as particularity, and we have to have the world in that sense" (*The World's Body*, pp. 158–59).

Linguistics, Mechanics, and Metaphysics: Anthony Burgess's *A Clockwork Orange* (1962)

Esther Petix*

The second half of the twentieth century has passively acknowledged the emergence of its most controversial gadfly, John Anthony Burgess Wilson: philosopher, critic, theologian, linguist, musician, academician, and author. Yet the seemingly facile task of the Burgess critic is not so much a matter of ascribing priorities within Burgess's various spheres of expertise, but rather (and amazingly) in shouldering the onus of redressing the dearth of any critical attention. Serious and exhaustive research reveals that Burgess's tremendous energy and soaring imagination have netted only moderate acclaim, a modicum of intellectual authority, and a quasi-reputation as one of the century's comic artists. For too long Burgess's literary precision and satire have been obscured beneath labels of precocious, light wit. While his contemporaries moved to the heights of fame and fortune, garnering critical attention, esteem, and aggrandizement, the wealth of Burgess's knowledge and ingenuity within the form of the novel remained ignored.

Most certainly Burgess has his following, but his disciples' enthusiasm (at times almost hysteria) has not diverted attention to his themes, nor has

*From *Old Lines, New Forces*, ed. Robert K. Morris (Cranbury, N.J.: Associated University Presses, 1976), 38–52. © 1976 by Associated University Presses. Reprinted with permission.

it acquainted large numbers with the universality of his traditionalism and messages. Perhaps, then, he is in need of one fewer disciple and one more evangelist. For as any devotee of Burgess knows, this is an era that enjoys the dramatic sweep of technocracy. Today one must introduce status (of any sort) from the point of volume rather than quality or essence, and by contemporary standards, shibboleths, and axioms, Burgess's work is not established. In terms of sheer physical output, Burgess ranks high. Compared with the popularity of contemporaries, however, Burgess's sales offer only tepid comparison.

That Burgess is not a top seller has many implications. First, and obviously, there are distinct implications for Burgess himself. As a professional author, he is certainly aware of market returns to his own purse; aware, too, that what and how much he sells has a material effect upon his own life-style, if not his *raison d'être*. Unyieldingly, however, he tends toward remoteness and obscurity, holding out in effect for principle over capital. Ideally, Burgess's stand is consistent with his philosophy.

The implications for the reading public are another matter. Why, for example, is Burgess considered intellectually obscure? Why, after nearly thirty books, must one still introduce him as "the author of *A Clockwork Orange*," and that reference only recognizable because of the barely recognizable film version (call it rather, perversion) of the novel? An obvious problem exists when an author who has so much to say and is possessed of such profundities is not widely read; is, in fact, dismissed as a perpetrator of violence or as a comic. But then, Burgess criticism is at best confused. It is further obfuscated by the fact that he holds sway over a devoted following (which includes some first-rate critics), yet does not hold commensurate stature among scholars. It is my contention that the major force of Burgess has been siphoned off into static frenetics rather than into direct qualitative evaluation. That a clouding of Burgess's fiction has occurred is patent; how and why it has occurred requires a deeper analysis of Burgess's fiction and mind, both of which are labyrinthine. The labyrinth, a symbol often invoked by Burgess himself, is charted with the aid of various threads and clues running through his fiction. And pursuing these leads, these seeming difficulties, these ambiguities, these strata and substrata brings the reader to the inner core of Burgess's central satire: the Minotaur's Cave.

As a maze-maker, Burgess challenges not only Dedalus in the manner of construction, but God in the act of creation—a device and theory he learned from Joyce. Yet such creations and constructs demand a more formal system, and often an elusive one. Like the protagonist, the reader is drawn through threads of the literal plot into the maze, formed often as not below the author's own hilarious crust of ego. Yet, concurrently, Burgess as readily hides himself in the center of his creation, sequestered and insulated by its vastness as well as its intricacies. Readers thus are invited, nay dared, to master the maze, to pick up the various threads and wander the labyrinth; but the same reader always comes to the mystical center—volitionally, and only after much effort.

Imperfectly read, Burgess is necessarily open to charges of philosophical bantering; misread he is often missed entirely. It remains, then, to follow those distinct, definitive threads designed by the architect himself which lead to the mind of the maze-builder, the "God-rival." For at the center the reader may discover an entire universe in which the author attempts to contain the human colony. As with all artists who attempt to match wits with God, Burgess provides only a scale model. Yet it is a model unique in many vital, identifiable ways. Stated as a more classical apostrophe, Burgess constructs his cosmogony to explain—there is no longer in the modern world any need to justify or vindicate—the ways of man to man: to see hope through failure; to set a course while adrift; to seek certainty in ambiguity. In following the threads leading into the center of the labyrinth, we are able to spin from Burgess's fictions something of our own identities.

Midway in Burgess's decade of authorship, and bleakest within his fictional cosmogony, are the years of the early sixties. It is a period marked by excessive concern with death (his own seeming imminent) and with protagonists only thinly disguised as alter-egos. Added to a medical diagnosis of (suspected) brain tumor were England's failures through socialism, her displacement as a world power in the aftermath of World War II, and her lack of character among the modern nations. All this greeted Burgess upon his return home from the Far East. In facing his own death, he also faced the demise of England. And the twofold bitterness is reflected in a twin-bladed satire so lacerating and abrasive that it goes beyond satire into black comedy.

In 1962 Burgess published his two dystopian novels, *The Wanting Seed* and *A Clockwork Orange*. Both are horrible visions of the future, predicated upon the present. In essence what Burgess does in the two novels is to project socialism and the excesses of the Welfare State (*A Clockwork Orange*) and historical behaviorism (*The Wanting Seed*) into a future that is at once nebulous and contemporary. Through such an extension in time he contends that socialism leads to a loss of the will and behaviorism leads to a loss of the soul. These companion novels consider the impact of original sin, abortion, cannibalism, violence, and free will on human beings who daily grow more will-less and more soulless.

However bleak the authorial outlook, however black the comedy, Burgess in his dystopian mood is Burgess at his most lucid. No longer are the protagonists culled from Establishment posts: Ennis of *A Vision of Battlements* was a soldier; Crabbe of "the Malayan Trilogy" was a civil servant; Howarth, of *The Worm and the Ring*, was a schoolteacher. Now the anti-hero of Burgess has become a full-blown rebel, and the quiescent, or slightly recalcitrant Minotaur is savage and obvious. One must keep this in mind in turning to *A Clockwork Orange*, for it is not only Burgess's best-known novel; it is Burgess at his most exposed, and perhaps most vulnerable.

The central thematic and structural interrogative of the novel comes when the prison "charlie" (chaplain) laments: "Does God want goodness or the choice of goodness? Is a man who chooses the bad perhaps in some way better than a man who has the good imposed upon him?"[1] Such a question, while it affords the concision necessary to a reviewer, is totally insufficient to the critic. For there is something at once delightful and horrible, dogged and elusive in *A Clockwork Orange* that even so profound a rhetorical question cannot contain. There is something about the novel so frightening that it demanded a new language, and something so immanent in the message of the novel that it refused to be separated from the language. Linguistics and metaphysics — the how and what of *A Clockwork Orange* — are the disparate, yet connected threads leading to the Minotaur.

A Clockwork Orange is in part a clockwork, not merely titularly, but essentially. Its cadence and regularity are a masterpiece of grotesque precision. The reader is as much a flailing victim of the author as he is a victim of time's finite presence. He is hurtled into a futuristic book of twenty-one chapters and comes to acknowledge that he, as well as the protagonist-narrator, Alex, is coming of age; that he, too, is charged with advancement and growth. This "initiation" aspect of the novel is not gratuitous — of course. For the novel is further divided into three parts, reminiscent of the three ages of man; and each of these three parts begins with the question scanning the infinite and the indefinite: "What's it going to be then, eh?" Added to both of these devices is the haunting and vaguely familiar setting of the novel that teases the reader into an absurdly disquieting sense of regularity — as numbers have a way of doing — all the more unnerving because such regularity conveys a sense of rhythm about to be destroyed.

The novel's tempo, and its overwhelming linguistic accomplishment is to a great degree based upon the language Nadsat, coined for the book: the language of the droogs and of the night. It is the jargon of rape, plunder, and murder veiled in unfamiliarity, and as such it works highly successfully. Anthony De Vitis asserts that Nadsat may be an anagram for Satan'd,[2] but Burgess insists on the literal Russian translation of the word for "teen." The novel makes a fleeting reference to the origins of the language. "Odd bits of old rhyming slang . . . a bit of gipsy talk, too. But most of the roots are Slav. Propaganda. Subliminal penetration" (p. 115).

Close examination of the language reveals a variety of neologisms applied in countless ways. First, there is the overwhelming impact of a Russianate vocabulary that is concurrently soothing and unnerving to the reader. It most certainly softens the atrocities of the book. It is far simpler, for example, to read about a "krovvy-covered plot" or "tolchocking an old veck" than it is to settle into two hundred pages of "blood-covered bodies" or "beatings of old men."[3] The author keeps his audience absorbed in the prolonged violence through the screen of another language. But the Russian has a cruelty of its own; and there are disquieting political undercurrents in Burgess's imposition of Slavic upon English, at least for the tutored ear.

Nadsat, like all of Burgess's conventional writing, harbors a number of skillful puns. People are referred to as "lewdies"; the "charlie/charles" is a chaplain; "cancers" are cigarettes, and the "sinny" is the cinema. There is, to be sure, little room for laughter in a novel as sobering as this, and Burgess's usual authorial grin is only suggested in this very bitter glimpse of tomorrow. Still, there is no absence of satire. In many ways Alex is still a youth, and the reader is repeatedly shocked by a profusion of infantilisms starkly juxtaposed with violence. Burgess flecks his dialogue of evil with endearing traces of childhood in words like "appy polly loggies," "skolliwoll," "purplewurple," "baddiwad," or "eggiwegg" for "apologies," "school," "purple," "bad," and "egg." It is necessary for Burgess to achieve an empathic response to Alex, and these infantilisms within Nadsat are reminiscent of Dickensian innocence — serving well as buffer zones (or are they iron curtains?) between the "good" reader and the "evil" protagonist.

Other clues to this grim future world are Burgess's truncated and mechanized synechdoches: The "sarky guff" is a "sarcastic guffaw." "Pee and em" are Alex's parents; the "old in-out-in-out" is sexual intercourse (generally rape!); a "twenty-to-one" (the number is scarcely fortuitous) is a gang beating; "6655321" is Alex's prison name, and "StaJa 84" (State Jail 84) is his prison address.

Closely linked with the mechanical hybrids used in Nadsat are certain words conspicuous by their absence. There are no words, for example, that give positive feelings of warmth or caring or love. When Alex wants to refer to goodness he has to do so by opting out of Nadsat and for English, or by calling evil "the other shop."

Yet the total effect of Nadsat is greater than the sum of its various parts. Alex, in the capacity of "Your Humble Narrator," uses the language to extrapolate a future both vague and too familiar. He sings of a time when all adults work, when very few read, and when society is middle class, middle-aged, and middle-bound. We are told only that 1960 is already history and that men are on the moon. The reader is offered no other assurances. And as the linguistic impact of Nadsat becomes more comprehensible, one is left to wonder if the world of clockwork oranges is so safely distant after all.

When one has truly and carefully followed the linguistic threads of Burgess's novel, the Minotaur guide can be heard arguing a matter deeply tragic in implications. By definition language, like its human author, man, has an essential right to reflect the fits and starts of a time-honed, familiar friend. There ought to be an ordered sense of choice, a spirit of chorus and harmony and solo. Jabberwocky is for fun; Nadsat is a very different construct and far more fearful. Though at times it can be beautiful, there is the lonely wail of tomorrow wrenched from the desperate sighs of today. In Nadsat one finds the Platonic form of mechanism: the cadence of a metronome and the ticking-tocking ramifications of humanity without its essence.

The deep and hard questions of *A Clockwork Orange*, however, are not veiled by the mechanical language. And standing richer when reviewed in light of the balance of Burgess's cosmogony, they stand even more specifically poignant when played against the panorama of all Burgess's writing. Through a reflective stage-setting, the reader is far more able to cope with the labyrinthine mind behind the dystopian clockwork.

Burgess is fond of envisioning himself as an exile. He has voluntarily absented himself from many situations with the voice of a vociferous (not a whimsical) outcast. He has politically removed his allegiances from Britain. He has removed himself from the aegis of the Catholic Church, voicing preference for a variety of heretical or mystical theologies. Burgess is truly a man of isolation, alone with his own thoughts and his fiction to espouse his maverick philosophy. The exclusive position that Burgess assumes lends his writing a metaphysically unique, if not philosophically original dimension.

Locked within that mind—that mental labyrinth—is a most clever approach to serious metaphysical questions. Burgess has fashioned and shaped a dualist system of eclectic, authentic origin and pitted it against the world of the past, the present, and the future. Burgess's theological contentions are amazingly astute from the point of authenticity, universality, and relevance.

Much of his metaphysics is genuine philosophy given a fresh approach. He has drawn upon Eastern and Western philosophies, concocting a novel brew of Eastern dualism, heretical Manichaeanism, Pelagian/Augustinianism, the cultural mythologies of ancient civilizations, the philosophy of Heraclitus, the implicit teachings of the Taoists, the Hegelian dialectic. The impact of Burgess's metaphysics, however, is not so much the clever jigsaw effect of a master eclectic; rather, it is that out of this syncretism Burgess has presented a serious allegory of the contemporary malaise, which has been diagnosed by all recent Existential and nihilistic thinking. He is answering through his writing the central paradoxes of life posed in Sartre's "nausea," Heidegger's "dread," and Kierkegaard's *Angst* and "fear and trembling."

Basically, twentieth-century man has come to live under the onerous speculations of recent philosophers. He has, in a sense, become a captive of his own (or what he used to feel was his own) universe. Ancient philosophers and artists were dedicated to the simple contention that the universe was a friendly home, divinely designed for mortal existence, and not incidentally mortal happiness. In varying degrees, yesterday's thinkers attempted to explain, rationalize, even challenge man's primacy upon earth; they seldom, however, questioned his right to be here or his natural relationship with the world in which he lived.

The last one hundred years saw the growing disaffiliation from the traditional acceptance of the world as benign. After thousands of years of philosophy dedicated to man's concentric sphere within the universe, nihilists and existentialists were now challenging not only man's place in the system but the entirety of the system itself. No longer was logic, or spirit, or mind, or even God the central force of the universe—these became only alternatives. The center of the universe was now existence; man's solitary life was enough just *in being*. Shockingly, this new paramount position of man left him not the conqueror of the universe but its victim. He was swamped by the very paradox that made his existence supreme. For in accepting and even reveling in the uniqueness of his own individuality, man was forced to accept that he was totally unnecessary. Adrift from the former Divine, or logical, or even scientific plan, adrift from Hegelian systems, humanity was presented with a position of supreme importance and, simultaneously, with the concept of its own total annihilation.

As the world more fully accepted that it was enough just to be, it became aware, too, that an individual existence, while central to that individual, was as nothing in the universe. With World War II and the prospect of total annihilation (not thousands, but millions of deaths and the promise of even greater debacle), the "nausea," "dread," and "fear" that had haunted the ivory towers of philosophers became a part of every living being.

Into this anxiety-ridden arena came the literature that chronicled, prescribed, and diagnosed a series of ways in which man could come to live with relative peace within himself. Yet always the paradox remained: each individual was a unique and single existence that had never been before and would never be again. Yet that same individual existence was nothing. It would die, never return, and the world would go on as before.

Burgess, for good or ill, has generally refused to enter the arena. Indeed, he has steered clear of the mainstream of the philosophical split alluded to above. He has removed himself as thoroughly and totally from this particular dialogue as he has from church and country. He is to be sure a chronicler of paradox. He, too, speaks and writes of polarity, ambiguity, juxtaposition. He does not, however, revile them; on the contrary—and this is perhaps what makes him unique among writers today—he seems to glory in them. Burgess's writing is dedicated to exposing the totality of the paradox and offering humanity an alternative to "fear and trembling." In a single shibboleth, Burgess demands that man first become aware of the paradoxes of life *and then accept them*. The injunction is neither so simplistic nor so naive as it may at first appear.

Burgess offers his readers a cosmogony spinning in exact parallel to their own world. Yet, rather than trembling in the face of paradox,

Burgess's cosmogony is energized by it. One is not at all surprised to find living side by side in *The Wanting Seed* "Mr. Live Dog" and "Evil God." "God" and "Not God" thrive in *Tremor of Intent*, and the following references from *A Clockwork Orange* show how energetic such dualisms can become:

> Hell and blast you all, if all you bastards are on the side of the Good, then I'm glad I belong to the other shop. (p. 71)

> But, brothers, this biting of their toe-nails over what is the *cause* of badness is what turns me into a fine laughing malchick. They don't go into what is the cause of *goodness*, so why of the other shop? If lewdies are good that's because they like it, and I wouldn't ever interfere with their pleasures, and so of the other shop. (p. 43)

Burgess advocates a pure dualism, reflected variously on earth as "X and Y," "left and right," "black and white," or "lewdies good and lewdies not good." The names and terms change with each novel, but the concepts are serious, unswerving, and consistent — head-to-head combat between equal but opposite deities who are the forces behind creation.

Although Burgess does not shout innuendos from the novel's lectern, he does posit dualism as a means for explaining the unexplainable. Garnered from fiction itself — for Burgess has never formally outlined his philosophy — the dualistic system works something like this:

Each of the two divinities created a sphere. The "Good God" created an ascendant, ethereal sphere. It became a world of light, and summer, and warmth. Contrarily, the "Evil God" set his stage. His was a descendant sphere of darkness and winter and cold. Thus the spinning universe contained the dual divinity and a massive panoramic background. One, the "Bog of the Good," all "gorgeousness and gorgeosity made flesh," gave to man a spirit, while the "God of the other shop" gave man his flesh — again, juxtaposition, ambiguity, paradox, and the need to choose.

The first and primary symbols of the Burgess cosmogony are the sun and moon. They are the mystical, mythical avatars that preside over the choosing upon the earth. Their qualities, both natural and allegorical, are the parameters of Burgess's fiction. Certain secondary symbols are, however, equally important for directing the protagonists' literal, as well as spiritual movement. From the partial list below, one can discern the two opposing spheres that directly relate to Burgess's dualistic universe, and the limbo sphere between them.

White ("Good God")	*Gray* ("Man")	*Black* ("Evil God")
sun	earth	moon
day	dawn/dusk	night
birth	life	death
creation	existence	destruction

grace	ambivalence	sin
past	present	future
soul	mind	body
summer	spring/fall	winter

Burgess uses this highly Manichaean and dualistic world for most of his principal settings. His protagonists are allowed to live out their lives until the moment they are embodied in the novels. That moment becomes the moment of choice, and Burgess forces them to exercise the dualistic option. This aspect of choosing and "the choice" mark every plot and direct protagonists from *A Vision of Battlements* to *Napoleon Symphony*. A novel like *MF* is (if one might forgive Burgess's own pun) riddled with choices. *A Clockwork Orange*, however, is unique of aspect in that Burgess is not working on a multiplicity of levels but concentrating on the *nature* of choice which, by definition, must be *free*. To underscore his message, Burgess is far more translucent about his symbolism in *A Clockwork Orange* than in most of his other novels.

The moon and the night and the winter are Alex's arena. Burgess has always attached allegorical significance to the night and never more heavily than here: "The day was very different from the night. The night belonged to me and my droogs and all the rest of the nadsats, and the starry bourgeois lurked indoors drinking in the gloopy worldcasts; but the day was for the starry ones and there always seemed to be more rozzes or millicents about during the day" (p. 45).

Scattered throughout the first section of the novel are innumerable references to the night as the time of evil. ("The Luna was up" and "it was winter trees and dark.") On Alex's final night raid that ends in death, treachery, and incarceration, Burgess is continually outlining in black and white: "So we came nice and quiet to this domy called the Manse, and there were globe lights outside on iron stalks . . . and there was a light like dim on in one of the rooms on the ground level, and we went to a nice patch of street dark. . . . They [the droogs] nodded in the dark. . . . Then we waited again in darkness" (pp. 60-61). Burgess continues the imagery — the black of the evening, the light from the windows, the white old woman, the pouring of white milk, the theft of a white statue of Beethoven. Nearly blinded by the most stupid of his droogs (significantly named Dim), Alex is captured by the police, brought through the black night to the white of the police station: "They dragged me into this very bright-lit whitewashed cantora. . . ."

Throughout the remainder of the novel Burgess employs a seemingly confused pattern of white and black. The white-jacketed doctors are evil, and as extreme versions of B. F. Skinner's behaviorists and advocates of "the Ludovico technique," understandably so. In their hands (or rather in their mechanical toils), Alex will become a clockwork orange: a piece of pulpless, juiceless flesh that acts upon command and not out of will.

Conversely, the chaplain is a drunk garbed in black, yet he is the only character within the novel who honestly questions the morality of this application of behavioral science.

The white of the doctors, the black of the prison cell, the white of the technicians, the black of the chaplain, the white of the interrogation room, the black of Alex's reentry into society—all are carefully balanced inversions. The reader has often to unravel such inversions—to work, that is, in and out of the maze—particularly within scenes with institutional settings. The same sorts of inversion occur in *The Doctor Is Sick* and in the hospital scenes from *Honey for the Bears*. Burgess generally inverts his black-white imagery in situations where the morality and ethics are prescribed and not chosen. Schools, prisons, military installations, and hospitals—all places calling for Burgess's use of color imagery—underscore, through studied inversion, his perception of a morally inverted, indeed perverted world.

In *A Clockwork Orange* Burgess has crafted a childmachine, placed him in the pit of tomorrow, and "voiced" him with the lament of a world so mesmerized by technocracy that it has lost its essence. Alex chooses to sin and the world cannot live with his choice. Dystopia takes away neither his sin nor his existence, but does take away his right to choose, and thereby his soul: "Badness is of the self, the one, the you or me on our oddy knockies, and that self is made by old Bog or God and is his great pride and radosty. But the not-self cannot have the bad, meaning they of the government and the judges and the schools cannot allow the bad because they cannot allow the self. And is not our modern history, my brothers, the story of brave malenky selves fighting these big machines?" (p. 43). Alex does what he wants to do, so the world takes away his freedom to choose. He becomes a programmed good machine and no longer a person. Yet there has to be room for freedom, for by design this is a world of man. We are all "malenky selves on our oddy knockies" and the price of freedom runs high. We are a medial element, both desperate and sublime, with our *only* distinction being our right to choose. The paradox is one of enormity, for the stakes are enormous; the only alternative is a mechanized hell.

Oddly enough, Burgess, as man and as writer, is caught in the same paradox he espouses. The mind does not journey far from the body; the medial element, the victimized chooser of Burgess's fictions, is really Burgess himself. The spirit as well as the body yearns for a place, a time to belong. The Far East, England, Malta, are all bridges he has burned behind him. Burgess has, through his fiction, his journalism, his determined stand, cut himself off in principle and in fact from much that he intellectually abhors yet emotionally loves. His church and his country go on, despite his verbal assaults. Like Gulliver, he might indeed be genuinely amazed that his satire of the human condition has not brought about immediate improvement of it. But then, like Swift—who, too, looks *down* to observe human nature, rather than *around*—he has been forced to pay for his olympian vision.

And, unfortunately, for his prophetic vision as well. Burgess's fiction is more alive today than even in the times it was written. One reads with amazement, if not indeed horror, that Burgess's prophesy has become fact. Zoroaster and Manes are dust now. Dualism is little more than an Eastern etiquette, permeating the life-style of Asia. Kierkegaard, Nietzsche, and Sartre are classics, venerable promulgators of the *Angst* and *nausée* that all of us have subliminally absorbed. But the dualistic paradox still continues to unwind itself, and we still throb in our gray cocoons, daring ourselves to opt for emergence into the day or into the night. Burgess would draw us out of ourselves and make us choose, would make us commit ourself to choice for choice's sake. Like Alex, we may become mere mechanism, or all will, incarnated in flesh and blood: a clockwork, or an orange. The responsibility is of course ours, and Burgess brilliantly instructs us how to shoulder the responsibility.

Notes

1. *A Clockwork Orange* (New York, 1962), p. 96. Subsequent references are taken from this paperback edition.

2. Anthony De Vitis, *Anthony Burgess* (New York, 1972), p. 56.

3. Translations are taken from Stanley Edgar Hyman's glossary of Nadsat appended to more recent editions of *A Clockwork Orange*.

Alex Before and After: A New Approach to Burgess' *A Clockwork Orange*

Philip E. Ray*

Most interpreters of Anthony Burgess' *A Clockwork Orange* have tended to follow the lead of such early commentators as Bernard Bergonzi, A. A. DeVitis, Carol M. Dix, and Robert K. Morris in defining the theme of the novel as the conflict between the natural and untainted Individual and the artificial and corrupt State.[1] Bergonzi's observation that "in its emphasis on the nature of human freedom in a totalitarian society the book has philosophical as well as literary importance"[2] is typical of the thinking that shaped the framework in which subsequent critical discussion has taken place. And this tendency has recently achieved a fitting culmination in the account of the novel that Burgess himself has pub-

*From *Modern Fiction Studies* 27 (1981): 479–87. © 1981 by Purdue Research Foundation. Reprinted with permission.

lished, an account which concludes with this dictum: "we may not be able to trust man — meaning ourselves — very far, but we must trust the State far less."[3]

This essay attempts to present a different approach to both the content and the form of A *Clockwork Orange*, an approach which complements rather than contradicts the other. This essay will, however, focus on the relations of Alex, Burgess' hero and narrator, with characters frequently neglected or overlooked by the critics: the owner of the cottage named "HOME" (p. 19);[4] his wife; and the unnamed and unborn male child whom Alex mentions only in the final chapter. In other words, characters who are the willing or unwilling agents of the State — for example, the prison chaplain, the prison governor, Dr. Brodsky, the Minister of the Interior — will receive less attention than they sometimes do. The specific thesis that this essay will argue for is twofold: that Burgess has the owner of HOME represent the person Alex will become, his future self, and the boy who does not yet exist represent the person he has already been, his past self, in order to express the view that human growth is inevitable;[5] and that the tripartite structure of the novel directly mirrors this chronological sequence of Alex's identities.

The three parts of A *Clockwork Orange* are of equal length, each having seven chapters, but they otherwise fall into an ABA pattern.[6] Parts One and Three are set in the city streets and country lanes of a future England so paralyzed by violent crime that it has surrendered them to the very teenagers who commit the crimes. Part Two is set in a prison — "Staja (State Jail, that is) Number 84F" (p. 77) — where the government is attempting to regain the upper hand by checking within the mind of the particular criminal the impulse toward violence. Alex, who has his own gang despite his mere fifteen years, is sent to jail for murder at the close of Part One; in Part Two he successfully undergoes the State's experimental Reclamation Treatment only to reenter, in Part Three, a world that is unchanged. Thus Burgess has Alex's adventures in Part Three — especially his return to his parents' flat, his encounters with "the crystal veck" and with Dim and Billyboy, and his visit to the cottage named HOME — duplicate or parallel those in Part One with this significant difference: whereas he earlier victimized others in committing robbery, burglary, assault, rape, and even murder, he himself is now the victim. With his natural instincts and drives artificially blocked, Alex is the "clockwork orange" of the title.[7] One part of the moral that Burgess wishes the reader to draw here is that, in attempting to transform the violent tough into the peaceful citizen, the State has succeeded in rendering Alex incapable of self-defense.

The other part of the moral is that the State has also rendered Alex incapable of enjoying the music of his adored "Ludwig van." To quote once again from Burgess' own account of the novel,

I imagined an experimental institution in which a generic young delinquent, guilty of every crime from rape to murder, was given aversion therapy and rendered incapable of contemplating, let alone perpetrating, an antisocial act without a sensation of profound nausea. . . . A lover of music, he has responded to the music, used as a heightener of emotion, which has accompanied the violent films he has been made to see. A chemical substance injected into his blood induces nausea while he is watching the films, but the nausea is also associated with the music. It was not the intention of his State manipulators to induce this bonus or malus: it is purely an accident that, from now on, he will automatically react to Mozart or Beethoven as he will to rape or murder. The State has succeeded in its primary aim: to deny Alex free moral choice, which, to the State, means choice of evil. But it has added an unforeseen punishment: the gates of heaven are closed to the boy, since music is a figure of celestial bliss. The State has committed a double sin: it has destroyed a human being, since humanity is defined by freedom or moral choice; it has also destroyed an angel.[8]

Thus the State has meddled destructively not only in the mundane area of morals but also in the higher realm of art.

But consider for a moment the notion that in figurative terms music is "celestial bliss" and Alex an angel. If this is so, then it is certainly logical to regard all of his utterances, the entire narrative related by him to the reader, as musical: if Alex is, in some sense, an angel, his story is, in that same sense, a song. And the question of what sort of song redirects our discussion to the matter of the novel's structure, for the ABA pattern in music is universally recognized as the distinguishing characteristic of the *da capo aria* in eighteenth-century Italian opera, a kind of aria which "consists of two sections followed by a repetition of the first, resulting in a tripartite structure ABA."[9] And it is perhaps no accident, then, that at one point in the story Alex listens with powerful emotion to what Burgess makes quite clear is an operatic aria: "One of these devotchkas . . . suddenly came with a burst of singing, only a bar and a half and as though she was like giving an example of something they'd all been govoreeting about, and it was like for a moment, O my brothers, some great bird had flown into the milkbar, and I felt all the little malenky hairs on my plott standing endwise and the shivers crawling up like slow malenky lizards and then down again. Because I knew what she sang. It was from an opera by Friedrich Gitterfenster called *Das Bettzeug*, and it was the bit where she's snuffing it with her throat cut, and the slovos are 'Better like this maybe.' Anyway, I shivered" (p. 27). One wishes that Burgess had provided more information about his imaginary composer of operas: when he lived, what kinds of operas he wrote, and so on. But he does provide enough so that certain parallels can be drawn later between Alex and the wretched heroine whose aria he now hears.

To return to the actual workings of the ABA pattern in the novel.

Burgess reinforces the reader's sense of the pattern by opening each of the three parts with the question "'What's it going to be then, eh?'" (pp. 1, 77, 135)[10] and by having Alex ask it in Parts One and Three and the prison chaplain ask it in Part Two. Thus, in the A Parts Alex is free to pose the question for himself, whereas in Part B someone else, significantly an employee of the State, must pose it for him. Similarly, the hero's name,[11] which (as one would expect) remains constant in Parts One and Three, is replaced by a prison identification number in Part Two: "6655321" (pp. 78, 81, 83, 84, 85, 95, 96, 97, 99). In the A Parts Alex can call himself by whatever name he chooses (it is surely important that he never once uses his surname); in Part B he is called by a number, not even a name, chosen by the State. As Alex describes the change, "I was 6655321 and not your little droog Alex not no longer" (p. 78).

Alex's name is significant in another, even more essential way because it provides the chief clue to the thematic function of the owner of the cottage called HOME. When in Part One Alex and his "droogs" break into the cottage, they not only vandalize it but also beat the owner and rape his wife, who later dies as a result. When in Part Three Alex returns, he does so alone and, having just been beaten himself, stands utterly defenseless before the man he has wronged. The latter fails, however, to recognize Alex (primarily because he was wearing a mask on the night of the break-in) and provides him with aid and shelter instead of punishment or revenge. The owner of HOME even manages, in thinking aloud about his dead wife, to identify Alex with her when he says to Alex, " 'Poor poor boy, you must have had a terrible time. A victim of the modern age, just as she was. Poor poor poor girl' " (p. 162). Alex, of course, does recognize the owner and, wishing to learn his name, searches for a copy of the book that he was writing, and that Alex read from, on that fateful night: "It struck me that I ought to get to know the name of this kind protecting and like motherly veck, so I had a pad round in my nagoy nogas looking for *A Clockwork Orange*, which would be bound to have his eemya in, he being an author. . . . On the back of the book, like on the spine, was the author's eemya — F. Alexander. Good Bog, I thought, He is another Alex" (p. 163). Having just been let out of prison, Alex has now ceased to be 6655321. He finds, however, that not only is he Alex again (with the addition of the "clockwork") but that someone else is Alex, too. He has somehow managed to encounter a second version of himself.

What, then, do Alex and F. Alexander have in common besides their names? Both, oddly enough, are authors of books entitled *A Clockwork Orange*. (Burgess keeps the reader aware of Alex's authorial role by having him frequently address his audience by means of the curious formula "O my brothers" and refer to himself as "Your Humble Narrator.") One important difference between the two authors is, of course, that, while F. Alexander is writing his book on the night of Alex's first visit to HOME and has a bound copy of it on his shelves during the second visit, Alex has not yet begun to write his. In the reader's eternal present, Alex is writing it now. But, precisely because he has already done what Alex will someday do, F. Alexander is being defined here as a future version of Alex's self.

At this point in the story, the second visit to HOME, Burgess hints at the theme of the inevitability of human growth, to which he returns in the final chapter. There he sounds it loudly by having Alex answer the oft-repeated question " 'What's it going to be then, eh?' " with the idea of getting married and having a son. As Alex himself puts it, "there was this veshch of finding some devotchka or other who would be a mother to this son. . . . That's what it's going to be then, brothers, as I come to the end of this tale" (p. 196). Once he has found and wed his "devotchka," Alex will, of course, have come to resemble F. Alexander in his role as a married man. But here it is not yet apparent whether growth, which will be inevitable for everyone else, will be so for him. Having "clockwork" in his heart and brain may mean that Alex will be the same forever.

There is, however, one other obstacle in the way of Alex's growing up to possess a future, and that obstacle is, ironically enough, F. Alexander himself. When he learns that Alex is one of those responsible for the death of his wife, he tries to force Alex to commit suicide. The attempt fails when Alex, having thrown himself out of an upper-story window, receives medical care that not only saves his life but also reverses the effects of the Reclamation Treatment. Thus Burgess underscores his irony by having F. Alexander insure that Alex will possess a future through the former's effort to deny the latter a present. Trying to murder Alex has the indirect result of bringing him back to human life, for F. Alexander manages to kill only the "clockwork" inside his head.

F. Alexander is clearly, in some sense, a father to Alex, albeit a murderous one. Before the attempt on his life, Alex sees F. Alexander as treating him in a parental manner, although he gets the gender wrong: he calls his host and comforter "this kind protecting and like motherly veck" (p. 163). And perhaps, when he discovered the name on the back of the book, he ought to have considered the first initial as carefully as the surname. If, as seems almost certain, it stands for "Father," then Burgess has arranged this reunion as one between Son Alex and Father Alexander.

There is further evidence for this view of F. Alexander in the facts that he is the owner of HOME (that significantly named dwelling) to which Alex as a latter-day Prodigal Son returns and is not punished but rather welcomed and feasted; that, unlike Alex's actual father (whom Alex would never think of striking and to whom he always refers contemptuously as "pee"), F. Alexander arouses powerful feelings in Alex; and that he is married to the most important woman in the story and in Alex's life so far. Burgess follows here the Freudian model of family relations by placing the father and the son in competition for the mother and by having the son's path to manhood lead directly through the father's defeat or death. Alex the son succeeds not only in possessing the mother but also in taking her away from the father, an event which intensifies the latter's natural desire to triumph over his rival into a rage for murder and revenge. But, of course, that act of violence brings about the more rapid displacement of the father by the son when Alex finds that his suicidal leap has resulted in the removal of the "clockwork" and in no permanent injury to himself.

The actual fate of F. Alexander, Burgess leaves obscure until Alex's conversation with the Minister of the Interior in the novel's penultimate chapter. Visiting Alex in the hospital to assure him that all is now well and to exploit the favorable political publicity, the Minister informs him that "There is a man . . . called F. Alexander, a writer of subversive literature, who has been howling for your blood. He has been mad with desire to stick a knife in you. But you're safe from him now. We put him away" (p. 182). The State now regards F. Alexander as it once regarded Alex. Certain phrases used by the Minister—"howling for your blood," "mad with desire"—would appear to be more appropriate if applied to a person both more animallike and more physically violent than F. Alexander. But, in any case, he has been declared "a menace" (p. 183) just as though he were roaming the streets at night with a band of "droogs." Therefore F. Alexander gets, at the end of Part Three, precisely what Alex got at the end of Part One: imprisonment in a State Jail. This fate also makes sense, because he is Alex's double as well as his symbolic or mythic father: thus the career of F. Alexander not only anticipates but also repeats the career of Alex.

But this relationship also contributes to the working out of the ABA structure. In the first A section Alex is simply Alex; in the B section he becomes both 6655321 and the "clockwork" man; and in the second A section he resumes his public identity as Alex but is not truly or fully Alex because he still has the "clockwork" within him. When, however, he meets again the owner of HOME, he encounters a father figure, an older and wiser Alex, a future version of the self, who unwittingly assists him in the task of removing the "clockwork" and becoming himself once more. The ill effects of his prison stay cannot, in other words, be overcome until our hero wrestles with and defeats his own image invested with Age and Authority, until the son replaces the father. What could provide a more striking illustration of the process of human growth?

If the vision of his future granted him in the final chapter holds true, Alex will accomplish something in life that F. Alexander did not: the begetting and raising of a son. He describes his prophetic moment in the following passage: "I kept viddying like visions, like these cartoons in the gazettas. There was Your Humble Narrator Alex coming home from work to a good hot plate of dinner, and there was this ptitsa all welcoming and greeting like loving. . . . I had this sudden very strong idea that if I walked into the room next to this room where the fire was burning away and my hot dinner laid on the table, there I should find what I really wanted. . . . For in that other room in a cot was laying gurgling goo goo

goo my son. Yes yes yes, brothers, my son" (pp. 194–195). The place Alex describes is obviously an idealized version of home, which means that he has just paid, although in "vision," his third and final visit to HOME. The fire and the dinner are the comforts that Alex destroyed on his first visit but will soon require for himself; the "ptitsa all welcoming and greeting like loving" is the mother transformed into a wife who will in no way resist his advances; and the father, who earlier attempted to block his path, is now absent. To complete the circle, however, there is the baby boy, who, like F. Alexander, will be "another Alex" and bear Alex's other name, whatever that may be. This son will be F. Alexander's opposite in that he will represent Alex's past, whereas F. Alexander represented Alex's future. Alex perceives this even now, as he concedes in advance that he will be unable to prevent his son from making the very same mistakes that he made: "My son, my son. When I had my son I would explain all that to him when he was starry enough to like understand. But then I knew he would not understand or would not want to understand at all and would do all the veshches I had done . . . and I would not be able to really stop him" (p. 195). Knowing the "veshches" or things his son will do, Alex also knows that he will be unable to prevent him from doing them, both the good and the evil. As his son grows up, Alex will behold his past being repeated just as F. Alexander beheld his. Everything human is inevitable, Burgess seems to say, both the good and the evil.

But Alex's tale is still a story of liberation: he has escaped from not only the literal prison of Staja 84F but also the figurative prisons of adolescent boyhood and "clockwork" humanity. And the reader who recalls that "music is a figure of celestial bliss" will want to translate "liberation" as "salvation." But it is the individual capable of growth — the " 'creature of growth and capable of sweetness' " (p. 21), as F. Alexander puts it in his typescript — that has been liberated or saved, not the group, the tribe, or the species. When he is born, Alex's son will not be free or blissful. He will be doomed, rather, to live through the error of his father's ways. Here, then, is that final flowering of the logic of the novel's structure: after A, B; after B, A again. After the freedom of the mature Alex, the imprisonment of his son. Could Alex somehow liberate his son, the structure of A Clockwork Orange would surely have to be ABC, which would signify progress without repetition.[12]

The da capo aria itself, if the reader chooses to think of either Alex or the heroine of Das Bettzeug as performing this sort of aria, represents the same lack of freedom: having sung A and B, the performer must sing A again. And it is precisely here that the meaning of this imaginary opera comes into clear focus. The surname of the composer, "Gitterfenster" (p. 27), is a German word best translated as "barred window," that is, the window of a prison. The heroine has sought presumably to escape this prison, whether literal or figurative, but, realizing that she can succeed only through suicide, has now taken that step: hence Alex's description, "it was the bit where she's snuffing it with her throat cut, and the slovos are 'Better like this maybe' " (p. 27). She is, therefore, in the very same situation as Alex when F. Alexander's friends leave him in their locked flat with the music turned on: "I viddied what I had to do . . . and that was to do myself in, to snuff it" (pp. 172–173). The window in this prison is not barred, however, because F. Alexander and his friends want Alex to jump: "the window in the room where I laid down was open" (p. 173). And they have even left behind a helpful hint in the form of a "malenky booklet which had an open window on the cover," proclaiming: " 'Open the window to fresh air, fresh ideas, a new way of living' " (p. 173). So Alex, saying in effect what the heroine said, goes to the window and jumps. And he succeeds, just as she may have, in achieving personal liberation — not through death, but rather through the return to life,[13] or, to put the matter somewhat more accurately, by the return to normal life after the nonhuman existence of a "clockwork" man, which is merely another formulation of the sequence "freedom"-"imprisonment"-"freedom"; that is, ABA.

Notes

1. Bernard Bergonzi, *The Situation of the Novel* (Pittsburgh, PA: University of Pittsburgh Press, 1970), pp. 182–185; A. A. DeVitis, *Anthony Burgess* (New York: Twayne, 1972), pp. 102–113; Carol M. Dix, *Anthony Burgess* (London: Longman, 1971), pp. 13–16; and Robert K. Morris, *The Consolations of Ambiguity: An Essay on the Novels of Anthony Burgess* (Columbia: University of Missouri Press, 1971), pp. 72–73.

2. Bergonzi, p. 185.

3. *1985* (Boston: Little, Brown, 1978), p. 96.

4. All parenthetical references in the body of the essay are to the first British edition of *A Clockwork Orange*, published in London by Heinemann in 1962. It is to be preferred to the American editions published by Norton and Ballantine because it contains a chapter they omit: the final one (Part Three, Chapter 7). For a discussion of this entire matter, see John Cullinan, "Anthony Burgess' *A Clockwork Orange*: Two Versions," *English Language Notes* 9 (1972), 287–292.

5. There is, of course, nothing new in the claim that the inevitability of maturation is an important theme in *A Clockwork Orange*. Long ago Burgess himself pointed out that "in the final chapter . . . Alex is growing up" (a 1972 interview published in *Rolling Stone* magazine quoted in Rubin Rabinovitz, "Mechanism vs. Organism: Anthony Burgess' *A Clockwork Orange*," *Modern Fiction Studies*, 24 [1978–79], 538). See also Cullinan, *passim*.

6. To some readers, ABA may seem to be an abbreviation for "Anthony Burgess Author." Others, who are more familiar with Burgess' rapidly increasing canon, will recall the fact that the title of his 1977 novel *ABBA ABBA* refers to the rhyme scheme of the octave of the Petrarchan sonnet. But, as I will attempt to demonstrate below, the primary significance lies elsewhere.

7. It is important to realize that Alex does come to think of himself as "a clockwork orange." Significantly enough, when the State puts him on display, Alex protests to the audience: " 'Am I like just some animal or dog? . . . Am I just to be like a clockwork orange?' " (p. 129). Thus Alex perceives that he has become something lower than an "animal or dog" because part of him, and a crucial part at that, is now mechanical. On the phrase itself, Burgess again comments helpfully in *1985* (p. 95): "The book was called *A Clockwork Orange* for various reasons. I had always loved the Cockney phrase 'queer as a clockwork

orange,' that being the queerest thing imaginable, and I had saved up the expression for years, hoping some day to use it as a title. When I began to write the book, I saw that this title would be appropriate for a story about the application of Pavlovian, or mechanical, laws to an organism which, like a fruit, was capable of colour and sweetness. But I had also served in Malaya, where the word for a human being is *orang*."

8. *1985*, pp. 94–96.

9. *The Harvard Dictionary of Music* 2nd ed. (Cambridge: Harvard University Press, 1969), pp. 51–52. The fact that Burgess first wanted to be a musician and continues to compose music is, I believe, so frequently mentioned as not to require documentation here. But a word is in order about Burgess' most ambitious and explicit use to date of musical structure in his literary work, the symphonic or four-part organization of his 1974 novel, *Napoleon Symphony*. The genesis of the novel he describes in a doggerel "Epistle to the Reader," which he appends to it:

> I was brought up on music and compose
> Bad music still, but ever since I chose
> The novelist's metier one mad idea
> Has haunted me, and I fulfill it here
> Or try to — it is this: somehow to give
> Symphonic shape to verbal narrative,
> Impose on life, though nerves scream and resist,
> The abstract patterns of the symphonist.

It is possible to argue, then, that *A Clockwork Orange* anticipates *Napoleon Symphony* because, as he composed it, Burgess attempted to give the "shape," the "abstract patterns" of the aria, to the narrative of Alex, whose single viewpoint stands in the same relation to the many viewpoints of *Napoleon Symphony* as the single voice of the aria singer to the many voices of the symphonic orchestra. [For further discussion of Burgess' use of musical form, see James Bly's essay elsewhere in this issue — Ed.]

10. I am indebted to Rabinovitz's thoughtful discussion of the question (p. 540).

11. Burgess provides an illuminating gloss on the name in *1985* (p. 95): "The name of the antihero is Alex, short for Alexander, which means 'defender of men.' *Alex* has other connotations — a lex: a law (unto himself); a lex(is): a vocabulary (of his own); a (Greek) lex: without a law. Novelists tend to give close attention to the names they attach to their characters. *Alex* is a rich and noble name, and I intended its possessor to be sympathetic, pitiable, and insidiously identifiable with us, as opposed to them."

12. For a comprehensive account of "linear" vs. "circular" symbolic patterns in the early Burgess, see Thomas Le Clair, "Essential Opposition: The Novels of Anthony Burgess," *Critique*, 12, iii (1970–71), 77–93.

13. Robert K. Morris makes this point in a more elaborate way when he writes that "Burgess brings in . . . one of the original archetypes through which Alex finds salvation: the fall, or in this case, the jump. . . . His try at 'snuffing it' becomes the last desperate exertion of a murdered will and, paradoxically, the means to its resurrection" (p. 73).

Politics and Modernity: The
Strategies of Desperation
George Kateb*

It is not strange . . . that the most common modes of thinking about
the future, in literature and in everyday talk, are extreme, often lurid.
That is but an indication that people know they are faced with tendencies
and forces that seem incompatible with the long life of what we have so
far learned to take as normality. There are signs here and there. And the
signs are most often read in two ways. Either ever greater and more
refined powers will come be be owned by small groups like the Inner Party
in *1984*. Or the problems of the world, some caused by new powers, others
insoluble by any new powers, will be too much for human effort, and the
world will have catastrophe, or a series of catastrophes, or some final
irretrievable breakdown — an apocalypse. That the contemplation of disaster is pleasurable by no means invalidates the pessimism. It is hard to keep
one's balance; it may turn out to be silly to have tried.

Silly or not, some futurists have tried. The most interesting of this
group are those who cling to their pessimism, but who moderate it enough
so that the world of the near future still appears to have some resemblance
to the world we know. The resemblance provides an admirable persuasive-
ness to the novelties. Not everything is new; not everything is malign; not
everything soon goes out of control; something decent struggles to survive
amidst circumstances not entirely bleak. The moral of the tale may have to
do with human resourcefulness in the presence of nearly intractable
problems, which are perhaps created or aggravated by man's own amazing
achievements, yet also palliated by them. It is a mixed moral, and really
does not reassure. But the teller of the tale does, so to speak, domesticate
the apocalypse, and thereby — rightly or not — earn greater credence.
These qualities are marvelously displayed in one of the handful of original
futurist works, Anthony Burgess's *The Wanting Seed*, published in 1962.[1] I
think that by paying attention to this book, we can come to a measure of
clarity about possible patterns of future experience. But also about human
experience as it always has been: we distort our discussion of modernity by
omitting continuities completely.

The Wanting Seed is one among many novels by this gifted Englishman.[2] It is not his only futurist novel: *A Clockwork Orange* (also 1962) is
about a time when gangs of young men have the run of the streets, and
society as a whole is in a condition of chilly *stasis*. But *The Wanting Seed*
can stand alone, and be examined by itself.[3] We must acknowledge at the
start, however, that it would be heartless and dull to turn Burgess into a
didactic novelist. He has an immense amount to teach, but he doubtless

*From *New Literary History* 3 (1971):93–111. © 1971 by The Johns Hopkins University
Press. Reprinted with permission.

wishes to be thought of as teaching through indirection. There is great exuberance in all his writing, especially when the matter is most grim, as it is in *The Wanting Seed* — great gaiety of language. The surface is glorious with inventive particulars. One feels a little guilty pressing such a book into the service of illustrating some thesis or other; one feels mean-spirited. For all that, we have to take our enlightenment where we can find it. I believe light is found in Burgess's novel. I propose to use the book: there are not many that can be as profitably used by anyone who is interested in the theme of the growth of human power and the growth of limitations on its effective use.

The Wanting Seed is a Malthusian fable. Just as futurist optimism, speaking through Marcuse, can say that a new conception of socialism "would mean passing from Marx to Fourier";[4] so futurist gloom, speaking through Burgess, can say that there must be a reinstatement of Malthus despite Marx. The central predicament of the future society is too many people, "the crisis of overpopulation" which has recently become one of the great anxieties of scientists and citizens. It is not, of course, a scientific treatment which Burgess gives. Indeed, the aim of the book is not to alarm: the book does not incite to any action. And if one of Malthus's motives in writing *An Essay on the Principle of Population* was to discredit the idea that there could be an indefinite "improvement of society," to discredit the utopianism of Godwin and Condorcet, the folly of utopianism is not one of Burgess's lessons. From the beginning it is made clear that overpopulation is a permanent fact of life, and that all life is determined crucially by that fact. No hope is held out that the severity of the determination can ever be softened: not even the mere possibility of utopia is part of the reckoning. The Malthusian law has again been enacted by reality at least up to a point. The checks on population have failed to the degree that the condition of life is defined by scarcity of food for *all* the people of the world. Not only the poor go hungry: in Burgess's world, class is irrelevant to consumption. The action of the book, schematically put, is the variation in intensity of scarcity. What does the world do when it does not have quite enough? Burgess's novel shows humanity going from one strategy of desperation to another.

In Malthus's analysis, there would be widespread famine if certain miseries and vices did not make their invaluable contribution to killing people off. "The vices of mankind are active and able ministers of depopulation."[5] Were it not for poverty with its diseases and depravities, were it not for plagues, and war, were it not for small-scale famines, numbers would soon increase beyond the means of subsistence, and many would die of starvation. ". . . premature death must in some shape or other visit the human race."[6] (In the second edition of the *Essay* [1803], Malthus added another sort of check, "moral restraint"; this prevents birth, rather than shortening life.) If, therefore, the "immediate checks" do not operate, the "ultimate check" will. "The ultimate check to population appears then to be a want of food, arising necessarily from the different ratios according to which population and food increase. But this ultimate check is never the immediate check, except in cases of actual famine."[7]

Malthus does not advocate that governments consciously use the immediate checks to keep population down. It must be obvious, however, how nicely Malthus's doctrine works to ease the conscience of those who, for example, make war: some have to die young anyway: why not in war? The only conscious check he allows for is the preventive check of moral restraint, which can be exercised only by individuals. The extent of governmental policy should be to avoid relieving the plight of the unemployed poor. Government should choose to let some people die when it could save them. (Malthus's influence on poor-law legislation is famous.) The heart of Malthus's teaching is, then, the idea that the most awful problem of life admits of no solution (one that would see every person's most fundamental needs satisfied), and that the problem is kept within (shall we call them "tolerable"?) limits only by different kinds of suffering. Put another way, the worst disease is incurable; it is hidden from sight or palliated in its effects only by other diseases. A secondary idea is that every advantage eventually turns into a disadvantage: temporary prosperity leads to depression, leisure to sloth, happiness to sorrow. Thus, only disease seem to cure; health is latent disease.

Burgess departs from Malthus in having all the checks issue from governmental policy. Government rewards those who practice the preventive checks; initiates policies which work as positive checks; and permits individuals to engage in peculiar positive checks. Part of the fun of the book comes from watching Burgess move his government this way and that. I have already said that Burgess is one of those who moderate their pessimism about the future. One of the things I meant is that in Burgess's world, horrible as it is, government is a largely benign force. It is undemocratic in the name of efficiency, but it is also completely devoid of the lust for power and aggrandizement. When it acts it acts solely for the general good. Some of the strength of Burgess's depiction comes from having a rather fussy decency in authority and responsible for the strategies of desperation. Government recognizes bounds; there is one obvious strategy of desperation it will not employ. The Prime Minister says: "Don't you see . . . that we could, if we wanted, kill off three-quarters of the world's population like that—" He snapped finger and thumb. "—Just like that? But government is not concerned with killing but with keeping people alive" (pp. 111–12). Nuclear weapons will not be used for mass extermination. (Malthus said that "Famine seems to be the last, the most dreadful resource of nature."[8] Man now has one yet more dreadful.) There are two superpowers, Enspun (English-speaking union) and Russpun: the world is pacified, or at least free of nuclear peril, and the two unions do not have Orwellian dealings with each other. War is not a *regular* feature of the system. In addition, there is one subtle strategy of desperation government employs only feebly. It does little to make people feel that they are superfluous; that for any individual no matter how gifted there are ten others as good or better; that for any individual there are many others just like him down to his idiosyncrasies; that to die is to be unmissed; and that it is best never to have been born. To be sure, corpses are used as fertilizer; and mourning is thought to be in bad taste. That is about as far it is goes. Burgess's is, in truth, a tamed apocalypse. But the future world as he imagines it is still awful, and awful according to a pattern that is Malthusian in many respects. Burgess has made Malthus vivid. There is virtuosity in the preventive and positive checks, and in the pattern of their qualified failure, of their successive desperation.

The pattern consists of phases in fixed order. In each phase there is a different strategy; each strategy is dictated by the inadequacy of its predecessor. The story opens in the *Pelphase*, goes through an *Interphase*, and ends in the *Gusphase*, which will one day yield again to the Pelphase and so on. The terms are those of the hero, Tristram Foxe, a history teacher in secondary school. He is the book's theorist as well as chief sufferer. The Pelphase takes its name from Pelagius, as the Gusphase takes its from Pelagius's great adversary, St. Augustine. Governmental benevolence lies behind all the checks in all the phases. One of the book's main lessons is precisely that. Starting with the best intentions, in a world of scarcity, yet a world in which scarcity is to be more or less evenly distributed, men try a wide array of strategies, contrary as these are to each other. Almost everything is tried; nothing really works; but life goes on. The relief a strategy brings lasts only a short time: either the strategy has to be given up because its moral cost is too high; or it is too much at variance with human nature; or the relief relaxes worry and thereby prepares the way for the return of the problem in all its acuteness; or some combination. A new strategy must then be devised that takes into account the experience of the previous one, and is a moral commentary on it. To the Malthusian "oscillation" of more and less is added a cycle of change.

Pelphase is the phase of liberal rationalism. The main checks to population are preventive, though there is one rather odious positive check. The citizenry carry the burden of prevention because their government trusts their rationality, supported by proper rewards and inducements. Government is a rather gentle presence, coaxing, frowning, persuading, praising. The presiding spirit is Pelagius, because the belief is that if men and women know what trouble they are in, they will all pitch in. They can save themselves through their own clear-eyed efforts. Which is to say they will see to it that there is no increase in the numbers of people alive. (Of course the curse of numbers is not enough food. But in a few brilliant strokes Burgess suggests yet another consequence of numbers — overcrowding. It is life in a closet: living quarters are tiny apartments in immense apartment buildings. There is almost no countryside left: London stretches to Brighton. Space, like other resources, is scarce.) Their diet is vegetarian and synthetic. Their very lives are as it were vegetarian: life has been pacified not only through the abolition of nation-states, the abandonment of the arts of war, and the socialization of production, but also through the mixing of races and colors. Everything is in such short supply that an abbreviated alphabet called "logograms" has been devised to save on paper. There is, then, great adaptability, comic as some of it is in its (to us) exaggeration. Some of these compressions and substitutions last through all the phases; but their spirit is really Pelagian. People, for a while, put up with much. Rationality seems to check scarcity, and thus keep famine away. In our terms, there seems to be a cure for the disease, and part of the cure comes from those new human powers which conduce to reaching, teaching, and governing large masses of people, and furnishing some of their needs through scientific ingenuity.

Looked at more closely, the cure is only a seeming cure, and is itself, in some of its parts, disease. Where Malthus's example of preventive check was moral restraint in the form of delayed marriage and sexual abstention, and thus unhappiness but virtuous unhappiness, Burgess's preventive checks, though rational in a manner of speaking, are of questionable rightness. These checks are readily available contraceptive pills (either sex can take them), and state-encouraged homosexuality and voluntary castration. Government also tries to disseminate the notion that family ties are best when they are matter-of-fact. Rational means cool, distant. So cool and distant that the one Pelagian positive (that is, post-facto) check is infanticide, tacitly approved and slyly or cryptically talked about. For consistency's sake Burgess should not make too much of this last method, because infanticide is not really Pelagian; and he does not. But even under Pelagius the gruesome must be given its due.

The check that is most dramatic and that Burgess obviously wants us to take as the very epitome of Pelagian response to the predicament of scarcity is clearly homosexuality. "It's Sapiens to be Homo" — a pun too bad not to be used. Burgess has a good time with this aspect of his future world. His joke is that large numbers of people, with just a little push, would take to the gay life rather easily. Naturally, his hero is not one of them. The self-seeking brother of the hero, Derek, only pretends to be. Beatrice-Joanna, the hero's wife and brother's mistress — the moral center of the book — is utterly feminine (by the conventional definition) and gets all of them into trouble by getting pregnant. (She had already had a child who died; one child, though dead, is enough, more than enough.)

Homosexuality as a preventive check lasts through all the phases. It is easy to turn on, but not off. But it goes best with liberal rationalism, which to Burgess's robust Chestertonian Catholicism, is anemic even in its heterosexual manifestations. In fact the ensemble of checks in the liberal-rational Pelphase is abhorrent especially to Catholicism (by the conventional definition). Contraception (and abortion), infanticide, homosexuality, family distance or enmity—all these are attacks, in one Catholic view, on the integrity of family life, and hence on the fundaments of natural law. Beatrice-Joanna's brother-in-law, Shonny, is an old-fashioned Catholic to his fingertips, and his rage at the practices of Pelphase is given full play. *The Wanting Seed*, however, does not vindicate Catholicism. There are practices in the other phases, at the furthest remove from effeminacy and individual isolation that are discountenanced equally. Burgess would have it no other way. Heterosexuality is the very cause of the predicament of overpopulation. The source of life is the source of too much life. Homosexuality is not a solution; but I think Burgess is saying that it is not as laughable as the straight mind would like to have it be. It is, after all, an effort at a solution. Nothing works any better. But though nothing works any better, Pelphase still has its own bitter lesson. That is: in seeking to be rational, in seeking to avoid coercion and terror, policy becomes unnatural. In the most dire circumstances the rational is the unnatural. The irony is that the affinity is almost as much a commentary on the unnatural (in its favor) as it is on the rational (in opposition to it).

The unnatural cannot last, any more than the natural can. There must be another phase, one in which rationality is dethroned, and cruder methods given a chance. The strain is too much. The successor phase, Interphase (in two parts), is consciously introduced. Those who govern give up their trust in people's capacities. It is too much to expect the world to go queer. The other techniques of rationality go only so far. The old urge of paternity lust revives; population presses ever more harshly on the means of subsistence. Liberal faith is lost through disappointment. As Tristram Foxe tells his students:

> "The governors," he said, in a reasonable tone, "become disappointed when they find that men are not as good as they thought they were. Lapped in their dream of perfection, they are horrified when the seal is broken and they see people as they really are. It becomes necessary to try and force the citizens into goodness. The laws are reasserted, a system of enforcement of those laws is crudely and hastily knocked together. Disappointment opens up a vista of chaos. There is irrationality, there is panic. When the reason goes, the brute steps in. Brutality!" cried Tristram. The class was at last interested. "Beatings-up. Secret Police. Torture in brightly lighted cellars. Condemnation without trial. Finger-nails pulled out with pincers. The rack. The cold-water treatment. The gouging-out of eyes. The firing-squad in the cold dawn. And all this because of disappointment. The Interphase." (pp. 18–19).

Another strategy of desperation is introduced. The world is moved from mock-utopia to semi-totalitarianism. The motives of the rulers stay good. The world's predicament is such, however, that terror can be used out of benevolent disinterestedness, just as homosexuality and infanticide can. Conduct which usually issues only from sick criminality now issues from good men trying to do their best. These are works according to the doctrine of the lesser evil. (Actually, Tristram overdoes the terror for the delight of his students. The narrative of Interphase does not live up to Tristram's promise of horrors. Enspun becomes more a police-state permitted to be squalid at the lowest levels of its officialdom, than the Nazi or Orwellian state; though it is no less epicene than the Nazi state.) The repression is directed towards the maintenance of rationing and, most important, the punishment of those who have babies in order to deter the fertility of others. The terror has no other aim. The monstrousness inheres in the necessity. As in the Pelphase, the purpose is restricting the number of births. The checks are characteristically preventive rather than positive.

Once again, human powers come up against their limits. The cure of repression is only a seeming cure. The seeming cure is itself a disease. This time, the metaphor of disease (which we have been using) turns literal. There is a blight that destroys crops (such agriculture as a crowded world can still afford) all over the world. Animals (and there is little animal life left in the world) die. Repression makes the world sick. The seed is wanting. Nature is in rebellion against the State's ferocious punishment of sexual potency and fertility. It punishes man in return by making his condition of scarcity all the worse: it punishes him for trying to combine the natural and the unnatural. It is almost as if nature resented enforced sterility more than homosexuality. The preventive checks of the first part of Interphase are sacrilegious, worse than those of Pelphase: to enforce the unnatural rather than merely permitting and encouraging it is not only to fail in yet another way, but to disturb the universe. "The governors become shocked at their own excesses" (p. 18). The state relents; it relaxes administration of the law; the terror ends, and with it the blight.

The second part of Interphase is the opposite of the first. The world is moved from semi-totalitarianism to anarchy, from unbearable discipline to unlimited permissiveness. Still another strategy of desperation is introduced. The strategy is to let nature take its course. The progression is thus from rationality mixed with infertile indulgence to force trying to make good the default of rationality, and now to the abandonment of rationality altogether and replacing it with nature. However, nature in anarchy seems infinitely more unnatural than rationality in society. Nature in anarchy means that heterosexuality is once again fashionable, and that copulation may thrive. It also means that people eat each other. What comes out, goes in. In Pelphase corpses are fertilizer; in the later part of Interphase, they are nourishment. In a Swiftian manner, the problem becomes the solution. The problem eats itself up. When some people become food, too many people become food for all. One of the cannibals says to Tristram in the course of a meal they share: "Man is a carnivore, just as man is a breeder. The two are cognate and the two have been long suppressed. Put the two together and you have no rational cause for suppression" (p. 165). The breeziness is Blimpish and superb. But of course cannibalism is no answer: even without cannibalism the state of nature is no answer. In a condition of scarcity, the natural turns into the savage. There is sex, friendship, affection in Burgess's nature, elements missing from Hobbes's loveless state of nature. Also missing from the latter is cannibalism: Hobbes did not go that far. Burgess does. At the same time he turns sex into orgy, a compulsive sacrament: the natural lapses into magic. The price of the natural is more bitter than that of the unnatural. The seed is wanton. The cure is only a seeming cure; it is in fact worse than the disease. Cannibalism violates the rules just as much as nuclear war would.

Burgess makes it very hard on himself by going further. In anarchic nature religion returns. Worship, copulation, and cannibalism are linked. An underground priest says, "They've done no good with their police, so now it's the priests they call on" (p. 141). Tristram sees ". . . that reason is only one instrument for running our lives." A return to magic ". . . seems very healthy to me" (p. 176). Religion is another device. Its appeal is greatest when self-control and political control are at the lowest level. Man is most religious when he is most animal. Burgess makes it appear that such a connection is more to the discredit of religion than to the credit of animality. Inevitably religion demands human sacrifice. The good Catholic, Shonny, loses his two children "on the altar of Baal" (p. 202). Tristram, not quite a liberal, tells Shonny: "It's people like you who've made this kind of world you say you no longer believe in. We were all safe enough in that old liberal society." He was talking of less than a year back. "Hungry, but safe. Once you kill the liberal society you create a vacuum for God to rush into, and then you unleash murder and fornication and cannibalism" (p. 204). Order is sterile; disorder is self-devouring. One leads to the other. Each must and will be tried and endured. Both are failures and symptoms of failure. Once begun, each goes to its limit, framed by scarcity: ". . . disappointment cannot sink any deeper. Disappointment can no longer shock the state into repressive action, and a kind of philosophical pessimism supervenes. In other words, we drift into the Augustinian phase, the Gusphase. The orthodox view presents man as a sinful creature from whom no good at all may be expected" (p. 23). Government re-emerges from the state of nature. Laws and regulations are made and obeyed again; order is restored. (People go along: the plasticity of the world is one of the most wonderful and least plausible aspects of Burgess's imagined world. Or it may be prophetic. People who are ready for anything, able to do anything, to go swiftly from one moral universe to another while still holding on to an identity, may have to be the people of the future. Picaresque pilgrims, like Tristram Foxe. It is like changing dress with the seasons.) In this phase government does not set itself up as teacher; the people are deemed unteachable. The ideology is laissez-faire. Little faith is placed in preventive checks. The seed wants. There must, therefore, be some positive check or checks. From the repertory of strategies of desperation war is plucked. It is not nuclear war, but limited, conventional war.

Gusphase is the phase closest to Burgess's heart. At first glance society seems to possess a comfortable normality. Tristram's brother can even stop pretending to be a homosexual. Women are encouraged to have babies. There is vigor in the air, and some private enterprise. Family relations are close. ". . . daring décolletages were *de rigueur* for evening" (p. 218). Above everything, state-supported morality does not intrude into every corner of life. But Burgess is unsparing. The cost of normality is a morally exorbitant artificiality, namely a strange kind of war. The state only permitted cannibalism as a method of eliminating life. In Gusphase it acts to eliminate life by making war. Once again, a disease is tried as a cure for the underlying disease of scarcity. The state's power shows itself in choosing which disease to use next.

Burgess gives war a fighting chance. Tristram muses (during the transition from Interphase to Gusphase): "This was the world, acquiesce in it: the mutter of love-making and the mass, the grinding of meat and the wheels of the military. Life. No, damn it, no. He pulled himself together" (p. 195). Tristram for the moment draws back. Later he thinks: "Was war, then, the big solution after all? Were those crude early theorists right? War the great aphrodisiac, the great source of world adrenalin, the solvent of ennui, *Angst*, melancholia, accidia, spleen? War itself a massive sexual act, culminating in a detumescence which was not mere metaphorical dying? War, finally, the controller, the trimmer and excisor, the justifier of fertility?" (p. 235). The idea is old and vulgar, and perhaps immortal. But Burgess sees to it that such a piece of romanticism has no place in the future world: the idea lacks seriousness. The only achievement of war is a useful number of deaths. To be sure, war and sex are compatible mates. Beatrice-Joanna says, "Sex. War and Sex. Babies and bullets" (p. 218). The connection, however, displeases the quintessentially feminine woman. The connection would be a sign of sex's weakness, not of war's beauty.

Beatrice-Joanna rejects the connection without knowing what kind of war it is that goes on. Tristram gives up the feeble romanticism as the truth dawns on him. (One of his adventures is to serve in the army, after negligently signing a paper that commits him to military duty. He signs in the belief that he is registering for food, which he then desperately needs.) The truth is that the war is entirely stage-managed by the state:

> "The end of war is the means of war. And *we* are the enemy."
> "Whose enemy?"
> "Our own." (p. 233)

The state has no enemies but the possibility of famine. It rounds up men and women, segregates them according to sex, trains them in far away places, moves them around in darkness, puts them on a battlefield within its own territory, turns up the sound system to produce the noises of war, sets off fireworks to produce the flashes of war, and then has two groups slaughter each other in ignorance of the facts. One group is men, the other women. The war between the sexes is made literal. (Tristram manages to survive.) At first the selection of people who go to fight is random. Then the state picks the anti-social types among the young. "Our age-groups for call-up will get progressively older—as far, of course, as the healthy and mentally normal sections of the population are concerned; the trash can go shortly after puberty" (p. 278).

Benevolent intentions are behind the war system as they are behind all the other strategies of desperation. However, it is true that just as war, of all the devices, seems least morally obnoxious, so Burgess's satirization of it seems the most unremitting. The force of the satire is commensurate to the intensity of the appeal of the thing satirized. There is an intimation of determined exorcism. With war, we are closer than usual to customary devices; its futurist rationale is uncomfortably similar to past and present shouts and whispers. The apologist says, among other things: "You see, what other way is there of keeping the population down? . . . Contraception is cruel and unnatural: everybody has a right to be born. But, similarly, everybody's got to die sooner or later" (p. 278). and, "The War Department is a bit like prostitution: it cleanses the community. If we didn't exist, a great deal of nastiness would bubble up in the State. . . . So long as there's an army there'll never be a police state, no more greyboys or rubber truncheons or thumbscrews or rifle squads at inconveniently early hours" (p. 279). Tristram remains unconvinced. The theory of war is far in excess of the reason for war. Besides, " 'It's all wrong,' said Tristram, 'All, all wrong.' " War is murder. The happy society rests on blood-sacrifice.

The punishment for success on these terms is to prepare for an early failure. If war is the device that comes nearest to being a solution, the reason is it lasts only long enough to become outmoded, but not long enough to generate the same sort of anxiety the other devices do. It touches only a small minority, yet enough to relieve some of the pressure on the means of subsistence. If it were to touch a larger number, it would become self-defeating: people would see through the game. As it is, the Malthusian oscillation will have its way. The relief war brings, leads to a rebirth of faith in rationalism, and the return of the Pelagian phase: The wheel is turned by both success and failure. Failure is failure, but so is success.

Tristram asks the apologist for war:

"Do you think people are fundamentally good?"
"Well," said the major, "they now have a chance to be good."
"Exactly," said Tristram. "Which means that it won't be long before the return of liberalism." (p. 279).

In short, power is powerless before the problem of scarcity induced by overpopulation. Scarcity is the one disease that is not a seeming cure; it may be the one disease without a cure; it is the parent of other diseases as it is the child of human powers. In Burgess's future world the diseased responses—the strategies of desperation—are each given a chance. All through the changes the intentions of the governors are steadily good. Their efforts, thanks to the reach of Burgess's talent, form a sequence of many of the major nightmares of this century's futurist imagination. Burgess's lessons are the more shocking precisely because his world is a world in which good men hold power. Would it be worse with worse men? Fortunately, Burgess's story leads us to believe it would. Good men are driven to try not anything but almost anything.

• • •

The strategies of desperation, as we have said, are works according to the doctrine of the lesser evil. It may be thought that no matter how great human powers grow, moral perplexities do not change their quality. The scale of woes may change together with the scale of power, but whatever the scale the world has always faced predicaments to which it often has responded with strategies as desperate, with lesser evils as evil as those in Burgess's future, or as they would be in anyone else's future. Indeed, what is war but a disease used to cure the disease of insecurity; conscience but a disease to cure the disease of vice; punishment but a disease to cure the disease of crime; inequality but a disease to cure the disease of sloth; marriage but a disease to cure the disease of sensuality; and so on? All these proposed cures are only lesser evils. The world has always used them, or devices like them. What differentiates modernity?

I think the answer to that question—and it is the answer implicit in *The Wanting Seed*—is that a point could be reached after which the greater the human advance the more primitive must the strategies of desperation become. The strategies are not unprecedented, as the powers are. But they seem to throw humanity back to much earlier times. They seem the more primitive because of the contrast to the novelty of the powers (that are either causing or failing to solve the problems.) The disappointment, to use Burgess's word describing the attitude of the governors in Pelphase, comes from the sense that what one thought humanity had outgrown once again finds a place. Infanticide, castration, cannibalism, human sacrifice, irrational religion, brute political control, war: we wish to forget that such things ever existed, and to remove them wherever they exist today. We want to define modernity in opposition to such backwardness. What would the revolution of human capacities amount to if these things remain, and remain in part because of that revolution?

Further, what other primitive strategies of desperation can be imagined for some future time? One fears that many of them would work to destroy the bourgeois conception of individuality. Out of a benevolent regard for human welfare what sacrifices of self-assertion, self-definition, self-exploration must be made if the world is not to explode or collapse or run down? Will it be back to the tribe in a technologically magical world? The more progress, the more regression: is that modernity's essence?

There is one particularly painful possibility. The advance in knowledge may lead to the unanswerable demand, or the need (by some humane definition), for censorship, or the prohibition of further inquiry; a return to the Inquisition. In Walter M. Miller's futurist novel, *A Canticle for Leibowitz* (1959), the survivors of massive nuclear war kill learned men and destroy books and take pride in the name of simpleton. It is as if all intellect shared responsibility for the holocaust. What of the possibility of previous restraint in the name of the global interests of humanity? In an interview, Herman Kahn said: "Now this is a very hard thing for me to say — 10 years ago I couldn't have said it, five years ago I began to think it — but the knowledge and technology that are now becoming available are very hard for society to absorb, so we may well need an index of forbidden knowledge. . . . A good deal of genetic engineering looks to me as though one might be better off without it. . . . Whatever the intellectual dangers of an index, they pall in comparison with the danger of not having one. A society that hasn't the moral capacity to absorb new knowledge without putting itself in mortal peril has to have restraints imposed upon it."[9] Knowledge is power; power is evil. Stop the evil at its source. Less progress means more progress. Some regression to avoid greater regression: will that be the heart of the future's strategies of desperation?

Notes

1. Anthony Burgess, *The Wanting Seed* (1962), (New York, 1963). All page numbers cited in the text refer to the Norton edition (New York, 1963).

2. For an excellent appreciation of Burgess, see William H. Pritchard, "The Novels of Anthony Burgess," *The Massachusetts Review*, VII (1966), 525–39.

3. Of course some of the moral concerns of this book figure in Burgess's other novels. What makes *The Wanting Seed* especially relevant is its concentration of moral sensibility.

4. Herbert Marcuse, *An Essay on Liberation* (Boston, 1969), p. 22.

5. Thomas Robert Malthus, *An Essay on the Principle of Population* (1st ed. 1798) in *On Population*, ed. Gertrude Himmelfarb (New York, 1960), p. 52.

6. *Ibid.*

7. Thomas Robert Malthus, *An Essay on the Principle of Population* (2nd and subsequent eds.) in Himmelfarb, *op. cit.*, p. 158.

8. Malthus, *Essay* (1st ed.), in Himmelfarb, *op. cit.*, p. 51.

9. An interview with G. R. Urban in *The New York Times Magazine*, (June 20, 1971), 24.

Speaking Himself in the Language of God: Burgess's *Tremor of Intent*

Francois Camoin*

What are we to make of this novel which closely follows the narrative conventions of the traditional spy novel, but which will not allow itself to be read as one? From the outset, it promises us Eric Ambler or John LeCarré—we have all the conventional baggage of the genre: the spy Hillier, called on for a final mission of great importance, the defecting scientist to be brought back home, the tools of the trade (the false passports, the ampoules of PSTX, that mysterious drug, the pistol and silencer, the coded message). And yet no matter how hard we try, this book will not allow itself to be read the way we read *A Coffin for Dimitrios* or *The Honourable Schoolboy*.

It defends itself against such a reading primarily by refusing to honor the conventions of realism. All the sub-genres—the detective novel, the western, science-fiction—are realist in technique. The language is transparent; the discourse assumes an external reality of which it is itself merely the notation. The text is descriptive—it is evenly divided between the description of things (or characters) and the description of actions. The genre novel always postulates that referential world and attempts to involve the reader in an experience of the "real" as little mediated by language as possible. But in *Tremor of Intent* the language is foregrounded, opaque, insistent on its own independence, its own freedom, its own *authenticity*. It will not let us indulge ourselves in the wonder of "the real." Reading this work is always a *literary* experience.

> For Roper all things are ready, including a new identity. John Innes, except [expert?] in fertilizers. The bearded face of that rubbery man from Metfiz looks sadly back at me from the Innes passport. He has been many things in his time, has he not, that all-purpose lay-figure? He has been a pimp from Mdina, a syphilitic computer-brain skulking in Palaiokastritsa, a kind of small Greek Orthodox deacon, J.R. Geist who had the formula, even a distinguished Ukrainian man of letters set upon for his allegations of pederasty in the Praesidium. And now he is John Innes, who is a sort of egg-cosy for soft-boiled Roper.[1]

There is too much in that catalogue that calls attention to itself, to the *act* of writing, for us to take it straight. Even if we attempt a recuperation by postulating an eccentric or slightly deranged narrator, a playful, literary spy, it won't wash. The rhythms are all wrong, too musical, too systematic; as Barthes has pointed out, system is in our culture the enemy of the realist illusion. Except for the most slothful of readers, it is not

*This essay was written specifically for this volume and is published here for the first time by permission of the author.

possible to ignore the surface of the book, to forget, as we must with Fleming, with Ambler, that this is a *reading*. This novel defends itself like a good soldier.

Nor, despite the seemingly parodic transformations of certain traditional narrative elements, will *Tremor* allow itself to be read as a parody of the James Bond epics (themselves perilously close to parody). The traditional feats of eating and sex are here replayed in exaggerated and distorted form, no longer quite intelligible if we read them straight;[2] but no possible reading of them will generate the special pleasures of parody.

> What now began was agonizingly exquisite, something he had forgotten existed. She gently inflamed him with the *mayil* or peacock embrace, moved on to the *matakatham*, the *poththi*, the *putanai*. Hillier started to pass out of time, nodding to himself as he saw himself begin to take flight. [. . .] The eighty-foot tower that crowed from his loins glowed whitehot and then disintegrated into a million flying bricks. He pumped the massive burden out. Uriel, Raphael, Raguel, Michael, Sariel, Gabriel and Jerahmeel cried with sevenfold main voice, a common chord that was yet seven distinct and different notes. (88–89)

Parody depends on the parallel experiencing of another text, on its deconstruction, in a sense, since the parallel text's literary codes are, by distortion and exaggeration, shown to *be* literary codes instead of transcriptions of the real. But there is no other text here to be mocked; there is only Hillier's language, Biblical, historical, anthropological, which writes itself furiously across the page, with gestures and acrobatics so interesting in themselves that we cannot look beyond them to the supposed act which is the occasion for them. Not only can we not ignore the surface of the book, we cannot even very well look past it. The text does not allow itself to be read as description.

The parallel text that *Tremor of Intent* consistently sets up alongside itself is not another literature, but the world, a world called real, in which real secret agents in the daily round of their business eat gourmet meals and sleep with women of great sexual gifts. The goal of the paralleling is not parody, but recovery— *Tremor* does not so much claim to be an imitation of the world as a language, a set of conventions and codes by which the world can be read. The novel doesn't choose to play itself out in the gap between real and fictional, as realist novels do. Ambler's novels, for example, derive their strength from the tension between the real business of spying and its fictional representation. Their paralleling texts are other spy novels which romanticize and falsify the real world of spies. (Both "real" and "fictional" are creations of the discourse and firmly located inside it— arbitrary signs made to look natural). Though Burgess plays with this internalized distinction (itself a convention not only of spy stories but of the novel in general, from Diderot and Defoe and Fielding to the present), the play cannot here be read as an affirmation of versimilitude, of the "truth" of the novel. Instead the real world is created as itself another text which the present text will, more or less successfully, decipher. Thus when Alan questions Hillier:

> "How do we know that you're not spying for the other side and that the danger comes from spies on our side who are disguised as spies on their side?" He accepted a Kunzle cake. "That you're trying to get back to Russia with secret information and somebody working for our side is already waiting to come aboard and get rid of you?"
>
> "Much too complicated. The whole thing could, theoretically, spiral to an apex where the two opposites embrace each other and become one, but it doesn't work like that in practice."

Alan's hypothesis is criticized both in terms of literature ("much too complicated") and of the world ("it doesn't work out that way in practice"), but the opposition between "real" and "literary" is fused rather than opened for us by Hillier's answer; within Burgess' discourse the real and the literary are one. When the novel does explicitly refer to other literary works, it is not in order to affirm its own reality, but to expose the other fictions as unsatisfactory codes for deciphering the world.

> Hillier tried to laugh, saying: "Imagine you're in a novel by Conrad. You know the sort of thing: 'By Jove, I thought, what an admirable adventure this is, and here I am, a young man in the thick of it.'"
>
> "Yes," said Alan. "A very young man. But ageing quite satisfactorily." (178)

The implication is not that Conrad painted a romantic picture of the world which the present novel will correct, but that Conrad's language was not adequate to decipher the world. *Tremor of Intent* neither adheres to the spy-story genre, nor parodies it. Instead the novel both explodes and exploits the conventions, just as Robbe-Grillet's *Les Gommes* both kills and caresses the traditional detective novel, and E.L. Doctorow's *Welcome to Hard Times* at once undermines and props up the Western.

Tremor of Intent must be read as a text which will enable us to decipher that other text, the world — in this case of course a world which, by the strange operations of literature, the deciphering text will itself create.

Like the last message Hillier receives from his employers, the novel contains a description of the mechanisms that allow it to *mean*. The message refers to the "November Goddess," and Alan, thirteen-year old veteran of American quiz shows, is able to read that as a reference to the accession of Elizabeth to the throne in November, 1558; this enables him to recuperate the message by substituting the fifth letter for the first, and the eighth for the fifth. Thus does "zzwm ddhgem" become "dear hillir." Misspelled, but recognizable, the misspelling affecting the appearance but not the meaning.

Throughout the novel we are treated to little paradigms of language theory.[3] Mechanisms of meaning are displayed; in a sense the novel can be said to contain images of its own methods, its own grammar. *Tremor* is anything but a naive text; reading it is like reading the *Oedipus* if it had been written by Freud. Or by Lévi-Strauss.

Thus a brief disquisition on arbitrary signs disguised as natural signs: "I looked at her with more attention [. . .] wide-mouthed (generous), gate-toothed (sensual), small-eyed (shrewd)" (47). It is the text's juxtaposition of signifier and signified, divided only by a parenthesis, that makes the point here. The emphasis is put not on Lucy's physical characteristics, but on Hillier's conventional reading of them.

On meaning through difference: Father Byrne, trying to recall the years when Roper and Hillier were students at Lancaster, says "that friend of yours, the clever one, God forgive him, Hoper or Raper or something?" (235).

On meaning as syntax: "Back in his cabin he restored, with much pain, his face to the face of Hillier. It was the expression more than the physiognomy that was adjusted. Jagger was the name of a function rather than a person" (114).

And in the Yarylyuk night Hillier overhears an American jazz tune, "*You Want Lovin' But I Want Love*" and wonders "Was that distinction possible in Russian?" (145).

Language is foregrounded in this novel, language *qua* language, the play of meanings which it makes possible, the mechanisms that allow meaning to be generated, the hero as sign, or the sign as hero.

The mechanisms of language are the mechanisms of the world. Hillier is branded on the flank with a capital S — S for sin, S for Salvation, S for satyriast and for spy, S for saint,[4] but most of all S for signifier, signified, and sign. The play of meaning is made explicit in a sequence of incidents which begins with Hillier being interrogated by Theodorescu:

> "Ah, yes" [Theodorescu] organ-stopped. "Accept only this brand. The genuine article." The S burned on wet nakedness; it was too late now to attempt to hide it. "Mr. Hillier," beamed Theodorescu. (91)

The morning after, Hillier muses on his own unmasking, on Theodorescu's stopping of the play of meaning which was the spy's career.

> No longer as Jagger. No longer as anyone. D. Wishart, sanitary engineer; F.R. Lightfoot, pediatrician; Heath Verity, the minor poet; John James Pomeroy-Bickerstaff, IBM man; P.B. Shelley, Kit Smart, Matchless Orinda — all would have an S on the left flank. He was known for that, the S-man, all over Europe, then. (105)

But Hillier reopens the play by shifting the S to another, whose identity has first to be erased. After the false steward Wriste has been killed by Alan, Hillier burns the S into the corpse's skin with the tip of his cigar, and leaves Roper to finish obliterating the dead man's face.

Going down the path to the coast-road, Hillier and Alan heard a very dull thud from the massage-hut. The S-man was now fully there. (178)

The play of signifier→signifier temporarily stopped by Theodorescu's seeing the face and the S together, is resurrected by the substitution of one of its terms. Hillier / HILLIR is now again free to become Jagger, Wishart, Lightfoot, P.B. Shelley, Qwerty Yuiop or anyone else he pleases, until, at the end of the novel, Hillier again ends the play, transforms the sign once more to index, by taking out an ad in (aptly) *The Times*, which will tell his employers, his enemies, his friends / fiends, where and who he is.

As a number of commentators have pointed out, one of the parallel texts of this novel is Augustine's *Confessions*. Plato insisted (or seemed to insist) that "to know the good is to do the good,"[5] and the *Confessions* can be read as a monumental exegesis of that single word "is" within Plato's sentence. Augustine knows early on what the good must be, but it is not until he chooses the language of Paul (or the language of Paul chooses him), that he can *do* the good. This passage from *know* to *do*, so short in Plato, so long in Augustine, is a passage through language. It is, we remember, a book left lying in a garden, and not a bolt of lightning that converts Augustine. The *Confessions* is not so much the discovery of a God as it is the discovery of a language, a way of speaking which will enable Augustine to make intelligible that other book, the world. A language the saint already knew, or he could not have learned it. What takes him so long is to learn to differentiate it from the other languages he already knew — the language of sensual love, the language of Greek culture, the language of the Manichees.

So it is for Hillier. He speaks the language of the Church from the beginning, deciphers the world by breaking it open with those very Catholic binary oppositions: good/evil, free will/predestination, soul/ body. But it is not until the end of the book that he begins to *understand* what he has been saying all along. Always there is the comparison with Roper, who abandoned the language of the Church for that of science, and, when that failed him, tried poetry, tried rational socialism.

That was a significant event in Roper's life, sir. I mean his going into the death-camp and seeing evil for the first real time — not the pruriently reported evil of the Sunday rags, but stinking palpable evil. For the sake of scientific rationalism he'd jettisoned a whole system of thought capable of explaining it — I mean Catholic Christianity; face to face with an irrational emptiness he'd made himself a sucker [. . .] for the first coherent system of blame that had been presented to him. (31–32)

But Hillier is spoken by other languages than that of the church. There is the language of the middle class, of *l'homme moyen sensuel*. "I have a dream of life, but one ideology will realize it for me better than any other. I mean a warm flat, a sufficiency of spirits, a record-player, the whole of *The Ring* on disc" (4).

The language of lust: "With athletic swiftness he turned her to the primal position and then, whinnying like a whole herd of wild horses, shivering as if transformed to protoplasm save for that plunging sword, he released lava like a mountain in a single thrust of destruction . . ." (90–91).

And that of love: "To ease her in gently to that world of release and elation which lay all before her, all too easily spoilt for ever by the boor, cynic, self-seeker, was surely a valid part of the office of almost-father he had assumed. This was an act of love" (205).

But ultimately all these prove as unsatisfactory as Roper's scientific, rational speech, and Hillier chooses, not the language of Augustine, but that language which Augustine rejected, the language in which good / evil is a true opposition, not collapsed by the logical necessities of monotheism. "The big war can be planned here as well as anywhere — I mean the war of which the temporal wars are a mere copy." (237)

This is not a new discovery for Hillier. Like Augustine he could not have learned this language if he had not already known it. (At the very beginning of the novel, he is already capable, after a description of conquered Germany, of describing life as a "bloody Manichean mess" [22]). Hillier's passage into sainthood, if it is that, is not a matter of giving up the sins of the flesh, of enlisting in the great battle, but of choosing to speak himself in a language that mandates purity, within which he can be nothing except a soldier in the army of the Lord. The book ends with a passage that can only be read in the new language, a language which no longer allows the possibility of the irony that earlier informed the novel.

> He fell without warning into a sudden deep pit of depression. His bed would be cold and lonely that night. The times ahead would be even harder than the times achieved. He was ageing. Perhaps the neutrals were right. Perhaps there was nothing behind the cosmic imposture. But the very ferocity of the attack of doubt now began to convince him: doubt was frightened; doubt was bringing up its guns. Accidie. He was hungry. (240)

Only within the language of the Church is the personification of *doubt* so automatic as to allow no comment. Only within the language of the Church does the "very ferocity" of this attack discount it. Here we have passed fully into the special grammar of hagiography. The language even transforms *hunger*, (earlier in the book a vice) into the symptom of his return to himself, of his victory over *accidie*. Hillier is hungry not because he is a glutton, but now because he has fought *accidie* and won. Like Augustine, Hillier is now speaking himself in the language of God.

Notes

1. Anthony Burgess, *Tremor of Intent* (London: William Heinemann, 1966), 2. All subsequent references are to this edition.

2. Geoffrey Aggeler, "Between God and NotGod: Anthony Burgess' *Tremor of Intent*," *Malahat Review*, no. 17 (January 1971):91–92.

3. We shouldn't be too surprised. Burgess is the author of *Language Made Plain*, a textbook of linguistics, and of a translation of the *Oedipus* which owes much to Lévi-Strauss and his studies of myths.

4. See Robert K. Morris, *The Consolations of Ambiguity* (Columbia: University of Missouri Press, 1971), 18.

5. Probably the most succinct discussion of this idea occurs in the *Protagoras*, where virtue is equated with pleasure and unethical behavior with pain. Socrates argues that since nobody would knowingly inflict pain on himself, men behave badly only out of ignorance.

Sonata Form in *Tremor of Intent*   James I. Bly[*]

The major aim of critical approaches to Anthony Burgess' novels has been to focus attention to thematic interpretations of the works. Valid though these may be in explaining the intellectual concerns that preoccupy Burgess, these approaches tend to skim over the impact that his musical sensibilities have had on his literary creations. For with Burgess, one is confronted by an author whose artistic view was shaped initially not by words but by the eye of a painter and the ear of a musician. "The creative impulse was strong in me as a child and an adolescent," he says, "but it never took a verbal form. I drew; I painted until I discovered I was colour-blind. I taught myself to play the piano and eventually to compose music. But I knew that my business was really with words."[1] Despite his current success as a word-man, music remains his first love, and he has expressed the wish that " 'people would think of me as a musician who writes novels, instead of a novelist who writes music on the side.' "[2]

Burgess' early experience with nonverbal forms of art and his self-emphasis on his role as a musician have no doubt contributed significantly to his concern with the novel as form. It is an issue to which he returns repeatedly: "I feel that we are already swinging to a new interest in form rather than content, and that that is where the significant pattern of the next ten years must lie."[3] And as a musician, Burgess looks at the potentialities of musical structure and technique to provide novel forms for his literary creations: " 'I still think that the novelist has much to learn from musical form: novels in sonata-form, rondo-form, fugue-form are perfectly feasible. There is much to be learnt also from mood-contrasts, tempo-contrasts in music: the novelist can have his slow movements and his scherzi. Music can also teach him how to modulate, how to recapitulate; the time for the formal presentation of his themes, the time for the

[*]From *Moden Fiction Studies* 27 (1981):489–504. © 1981 by Purdue Research Foundation. Reprinted with permission.

free fantasia.' "[4] The purpose of this study is to examine how Burgess has utilized sonata-form as the base structure of *Tremor of Intent*.[5]

Thematically, most critics agree, the novel is a quest for spiritual commitment, a search for a spiritual home.[6] And Burgess himself, in an essay published the same year as *Tremor of Intent*, discusses the validity of using religious themes in works of fiction. He concludes: "A legitimate source of fascination is the process which turns a sinner into a saint – not by sudden Pauline conversion . . . but by the working of some slower Augustinian ferment."[7] Burgess' fascination with the "process" of the transformation leads one directly to the structure of the novel, for he is as much concerned with the form of the movement as he is with making a statement of "what" it is.

One of the more complex musical forms and the one used as the base pattern for *Tremor of Intent* is sonata-form. The four major divisions of this form, which correspond to the four parts of the novel, are the exposition, the development, the recapitulation, and the coda.[8] Each of these major sections has internal compositional principles that govern such elements as the introduction of thematic subjects, fragmentation of motifs, and transformations in the re-presentation of subjects. An analysis of the novel shows that Burgess utilizes not only the broad structural divisions but also adapts the internal principles of development to his work.

Fleming and Veinus describe the movement of the exposition section in three stages: the first subject, the second subject, and the closing section or codetta. The first subject, which may be preceded by a short introduction, establishes a home base and may become the main subject of the entire sonata. A short transition or bridge leads into the second subject, which might vary from a strong contrast to close identity with the first subject. A short coda follows, giving the exposition a sense of unity (*UM*, pp. 123–124). Burgess himself discusses the exposition section of sonata-form in a work of literature in his analysis of James Joyce's *Ulysses*. His comments provide a helpful perspective to this structural technique: "In the exposition section of a movement in sonata-form there are usually two main contrasting subjects around which cluster groups of subsidiary themes. In *Ulysses* we have had the equivalent of these in Bloom and Stephen, each with his many satellites of characteristic preoccupations."[9]

As illustrated in Figure 1, Burgess closely follows this compositional sequence in Part I. The story opens with a brief introduction (pp. 9–11) in which the two main subjects, Hillier and Roper, are swiftly juxtaposed. After a very brief sketch of Hillier as the first subject (pp. 11–12), the narrative shifts to the past; and for the rest of Part I the emphasis centers on Roper as the second subject. The closing four paragraphs (pp. 52–53) return the reader to the present, Hillier's stateroom in which the novel opened, thus giving the section a sense of unity and bringing it to a close.

The two subjects of a sonata, as suggested earlier, may be in strong opposition or nearly identical. Burgess seems to have it both ways. Several

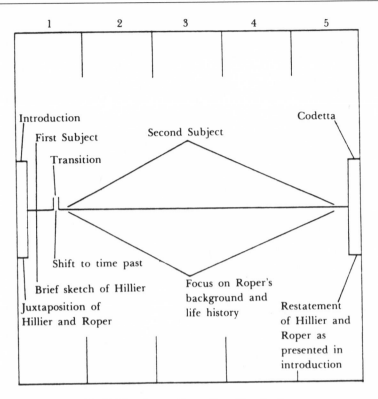

FIGURE 1:   *Sonata Form: Exposition Section*

factors support the idea that there is an essential identity between Hillier and Roper, that instead of polarized thematic subjects, one is dealing with one subject split into two parts—the transformation of sinner into saint as represented by the head (Roper) and heart (Hillier).[10] Burgess has described his own religious agonies in his separation from the Catholic Church in these terms: "But for a cradle Catholic to leave his Church is like the wrenching of palpable bone and muscle—it is like the draining of the very content of the skull. To me . . . it was unavoidable agony because it seemed to be happening totally against my will. . . . Anyway, it seemed to me that what I called reason was tugging one way, and emotion, instinct, loyalty, and fear were tugging the other."[11]

Lending strength to the reason-emotion dichotomy within the novel is the care with which Burgess establishes nearly identical backgrounds for the two characters in the exposition section (pp. 12–13). As Hillier and Roper share similar experiences, their responses begin to differ more markedly until their Augustinian-Pelagian oppositions fully emerge. Although the two go separate ways for much of the novel, their personalities frequently interpenetrate (pp. 26, 35, 76, 79, 103, 141). They are joined together at Yarylyuk, where their last pretensions are jointly exposed, and together they face death. Again they separate, the heart cleaning itself through a scapegoat ritual — the death of Theodorescu — and entering the priesthood. The head, meanwhile, perhaps harder to convince, moves from the Soviet Union to East Germany. The head's ultimate reunion with the Church is foreshadowed in IV.2 when Father Byrne, who collapses Roper's and Hillier's identities into "Hoper," castigates Roper for his godless science. He is told by Hillier, "Wait" (p. 216), implying Roper's eventual return. Without these points of identity, Hillier's comment would be tenuous at best.

The development section of sonata-form is one in which "material selected from the exposition is broken down into its smaller components, and the inner resources of the material made explicit by working with these smaller units or motives" (*UM*, p. 124). In his discussion of *Ulysses*, Burgess, gives this definition: "The exposition will not make sense until it has been followed by a development section in which the subjects combine, lend each other their subsidiary motifs, swirl about each other in an area of dreamlike fantasy, bump into each other drunkenly, melt into each other on the discovery of previously unguessed affinities" (*RJ*, p. 158).

This technique is used in Part II as Burgess, concentrating now on Hillier as the first and main subject, engulfs Hillier in a blizzard of fragments. The process involves three stages: presentation of subsidiary themes or images in Part I; fracturing these motifs into smaller units in Part II, swirling them around Hillier and sometimes joining them with other units in surprising ways; and restoring order in Part III (Figure 2). The technique, particularly in the development section, serves both to enhance the surprise element necessary for spy fiction and to suggest the chaos of Hillier's world.

Burgess develops a variety of methods to adapt this technique to the novel. Most prominent is his tossing the motif from character to character, paralleling a musician's use of different orchestral instruments. For example, Hillier's Aiken gun is transferred from Hillier to Theodorescu to Alan and back to Hillier, appearing and disappearing in surprising ways and timely fashion; and the stripping of Hillier's Jagger disguise moves progressively from Wriste to Alan to Theodorescu to Alan to Devi and finally to Theodorescu again. A second technique is to present the motif in different combinations: the year 1558, for example, appears as two minutes to four, as 15:58 Continental time, and as the binary code the first is the fifth and the fifth is the eighth. This technique might resemble the musician's presenting the motif at different pitches or with different harmonies. And a third variation is to link motifs together in surprising ways, perhaps as a musician might take snatches of melodic lines from two songs to create new chords or new melodies. The motif of burning, for example, is

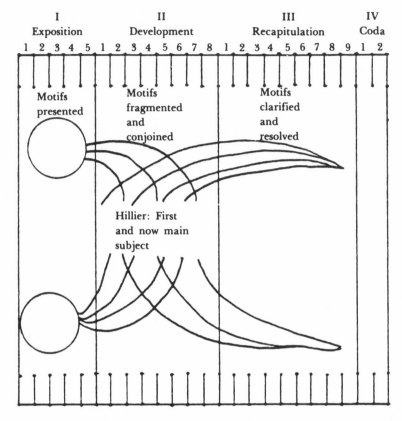

FIGURE 2:   *Sonata Form: Development Section*

associated with Father Byrne and his damnation of lust; it is an element of Edward Roper's martyrdom; it is the burning of Hillier's S-brand; and it is the means by which the S-brand is transferred to Wriste.

A full illustration of the motifs, their fragmentations and lines of interrelationship is nearly impossible. However, Figure 3 illustrates some of the potentialities. No attempt has been made here, aside from placing "home" as the central theme, to organize the patterns within the structural sequence of the novel. Rather, several of the major thematic images have been placed within the circles, with circle-to-circle lines suggesting some of their interrelationships, and other lines that indicate the development of motifs or fragments from the larger circles. Thus as Roper and Hillier drift from their spiritual home, each sets up his own "house." Father Byrne, representative of the original spiritual home, condemns both Roper's intellectual pride (sickness of mind) and Hillier's lust (sickness of body). The name "Byrne" is connected to Edward Roper's martyrdom; and the year in which that occurred, 1558, is linked with the coded letter sent to Hillier. As the fragmentation progresses into smaller and smaller units and

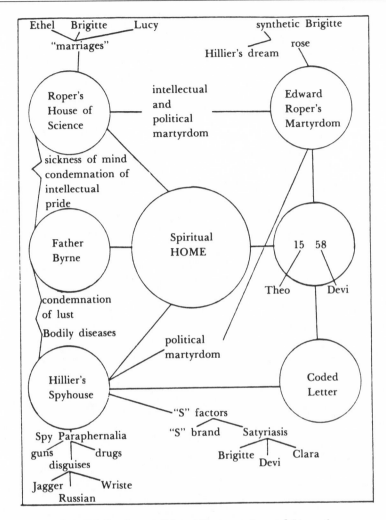

FIGURE 3: *Potentialities of Fragmentation and Lines of
Interrelationship*

as these units become fleetingly interlinked, one becomes aware of the
chaos of Hillier's world, which drives him to despair and nearly to death.

Space here allows the tracing of only one strand of these subsidiary
themes, and even then the interrelationships must be curtailed. Edward
Roper's martyrdom is a thematic referential point for the entire novel. His
story, recounted in Part III (pp. 145–146), is brief, but pregnant. He was
burned at the stake for his faith in 1558, but before he died he expressed
his patriotism by throwing a rose, symbol of the ruling Queen, to the
crowd so that it would not be destroyed with him; and in his flaming
death he became a witness to the light. Thus he is a symbol of the

spiritually committed person, the kind Hillier and Roper are struggling to become. Therefore, it is not surprising that Burgess selects both "burning" and the "rose" as aspects of the fragmentation process.[12] But the 1558 fragmentation has been selected for development here.

Presented early in the exposition, the number 1558, innocuous in itself, develops considerable potency as it is fragmented, conjoined with other motifs, and finally clarified. It appears three times in the exposition section: first in disguise as "two minutes to four" (p. 10) in Roper's last letter to Hillier; then as the year of Edward Roper's death (p. 29); and finally again as "two minutes to four" (p. 53) as Hillier notes the time before his adventures begin. The number is thus linked to both Roper and Hillier, emphasizing their close thematic and personal identity, and also conjoined with martyrdom, buttressing the spiritual theme of the novel as a quest for the kind of commitment evident in past ages.

The number is fragmented and yoked with other motifs in the development section. Its first appearance is oblique, contained in the "November goddess" reference in the coded letter Hillier receives from his superiors (p. 61). The reference is to Queen Elizabeth I, who ascended the throne in November 1558. It next is fragmented into 58, the number of Devi's cabin (p. 83), only to reappear in full bloom during Hillier's ecstatic vision in his tryst with Devi (p. 86). This time the number receives its full political significance, explaining both the relationship of Queen Elizabeth to the November goddess and yielding the binary code "the first is the fifth and the fifth is the eighth" to decode Hillier's letter. A second fragment, 15, comes next in Theodorescu's Istanbul address (p. 99). And its final appearance in this section is as a vague "number" that Hillier associates with the idea of home, another motif (p. 102). Thematically one might suggest that Hillier's 1558 faith lies in political commitment (November goddess), but his own laxity as a spy in failing to decode his letter, combined with the fragmented powers (Devi and Theodorescu) of the modern world, incapacitates him (he is unable to realize the significance of his vision in Devi's room) and leads to his political martyrdom (treason). He is left, then, with the vague feeling that a "number" and "home" are meaningful, but he does not yet know in what way (p. 109).

The motif is picked up immediately in Part III and brought to an ultimate resolution. Alan Walters, Hillier's protégé, utilizes the 1–5–5–8 binary code to decipher part of Hillier's letter; but Hillier, who already has suffered political martyrdom, is no longer interested in the letter and associates the number instead with Roper's martyred ancestor (pp. 119–120). Roper joins the game in Yarylyuk by giving the symbolic meaning of the number: "Edward Roper's clock stopped at two minutes to four. Fifteen fifty-eight. Martyrs are witnesses for the light. . . . The dream of a world society with man redeemed from sin" (p. 144).

But then Hillier's knowledge that Queen Elizabeth did not ascend the throne until November 1558 proves to Roper that his martyred ancestor was a Protestant instead of a Catholic, as Roper had originally believed (p. 147). References to the number continue as Wriste notes Hillier's slackness as a spy in not decoding the secret letter when he first received it (p. 152), and it appears a final time in Roper's memoirs as 15:58 Continental time (p. 184), bringing the motif full circle to its initial appearance as "two minutes to four." The coded letter's message, written in disappearing ink, also vanishes (p. 193), suggesting the severance of Hillier from his political commitments as he moves closer to his spiritual home.

Thematically the motif in this section indicates Hillier's shift from political to spiritual concerns and becomes the focal point also to jar Roper loose from his self-pitying attitude into more active participation in spiritual struggles. The final references to the number and coded letter complete the cycle of these motifs and give a sense of structural unity to the novel, although both Hillier and Roper have work yet to do.

The purpose of the recapitulation section in sonata-form is to bring back the two subjects originally presented in the exposition, but not as they were before. Burgess says: "After that—in the recapitulation section—they can appear soberly and singly, properly dressed and tidied up, but they cannot be as they were before, in the exposition. They have learned strange things about each other and about themselves, they have had a night out together" (*RJ*, p. 158). It is also standard form, according to Fleming and Veinus, for the first subject to dominate the recapitulation section and to allow for new developments to clear up any remaining problems from the development (*UM*, p. 125).

As illustrated in Figure 4, Burgess conforms fairly well to this pattern in Part III, reintroducing his first subject in chapters 1–3, merging his two subjects in a literal night out in chapters 4–6, presenting the second subject singly in chapter 7, and then returning to Hillier in chapters 8–9 as he undergoes his final acts of purification before entering home.

A major requirement of the recapitulation section is the transformation, however slight, of the subjects from the exposition section. In this novel, the transformations are well marked. In the exposition, Hillier was presented as a void, a dark sack crammed with skills. He was performing his last assignment for its cash reward, in effect a slack spy, concerned with his dreams of retirement more than with the task at hand. The beginnings of Hillier's metamorphoses are clearly outlined in III.1–3. Though still in the dark, he curbs his gluttony on a diet of bread and cheese, and his satyriasis through a fatherly attitude toward Clara. He is disgusted by the lust of the Russian officer lured into Clara's cabin, perhaps seeing in him the reflection of his own old nature. His wanderings in Yarylyuk prompt thoughts of home and spiritual regeneration, but he still retains elements of the old S-man.

Hillier and Roper are brought together in chapters 4–6, and their meeting set off a series of shocks in each. Roper, though still the scientist, has changed physically; he is sick and has been marked by age. It is with

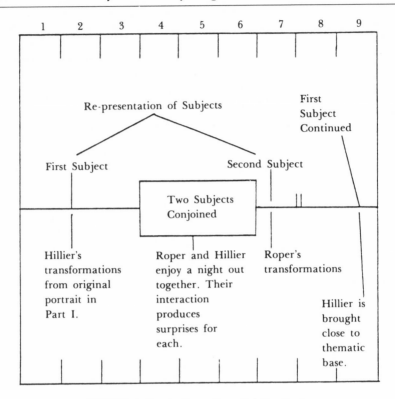

FIGURE 4: *Sonata Form: Recapitulation Section*

surprise that Hillier learns that Roper's defection has had historical-religious rather than political roots, contrary to his assessment of the defection in Part I. And it is with equal surprise that Roper learns from Hillier that his suppositions regarding the martyrdom of Edward Roper have been incorrect.

Wriste contributes to the enlightenment process in chapter five by telling both men things about themselves and each other that they had not known before. The knowledge is deflating to both egos. Wriste reveals the existence of Roper's confessional memoirs, that Roper was merely a lure to get Hillier to Russia, and that Roper's death warrant had been purchased by Cornpit-Ferrers, who feared his return to England. Hillier discovers the duplicity of his own department; his terminal bonus was to be really terminal. It is a cruel stripping process, baring hidden secrets to both men and to each other. Together they face death, and as their moment of truth arrives, Hillier's latent spiritualism, a tremor of intent, asserts itself, and his act of contrition is a shock to Roper as well as to himself.

This shared humiliation and confrontation with death makes both men aware of deeper currents within themselves and within the other. In this context Hillier's remark that Roper will eventually return to the

Church contains a prophetic undertone to its bantering surface (p. 162). And Roper's actions serve to reveal his tremor of intent: he gives Hillier the final chapter of his memoirs, aids in the mutilation of the S-man Wriste, and reasserts his Englishness (p. 164). Their night out together has advanced both men on their return trip to their spiritual home.

Roper, as the second subject, is the focus of chapter seven, and he, too, is seen as having changed from the earlier view in the exposition. At the close of Part I, Roper appeared to have finally attained a haven of peace. As Hillier said of him: "He seemed happy. He seemed to have got over sin. He was safe, sir" (p. 52). But the apparent serenity of his existence, one discovers in III.7, was a façade that covered a deep pit of sexual-spiritual emptiness. Lucy Butler was no substitute for Brigitte, and Roper's search for his lost wife is interpreted by Hillier in the footnotes as an indication of his spiritual quest (p. 173).

The last two chapters again focus on Hillier as he undergoes his final acts of purification in preparation for his entry home. Chapter eight continues the process of respiritualization through love that was begun in III.1–3, but Hillier experiences with Clara a reminder also that he needs death before regeneration can be complete. His identification by Alan as a neutral also reminds him that his political gamesmanship has been a poor substitute for spiritual commitment and that his dream of retirement is a neutralistic opting out of the conflict.

Symbols of Hillier's approaching regeneration are emphasized in chapter nine, both in the three-day waiting period (the Biblical resurrection) and in his lodging at the Sublime Porte Hotel, the gateway to his spiritual homecoming. The waiting period gives him time to reflect "on how wrong he had been about things, believing too much in choice and free will and the logic of men's acts; also the nature of love" (p. 194). But he knows now what he must do, and he carries out his last acts of purification — the sloughing off of his old lustful Adam in his final encounter with Devi, and the drowning of his spy past and of Roper's memoirs in the death of Theodorescu. Thus cleansed, he is ready for home.

The recapitulation fulfills the demands of sonata-form structure, representing the two main subjects, both singly and together, as they have been transformed by their experiences. The motifs laid out in the exposition and fragmented in the development are resolved, except for the conclusion of the "home" motif. The sinful S-factors have been spiritualized. The slow fermentation process by which a sinner is transformed into a saint has been quietly at work, sturdily supported and carried out by the intricate patterns of sonata-form.

Although Burgess' definition of sonata-form in *Re Joyce* does not include a comment on the closing section, a coda is traditionally a part of the entire design, and Part IV serves that function. Fleming and Veinus say the coda "must now sound like the close of a whole movement. . . . A few additional measures may be sufficient" (*UM*, p. 125). In *Tremor of Intent* the last brief section fulfills the thematic quest, for here Hillier achieves a new allegiance to the Church: he has returned to that home base from which he had strayed. Burgess, who has prepared the reader throughout the novel for this climax, closes out the old life and initiates the new with remarkable brevity: 'I'm home, Mrs. Madden,' he called. The word no longer seemed forced or conventional. Soon he would be deeper home" (p. 214). Hillier's long journey has come to an end.

The last chapter winds up loose strands and launches Hillier in his new life. In the five seasons that have passed since his commitment to the Church, Hillier has been renewing his energies within the discipline of religious order. He is no longer simply a void crammed with skills; he discovers that he "had been discharged dead, after all. Only after death, he had once said, was regeneration possible" (p. 216). He has met Father Byrne and told him of Roper's eventual return to the Church, and Hillier now waits for a reunion with Alan and Clara.

This last scene portrays the growth of all three characters. Clara's immature obsession with sex books and the arts of lust is to be matured in the sanctified love relationship of marriage. Alan is anticipating medieval studies, to be grounded in an age in which spiritual realities were more clearly defined. And Hillier, his satyriasis and gluttony now firmly controlled, exercises his Fatherly role with a last sermon on the nature of the cosmic war between the forces of God and Notgod, a war in which he is now fully committed.

As has been demonstrated, the sonata-form structure controls not only the broad divisions of the plot sequences — exposition, development, recapitulation, and coda — but also internal dynamics such as the order in presenting the thematic subjects and subsidiary motifs, the fragmentation process and clarification of developments. The discussion, however, would be incomplete if one failed to note two complementary patterns: the falling-rising linear development of the two main characters and a series of triadic progressions associated with each. The sonata-form and linear patterns are juxtaposed in Figure 5.

Hillier's falling-rising pattern neatly bifurcates the plot, with his descending line extending from I.1–II.7. Although Part I focuses primarily on Roper, Hillier suffers a slow drift from the Church that creates a spiritual vacuum that he attempts to fill by his political commitment as a spy. In Part II, Hillier's dream of retirement and his susceptibility to the sins of the flesh offset his wariness as a spy so that he is entrapped by Devi and Theodorescu and forced to commit treason. His ascending pattern begins with II.8 as he struggles to find meaning in life, first by rededicating himself to his rescue mission and later by recognizing his need for spiritual commitment. The return home is intensified in Part III as he becomes aware of his moral guilt and confronts death. His prayer for

A. Sonata Form Plot

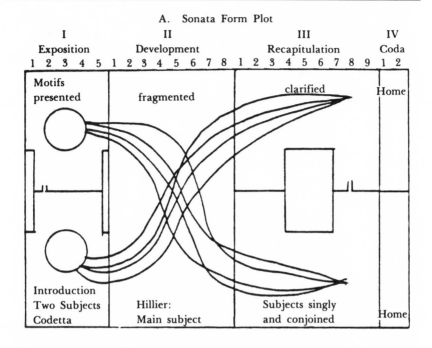

B. Linear Patterns: Character

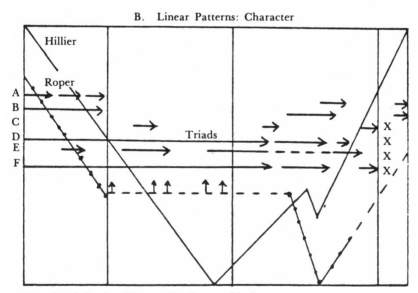

Roper's triads: A—Woman; B—Geographical.
Hillier's triads: C—Ocean as vomitorium; D—Disguises;
E—Women; F—Geographical.

FIGURE 5: *Juxtaposition of Sonata-Form and Linear Patterns*

forgiveness moves him on to Istanbul for the completion of the purification process, and he ends back home in the Church to begin his new life.

Roper, as second subject, has a broken linear pattern, one that achieves only the promise of completion by novel's end. Like Hillier, Roper moves away from the Church, suffers a stripping process, and is jarred into motion toward a return to the Church. His decline is the focus of Part I, tracing his early skepticism, his intellectual retreat into the idea that evil is only lack of knowledge, and his affirmation of scientific rationalism as the hope of mankind. His appearances in Part II are as fragmented pieces of Hillier's vision, but his descending pattern continues in III.4–5 as he is stripped of his intellectual security and his self-pity as a political/ religious martyr. The effect of the stripping process is to jolt him into action in aiding Hillier (III.6), thus beginning his ascending pattern. The spiritual uneasiness underlying his surface serenity is seen in III.7 and lends support to Hillier's prophetic words that Roper will eventually return to the Church.

The triadic progressions might be considered as variations on a theme in sonata-form, but they have been separated here as a structural entity because of their close correlation with the linear progress of the characters from sin to salvation. Both Hillier and Roper are associated with these triads, but Hillier, as main subject, displays the most complete pattern. His triads involve three women, three regurgitations into the ocean, three geographical locations, and three disguises. Each of these triads is completed within the three main parts of the novel, and each culminates in a fourth stage in the coda, thus both ending the old cycle and beginning a new one. As second subject, Roper has fewer triads. Like Hillier, he is associated with three women and three geographical locations, but the fourth stage is not achieved.

Hillier's triad of women are Brigitte, a sexually indiscriminate person (the *Urmutter*, p. 35) who represents a universe void of spiritual distinctions between good and evil; Devi, the dark goddess of sex; and Clara, the light goddess of spiritualizing love.[13] Structurally Burgess uses these women as focal points for the three major divisions of the novel, and Hillier's relations with each indicate the stages of his spiritual growth. He rejects Brigitte and her philosophy in Part I, becomes ensnared by Devi in Part II, and is respiritualized by Clara in Part III. His spiritual quest reaches a chaste climax in his role as Father in Part IV.

Hillier's purification process also is reflected in his use of the ocean as vomitorium. He begins the novel burdened by sins of gluttony and satyriasis, but, in addition, his life as a spy has become a weight that he needs to unload, a false faith that has turned into a spiritual void. His sin of gluttony is heaved overboard after his gourmet battle with Theodorescu (II.3). Similarly, Clara's sex books remind him of the multitude of fleshly pleasures with which he has defiled his body, and he consigns her books and his satyriasis to the sea (III.3). Finally, he regurgitates his entire spy past onto the scapegoat Theodorescu and commits it to the sea (III.9). Thus cleansed, he is capable of exercising self-control in Part IV.

The three geographical movements and disguises are closely aligned. Both the England-Yarylyuk-Istanbul pattern and the Jagger-Polotski-Wriste disguises bring Hillier into contact with the political options of modern life: commitment to West, East, or neutralism. Hillier discovers both through his geographical movement and through the piercing of his disguises that his service in obedience to the powers of politics is a surface gamesmanship and an inadequate substitute for faith. As a lax Western spy, his disguise as Jagger is stripped (II.5). His cover as the Russian officer Polotski is pierced with equal ease by the kitchen worker in Yarylyuk (III.3). And after adopting the dress of Wriste, Hillier is viewed by Alan as a neutral (III.6, 8). Each of the alternatives is found wanting, and after disposing of his political commitments through the death of Theodorescu, Hillier moves to his fourth stage and new beginning as a priest.

Roper's feminine triad — Ethel, Brigitte, Lucy — contains strong parallels with Hillier's triad. Ethel, like Clara, is a fair-haired, wholesome person; and Roper, like Hillier, has incestuous thoughts about her (compare pp. 25, 58, 187). Both men share Brigitte. And Lucy, like Devi, is dark-haired (p. 49). But Roper's triad represents a descent into intellectual sterility as he moves from Ethel (I.2) to Brigitte (I.3) and finally to Lucy, the computer operator who is no more than a good friend (I.5). By novel's end, however, Roper has returned to Brigitte (p. 216), a wife he has confused with the Virgin Mary (p. 47). The implication in Part IV is that Roper will eventually discover his error and return to the Church.

The second triad follows Roper's movement from the West to the East and, in the coda, to East Germany. Like Hillier's geographical movement, the triad illustrates Roper's disillusionment with political commitments, and his return to East Germany and Brigitte may be only temporary, a half-way house in which time will restore his true perceptions of life's spiritual meaning.

The linear pattern, in summary, complements the sonata-form plot structure by establishing a falling-rising pattern for the characters and by creating a series of triadic progressions that reveal the stages of their spiritual transformation. That Burgess is capable of maintaining the simultaneous flow of each pattern without bringing them into a collision course is a tribute to his fine craftsmanship and indicative of his deep concern with the novel as form. That the novel also makes delightful reading is a tribute to his art as a storyteller and as a master of words.

Notes

1. Anthony Burgess, *Urgent Copy* (New York: Norton, 1968), p. 257.

2. Walter Clemons, "Anthony Burgess: Pushing On," *New York Times Book Review*, 29 November 1970, p. 2.

3. *Urgent Copy*, p. 155. See also Burgess' emphasis on form over content in "A Novelist's Sources Are Myth, Language and the Here-and-Now," *New York Times Book Review*, 19 July 1964, p. 5; "Speaking of Books: The Writer's Purpose," *New York Times Book Review*, 1 May 1966, p. 2; and *The Novel Now* (New York: Pegasus, 1970), p. 206.

4. "The Writer and Music," *The Listener*, 3 May 1962, pp. 761–762.

5. *Tremor of Intent* (New York: Ballantine Books, 1967). All references are to this edition of the novel. A study of musical patterns in Burgess' novels was stimulated in part by the suggestion in the "Preface" of A. A. DeVitis' *Anthony Burgess* (New York: Twayne, 1972).

6. See, for example, Charles F. Duffy, "From Espionage to Eschatology: Anthony Burgess's *Tremor of Intent*," *Renascence*, 32 (Winter 1980), 87; William P. Fitzpatrick, "Black Marketeers and Manichees: Anthony Burgess' Cold War Novels," *West Virginia University Philological Papers*, 21 (December 1974), 85; DeVitis, *Anthony Burgess*, pp 155–156; Geoffrey Aggeler, "Between God and Notgod," *Malahat Review*, 17 (January 1971), 101; and Robert K. Morris, *The Consolations of Ambiguity* (Columbia: University of Missouri Press, 1971), pp. 18–20.

7. "The Manicheans," *Times Literary Supplement*, 3 March 1966, p. 154.

8. William Fleming and Abraham Veinus, *Understanding Music* (New York: Holt, Rinehart and Winston, 1958), pp. 123–125. Subsequent references to this edition will appear in the text abbreviated as *UM*.

9. *Re Joyce* (New York: Norton, 1968), p. 158. Subsequent references to this edition will appear in the text abbreviated as *RJ*.

10. Thomas LeClair notes the Hillier-Roper opposition as one between an Augustinian heart and Pelagian head, but he does not mention their potential union in one person: "Essential Opposition: The Novels of Anthony Burgess," *Critique*, 12, iii (1971), 90–91.

11. "Silence, Exile, and Cunning." *The Listener*, 6 May 1965, p. 662.

12. See references to the rose in Hillier's crucifixion dream (p. 55); in the scent of roses in Yarylyuk (p. 132); in Roper in the rose garden (p. 140); and in Brigitte's synthetic smell of roses (p. 174). The rose is, as Hillier explains, a symbol of pledges "that life went on in universal patterns below the horrors of power and language" (p. 132).

13. Several critics have discussed Hillier's women, focusing primarily on the characters of Devi and Clara as the dark and light figures of Manichean opposition. None, however, has noted Roper's parallel series of three women. See Morris, *The Consolations of Ambiguity*, p. 20; Jean E. Kennard, *Number and Nightmare* (Hamden, CT: Archon books, 1975), p. 142; and DeVitis, *Anthony Burgess*, pp. 160–161.

Incest and the Artist: *MF*   Geoffrey Aggeler*

In a number of his novels, notably *The Wanting Seed, The Eve of St. Venus, The Worm and the Ring*, and *Enderby*, Burgess builds deliberately upon mythic frames and, like his master Joyce, even reveals some mythopoeic tendencies. Many of Burgess's characters are ironically modified archetypes who undergo archetypal experiences or ironic parodies of such experience. In addition, we find literal goddesses as well as goddess figures intervening in human affairs in order to revive and regenerate. However,

*From *Anthony Burgess: The Artist as Novelist* (University: University of Alabama Press, 1979), 195–207. © 1979 by the University of Alabama Press. Reprinted with permission.

none of these novels fits wholly within a mythic frame, presumably because Burgess found such archetypes too confining for his purposes. In *MF* he seems to have found a framework large enough to accommodate his total artistic design. He has fused incest myths—Algonquin Indian and Greek—and given them new meaning as a devastating satiric indictment of contemporary Western cultural values that goes well beyond the criticisms levelled in the *Enderby* novels.

The novel's title, *MF*, derives in part from the initials of the narrator / protagonist, Miles Faber. It also stands for "male / female," a valid human classification that the book implicitly contrasts with various false taxonomies, and it has another, related significance with reference to the all-encompassing theme of incest, especially when certain racial factors, bases of false taxonomies, are revealed in the conclusion. As everyone knows, the term *motherfucker* has a wide range of usages in the North American black idiom, and Burgess reveals that the range can be widened further to encompass totally the maladies currently afflicting Western culture.

As the novel opens, Faber is recalling a scene in a room of the Algonquin Hotel in New York City. He had been young then, an affluent orphan not yet twenty-one, and a student at an American Ivy League university. Like many of his fellow students, he had been perpetually filled with moral outrage by various more or less vaguely defined social and political injustices—"tyrannical democracies, wars in the name of peace, students forced to study . . . skeletal Indian children eating dog's excrement" (*MF*, 4)[1]—and on one occasion he had sought to express his outrage in an unoriginal, ineffectual, yet satisfying manner—by public copulation in front of the university library. Like the creator of a recent play featuring copulation on the American flag, he and his cheering student supporters had apparently hoped to make the American establishment see that this form of "obscenity" was much less obscene than its own obscenities of social and political injustice. His social conscience was not, however, his only or even his strongest motivation. To be able to protest one type of naked obscenity by means of another, using one's social conscience as an excuse, is an exhibitionist's dream, and Faber, as he readily admits, is a sexual exhibitionist. The exotic flesh of his partner in protest, Miss Ang, was another major stimulus to his social conscience.

As Faber casually defends his actions to the lawyer in charge of doling out his inheritance, we find he has been gifted with an Oedipean skill as a riddler. This talent in itself emphasizes his role as an archetypal MF, and it becomes more and more important as the mythic design of the novel is revealed. Like "that poor Greek kid" who had been crippled and left to die, he is propelled unwittingly but inexorably toward a solution to the riddle of his own origins and destiny. The gods have managed to place him under the influence of a professor who introduces him to the works of one Sib Legeru, a poet and painter who had lived, created, and died in almost total obscurity on the Carribean island of "Castita." The samples he has seen of Leguru's work lead Faber to hope that the main corpus will reveal the "freedom" he passionately yearns to see expressed in art — "beyond structure and cohesion . . . words and colors totally free because totally meaningless" (*MF*, 11). To be vouch-safed this vision, he must make a pilgrimage to the island and seek out a kind of museum where Legeru's works have been decently interred.

The process of reaching this shrine is long and arduous. Initially, Faber is delayed by the efforts of the lawyer, who, it turns out, is seeking to prevent fulfillment of a curse of incest that hangs over the house of Faber. The young man is told that he is the offspring of an incestuous union of brother and sister, and that this same union has produced a sister he has never been allowed to meet. One of the chores laid upon the executors of his will by the remorseful incestuous father has been to maintain a safe distance between young Faber and his sister. By what would seem to be an incredible coincidence, her hiding place happens to be the island home of the late Sib Legeru. Actually, as Faber is destined to discover, there is much more than coincidence involved.

Prodded on by the insatiable curiosity of a riddler, he will not be persuaded to delay his pilgrimage until the occasion of sin can be removed. His haste is stimulated to some degree by a desire to see the sister who has been so deceitfully hidden away from him, but this does not overshadow his main goal, that of visiting the Sib Legeru shrine, there to imbibe true artistic "freedom." This experience will, he hopes, enable him to liberate his artistic energies, which will in turn enable him to cram together all the masses of inconsequential, unrelated data whirling about within the "junkshops" of his young brain so "inconsequentiality" will be forced to "yield significance." His choice of a medium to express his vision is dictated by his exhibitionism. He will write a play, the like of which, he fancies, has never been written. It will contain such memorable glimpses of the inconsequential as this scene:

> GEORGE: Half-regained Cimon the spider-crab.
>
> MABEL: A pelican fish of herculean proportions. The three Eusebii in baskets, I mean Basque berets.
>
> GEORGE: Yes yes. The thundering legions.
>
> These words to be spoken on a bed, with copulation proceeding. The significance, of course, would lie in the inconsequentiality. (*MF*, 57)

As he looks back on this youthful dream, Faber realizes that such scenes, charged with this sort of "significance," would hardly have made him one of the avant-garde among twentieth-century dramatists. But he had been young then, filled with blinding, formless "vision" and, like so many of his form-despising peers, utterly unable to grow in wisdom. Only after he has completed his pilgrimage and unravelled the great Sib Legeru riddle will he be able to see things clearly and divine the real "significance" of "inconsequentiality."

On the last leg of his journey to Castita, Faber sails as a galley hand on a yacht with two homosexuals who have little to do besides cruising about the Carribean in "desperate sexual bondage to each other" (*MF*, 55). One of them, the skipper, is a woman-hating ex-fashion designer. His faithless, helpless mate is a would-be poet. *MF* is not really a "contrived" book, but this voyage, like everything else in it, fits within the archetypal framework. Its archetypal function is emphasized during a storm, which very nearly finishes all three voyagers and which Burgess manages to draw with Conradian vividness and authenticity:

> God, like a dog, hearing his name, leapt in a great slavering joy upon us. The sea cracked and ground at the bones of the bows in a superb accession of appetite. We rode rockinghorse the quaking roof of the waves. Aspinwall cried:
> — God Jesus Christ Almighty.
> There was an apocolyptical rending above us and then the thudding of wings of a tight and berserk archangel. Aspinwall bounded for the deck, sandwich in hand, and I lurchfollowed. Brine spray spume jumped on us ecstatically. He threw his sandwich savagely into the rash smart slogger, which threw it promptly back, as he gaped appalled at the fluttering flagrags of old laundry on the bolt ropes, stormjib eaten alive, trysail sheetblocks hammering. He had time to look at me with hate before yapping orders that the wind swallowed untasted. A war, a war, or something. No, a warp. But what the hell was a warp? He tottered to the forecastle himself, cursing, while I clung to a rail. Then I saw what a warp was: a sort of towline. He and I, he still going through a silent-movie sequence of heavy cursing, chiefly at me, got the trysail down and then furled it with this warp to the main boom. There was no sail up at all now. The yacht just lolloped moronically in the troughs. It was a complicated torture of an idiot child tossed by one lot of yobs in a cloth, another gang of tearways singing different songs loudly and pounding him, her, it with ice-lumps that turned at once to warm water. Night, as they say, fell. At the helm I left Aspinwall, whipped by warm water that broke in heads of frantic snowblooms, and went below, being scared of being washed overboard. (*MF*, 62–63)

Shortly after he goes below, Faber is knocked unconscious by a piece of loose furniture, but just before he goes under, he senses the significance of what is happening to him. The would-be poet is cringing below, not actually praying but wearing a sports shirt patterned with the utterances of mystical writers that seems to pray for him. One saying that catches Faber's eye expresses resignation and hope in the Resurrection: "*If He is found now, He is found then. If not, we do but go to dwell in the City of Death*" (*MF*, 63). Immediately after Faber notices this, the "oyster-ballocked poetaster" expresses both his terror and his sense of the archetypal in one brief exclamation: "Jonah." At first Faber seems to reject the notion of himself as a "Jonah," but a few moments later, as he is plunging into insensibility, he accepts the role: "that inner pilot was doused as I went down into slosh and debris, the belly of Jonadge, black damp whaleboned gamp" (*MF*, 64). Faber is, in fact, going through an essential stage in his progress toward knowledge. According to Joseph Campbell, who has managed to discern a single archetype behind Jonah, Oedipus, Hiawatha, Finn MacCool, and a thousand other faces in world mythology, such plunges into darkness signify a hero's arrival at a "threshold" of awareness: "The idea that the passage of the magical threshold is a transit into a sphere of rebirth is symbolized in the worldwide womb image of the belly of the whale. The hero, instead of conquering or conciliating the power of the threshold, is swallowed into the unknown, and would appear to have died."[2]

Faber emerges from the dark womb of unconsciousness to clear daylight and the landfall that means Castita. As he gropes about below deck, an utterance that seems to be from the poetaster's shirt impinges itself upon his brain: *"The fear of solitude is at bottom the fear of the double, the figure which appears one day and always heralds death"* (*MF*, 66). Significantly, he can't find this text anywhere on the shirt itself. It is in fact a message from the unknown revealed to him while he was on the threshold of awareness awaiting a rebirth of consciousness. It will have no meaning for him until he has solved the riddles of Castita.

It is useful to review briefly the myths that Burgess has fused in constructing his archetypal framework. His fusion of Algonquin Indian and Greek incest myths has been noted. The Greek myth, the story of Oedipus, is quite well known. Depending upon one's own assumptions, one can say it has thrown both light and darkness over the fields of psychoanalysis and literary criticism. There is something irresistibly fascinating about the story of the brilliant riddler doomed by the gods, his own weaknesses, and his own cleverness to parricide and an incestuous marriage. Everyone, including Oedipus himself, is determined to prevent fulfillment of the curse, but everyone plays completely into the hands of the gods. As many commentators have pointed out, it is not merely Oedipus's skill as a riddler or the various coincidental happenings that lead to his entrapment. He is trapped from the moment of his birth by the very blood in his veins. The son of a king can hardly be expected to exhibit meekness when he is rudely ordered off a road by a surly charioteer, and later, when he is offered a crown, the regal blood in his veins will not let him refuse. All that is needed in addition is his instinctive skill as a riddler, which enables him to destroy the Sphinx, but which also accelerates the process of his own destruction by driving him on to solve the riddle of Laius's murder and the plague afflicting Thebes.

The inevitability of the whole process and the inescapableness of the act of incest are perhaps the most stimulating aspects of the myth. Joseph Campbell views this and other incestuous unions in mythology as indicative of the hero's arrival at a summit of awareness beyond the "threshold" previously described: "The mystical marriage with the queen goddess of the world represents the hero's total mastery of life; for the woman is life, the hero its knower and master. And the testings of the hero, which were preliminary to his ultimate experience and deed, were symbolical of those crises of realization by means of which his consciousness came to be amplified and made capable of enduring the full possession of the mother-destroyer, his inevitable bride. With that he knows that he and the father are one: he is in the father's place."[3] However, neither Campbell nor Lord Raglan nor Sir James Frazer nor even Emile Durkheim has satisfactorily accounted for all aspects of the Oedipus myth.[4] They have not, for instance, suggested any logical connection between the hero's gift of riddling and his incestuous entrapment. Establishing this connection was a task that remained for Claude Lévi-Strauss. In developing his theory, Lévi-Strauss was proceeding from his own doctrine that archetypal myths are shared by cultures so widely separated that there could be no direct exchange of ideas between them — as widely separated as, say, aboriginal New England and Greece. His conclusions with regard to this particular myth are most convincing, and one of the people he has convinced is Anthony Burgess.

Burgess seems to have first encountered Lévi-Strauss's theory in the latter's inaugural lecture as a newly appointed professor of the Collège de France. In that lecture, subsequently translated into English as *The Scope of Anthropology*, Lévi-Strauss recounted the following piece of Algonquin Indian folklore:

> The Iroquois and Algonquin Indians tell the story of a young girl subjected to the amorous leanings of a nocturnal visitor whom she believes to be her brother. Everything seems to point to the guilty one: physical appearance, clothing, and the scratched cheek which bears witness to the heroine's virtue. Formally accused by her, the brother reveals that he has a counterpart or, more exactly, a double, for the tie between them is so strong that any accident befalling the one is automatically transmitted to the other. To convince his incredulous sister, the young man kills his double before her, but at the same time he condemns himself, since their destinies are linked.
>
> Of course, the mother of the victim will want to avenge her son. As it happens she is a powerful sorceress, the mistress of the owls. There is only one way of misleading her: that the sister marry her brother, the latter passing for the double he has killed. Incest is so inconceivable that the old woman never suspects the hoax. The owls are not fooled and denounce the guilty ones, but they succeed in escaping.[5]

As Lévi-Strauss observes, the thematic parallels between this myth and the story of Oedipus are startling. For one thing, "the very precautions taken to avoid incest actually make it inevitable." Moreover, in both myths, much depends on the fact that two characters, supposedly distinct, become identified with each other. In the Indian myth, the hero is not technically related to his double; yet he and the double are one to the extent that the murder is a kind of suicide. Similarly, Oedipus has two distinct personalities—a condemned child long thought to be dead and a triumphant hero. Lévi-Strauss views the incest between brother and sister of the Iroquois myth as "a permutation of the Oedipal incest between mother and son." These parallels might of course be purely coincidental. More proof that we are dealing with the same archetype is needed, and Lévi-Strauss provides it by establishing that the owls in the Indian myth are a transformation of the riddling Sphinx destroyed by Oedipus. He notes that puzzles, proverbs, and riddles are rare among North American Indians. There is, however, in the Southwest a Pueblo ceremony in which clowns set riddles to the spectators. According to Pueblo myths, these clowns were born of an incestuous union. More significant perhaps is the fact that among the Algonquins themselves are "myths in which owls, or sometimes the ancestor of owls, set riddles to the hero which he must answer under pain of death." The fact that the sorceress in the myth is a mistress of owls, rational creatures capable of solving the riddle of her son's murder, strongly suggests a correlation between riddling and incest.

The nature of the correlation can be seen if one considers what a riddle is. It may, according to Lévi-Strauss, be defined simply as "a question to which one postulates that there is no answer." To make the definition more all-embracing, one may consider all the possible transformations of it. One may even invert its terms to mean "an answer for which there is no question." He points out that there are a number of myths that derive their dramatic power from this "symmetrical" inversion. The death of the Buddha follows inevitably upon the failure of a disciple to ask an expected question, and in some of the Grail myths, much depends upon the timorous reluctance of heroes in the presence of the vessel to ask, "What is it good for?"

Riddling and incest have become associated in myth because they are both frustrations of natural expectation. Just as the answer to a riddle succeeds against all expectation in getting back to the question, so the parties in an incestuous union—mother and son, brother and sister, or whatever—are brought together despite any design that would keep them apart. One can see the relation as well in that the hero himself is a living riddle whose solution is simultaneously a discovery of incest. Frequently, as in the case of Oedipus, discovery is hastened by the reaction of an outraged Nature: "The audacious union of masked words or of consanguines unknown to themselves engenders decay and fermentation, the unchaining of natural forces—one thinks of the Theban plague—just as impotence in sexual matters (and in the ability to initiate a proposed dialogue) dries up animal and vegetable fertility."[6]

Burgess was greatly stimulated as well as convinced by Lévi-Strauss's argument. In an essay entitled *If Oedipus Had Read His Lévi-Strauss*, he observes that a theme common to both the Algonquin myth and the story of Oedipus — that one may avoid incest by avoiding riddles — is also developed in Joyce's *Finnegans Wake*. Guilt-ridden Earwicker, whose name during his waking hours is Porter, transmits his obsessive passion for his daughter to his two sons, Shem and Shaun. Shem, who is to be identified with Joyce himself, is saved from incest with his sister by his inability to solve a riddle put to him by a chorus of angelic, "not quite human" girls. His failure is a humiliation, but it removes him from temptation. If Oedipus had not humiliated the Sphinx, he would have been devoured, but he would have been saved from incest. Burgess found additional evidence that the "riddle-incest nexus" is deep in human consciousness in his own writing. In his eschatological spy thriller *Tremor of Intent*, the hero is saved from a kind of incest by his refusal to listen to the decoding of a message.[7]

The riddle / incest bond was not one of Burgess's major concerns in *Tremor of Intent*. As with some of the most interesting themes in Shakespearean drama, it seems to have emerged on its own while the author was consciously preoccupied with something else. In *MF*, however, the theme of incestuous entrapment through riddling is everything. The adventures of Faber parallel both the story of Oedipus and the Algonquin myth. One may even discern figures of the Algonquin owls and the Theban sphinx. Professor Keteki (Sanskrit for "riddle"), who introduces Faber to the works of Sib Legeru, is remembered by him in very feathery terms, "crane-like in body, owl-headed, ululating a mostly intelligible lecture, with the smell of Scotch as a kind of gloss" (*MF*, 6). The fact that he is engaged in a study of "Volitional Solecisms in Melville" seems to tie up with the novel's Jonah theme. Like one of the Algonquin owls, Keteki puts a riddle to his class that Faber manages to solve by an incredible suprarational process of association. Later, when Faber finds himself answering riddles to stave off starvation on Castita, he faces Dr. Gonzi, a riddling creature whose appearance is more lionlike than human. It is the misery of looking less than human, rather than the humiliation of being outwitted by Faber, that causes this creature to follow the example of the Theban sphinx in self-destruction.

Having overcome this latter riddling peril, Faber is led inexorably on toward a meeting with his double, a repulsive, foul-mouthed creature named Llew, whose taste in art runs to pop songs and pornography. What Llew represents is suggested by his mispronunciation of the name of the street where Faber is looking for the Sib Legeru museum. Llew encounters and attempts to rape Faber's sister in a house on the same street. Its name, "Indovinella," is Italian for "riddle," but Llew gets it out as "indiarubber," suggesting that he himself is a plastic creation, erasable, and dedicated to infertility, rather than a man. Llew's death at the hands of the girl's protector causes Faber little grief initially, but it is destined to force him into abandoning his identity and being trapped in incest.

As in the Algonquin myth, Faber is tested by a mistress of birds and is threatened by the birds themselves. Eventually, the curse of incest is exorcised. When this is accomplished, the real "meaning" of *MF*, the connection between incest and the maladies currently afflicting Western culture, especially art, is made clear. Although an awareness of the mythic framework and the influence of Lévi-Strauss is useful, such information is not essential to an appreciation of *MF*, any more than, say, a knowledge of Vico's theories of history is essential to an appreciation of *Finnegans Wake*. No writer of lasting quality is dependent to any degree on the exegesis of academic critics.

One way or another, Burgess reaches those who are capable of responding to serious literature with or without glosses. The most useful service an academic critic can perform for readers of a novel such as *MF* is to provide them with hints to aid them in increasing the sensual and intellectual enrichment they may find in any event. Such a truism may be a kind of reassuring answer to one of Faber's asides to the reader near the end of the novel: "Don't try distilling a message from it, not even an expresso cupful of meaningful epitome or a sambuca glass of abridgement, *con la mosca*. Communication has been the whatness of the communication. For separable meanings go to the professors, whose job it is to make a meaning out of anything. Professor Keteki, for instance, with his *Volitional Solecisms in Melville* (*MF*, 240–41). As a member of the scribbling, riddling crew "whose job it is," I want to declare the purity of my intentions in presuming to discuss and evaluate *MF*. I would not attempt to extract any "separable meaning" from it, any more than I would try to distill one from *The Wanting Seed*.

Like *The Wanting Seed*, *MF* is an invitation, an exhortation perhaps, to view Western culture within an illuminating framework. Just as it is easier to comprehend two radically different, yet similar, philosophical and political avenues to insanity within the framework of an archetypal theological debate, so it is easier to see much of what ails Western culture within the framework of archetypal myth. If the academic exegete has any useful function at all, it is merely to encourage the reader to accept the invitation and test the adequacy of the framework even as he experiences the vision.

Burgess's mythic framework encompasses much of Western culture and especially those branches that seem to be flowering currently in North America. It is clear that Burgess's American experiences, perhaps as much as his reading of Lévi-Strauss, have had a great deal to do with generating his vision of incest. According to Miles Faber's grandfather, who may or may not be expressing Burgess's point of view, incest "in its widest sense" signifies "the breakdown of order, the collapse of communication, the irresponsible cultivation of chaos" (*MF*, 235). This same character, who has a Tiresian vision of the world's corruption as a result of a long lifetime's immersion in it, observes that the totally free (because totally meaningless) "works of Sib Legeru exhibit the nastiest aspects of incest. . . . In them are combined an absence of meaning and a sniggering boyscout codishness. It is man's job to impose order on the universe, not to yearn for Chapter Zero of the Book of Genesis. . . . Art takes the raw material of the world about us and attempts to shape it into signification. Antiart takes that same material and seeks insignification" (*MF*, 235).

For a number of reasons, one is liable to suspect these are Burgess's own sentiments. For one thing, they echo sentiments expressed by the autobiographical Shakespeare (WS) in *Nothing Like the Sun*. In refusing to support Essex's revolt, WS explains that "the only self-evident duty is to that image of order we all carry in our brains," and this duty has a special meaning for the artist: "To emboss a stamp of order on time's flux is an impossibility I must try to make possible through my art, such as it is" (*NLS*, 199). We might also recall the opposition between the honest, technically competent poetry of Mr. Enderby and the utterly chaotic, meaningless drivel of the chaos and acid-inspired makers who scorn him. But one need not go beyond *MF* itself to find Burgess's sympathies with the view that art demands discipline, not an incestuous abandonment to an illusion of freedom. One need only look at young Faber himself, a pedantic, thoroughly obnoxious, confused product of a culture that exhibits a curious fondness for chaos, which it tends to equate with freedom. In the realms of art especially, there is a reluctance to label the chaotic and undisciplined according to data gathered by sense and intellect. Take, for instance, the case of the linguistic team who gave their computer a free hand in turning out a volume of "poetry" and then sent the volume around to some *soi-disant* literati. One set of readers offered the "poet" a full university scholarship. Others expressed concern for his mental and emotional well-being. Happily, a few *poets* were able to tell that the verse had not been written by a human being. Or take the case of the painter who spreads his oils with the rear wheel of his motorcycle. Or the respected composer who offered an audience a symphony of total silence. As *MF* suggests, this chaos obsession and reluctance to call *merde* by its proper name shows itself most insidiously on the campus, frequently in the attitudes of people such as Professor Keteki who should know better because they have the cultural yardsticks of the past at their command. All too frequently, the students are seriously taken in by works such as those of Sib Legeru, but occasionally they are not. Recently, I was delighted to overhear two undergraduates extemporizing between fits of laughter a scene from an imagined play by a respected Legerulike writer. It sounded quite a bit like the scene Faber imagines in his projected play. Their healthy laughter was one of the most reassuring sounds I have heard in months.

The focus of *MF* is broader than art — much broader. The whole pattern of Western culture, as Burgess sees it, is incestuous. Race consciousness in particular, which has in no way diminished in recent years, is symptomatic of an incestuous pull. In Burgess's view, "the time has come for the big miscegnation."[8] All of the races must overcome their morbid preoccupation with color identity and face the merger that is inevitable in any event. As *The Wanting Seed* suggests, population pressures will make any notion of racial compartmentalization utterly absurd in the not-too-distant future. But aside from this, Burgess sees race consciousness itself as fundamentally absurd, and he has illuminated the absurdity in a number of books. In *A Vision of Battlements*, for one, he has Richard Ennis imagining how life in postwar England would be for him and the beautiful Spanish girl he loves: ". . . Concepción in the fish queue, the "bloody foreigner" in the English village, the "touch of the tar brush" from the tweeded gentry. He foresaw the ex-prisoner-of-war Luftwaffe pilot, flaxen, thick-spoken, absorbed into the farming community playing darts with the boys ("That were a bloody good one, Wilhelm"), Concepción and himself in the cold smoke-room ("That foreigner that there Mr. Ennis did marry") (*AVOB*, 71). Throughout the *Malayan Trilogy* race consciousness is shown to be the major factor that will inhibit cultural progress in the new Malaysia. In *MF* Burgess focuses on what he regards as the absurd and incestuous black preoccupation with race. Some months before he began writing *MF*, he observed "that it's about time the blacks got over this business of incest, of saying they're beautiful and they're black, they're going to conquer, they're going to prevail."[9] In *MF* itself, he attempts to jolt the readers out of their race consciousness by allowing them to finish the entire novel before he reveals a racial factor that most writers would feel compelled to clarify on their first page.[10] One of the "alembicated morals" he mockingly offers the reader is "that my race, or your race must start thinking in terms of the human totality and cease weaving its own fancied achievements or miseries into a banner. Black is beauty, yes, BUT ONLY WITH ANNA SEWELL PRODUCTS" (*MF*, 241).

Burgess has invited us to recognize, if we can, the incestuous pattern on the racial plane as it mirrors the incestuous yearning in art or, rather, antiart. The two are directly related in that they both reveal a colossal willed ignorance and laziness on the part of Western man. Just as it's a good deal easier to shirk the burdens of true art in the name of "freedom," so it is easier to allow oneself to be defined and confined by a racial identity so the search for truths that concern "the human totality," truly a "man's job," can be put off. Both the "freedom" of the artist who incestuously allows his own masturbatory "codishness" to create for him and the "identity" of the black or white racial chauvinist are pernicious illusions that the artist, perhaps more than anyone else, is bound to expose.

To the extent that it deals with the role of the artist, *MF* can be seen as a continuation of the explorations in *Enderby*. The works of Sib Legeru, like the insipid wailing of Yod Crewsy or the supposedly "relevant" babbling of the acid heads, are pseudoart or antiart. Their acceptance as real art has been encouraged by such revered "prophets" as Marshall

McLuhan, but, as an *Enderby* persona suggests, we need not fear that posterity will be fooled. *MF* reassures us of the same thing by affirming a faith in basic sense experience. All the spurious creation of Sib Legeru "stinks" in a metaphorical sense, and some of it stinks quite literally, and only a pseudointellectual little wretch like Faber, or one of his professors like Keteki, could be taken in indefinitely.

MF can also, as suggested, be seen as a continuation of those novels in which Burgess focuses on Western man's myopic view of his own nature. In his dystopian books *A Clockwork Orange* and *The Wanting Seed* especially, he focuses on Western mans' insane compulsion to generalize about the nature of "man" at the expense of any true understanding of human problems. As social order is sought on the basis of preconceived "Pelagian" or "Augustinian" notions about the nature of man, society is propelled toward moral chaos. Similarly, in *MF* we see that the yearning for freedom through chaos is actually a yearning for slavery. Another "alembicated moral" Faber offers his readers is that "a mania for total liberty is really a mania for prison, and you'll get there by way of incest" (*MF*, 241). Taking the application of this at its broadest, one realizes that Western man's failure to understand himself causes him to develop a spurious concept of freedom and to seek ruinous avenues to that freedom. Narrowing the focus to America (and *MF* invites this focus), one can see a strong tendency to preserve "freedom" through incestuous avenues. The "yellow horde" must be kept back in Asia and controlled in Latin America. Non-American cultures must either be resisted or Americanized. World federalism, the concept of world government, is viewed as un-American and dangerously subversive. This incestuous tendency of America, this feeling that it can be saved only if it turns in upon itself and either excludes or converts the corrupting influences from the great world outside, is not an avenue to freedom. It imprisons America. Many supporters of the recent "crusade" in Indo-China, who considered it essential to the preservation of American liberty, would like to see Washington politicians replaced with generals. Only in this way, they feel, can America be "free."

Some readers may think: "You're reading all of this into Faber's 'alembicated moral?' He was only talking about the 'mania for liberty' and the incestuous impulse in art, and, to some extent, race consciousness." However, as Burgess says, we may take what we please from his story, "any damned nonsense" we "happen to fancy." He has defined incest for us and invited us to find it where we will. Some readers will find it elsewhere in the American or Western consciousness. The only thing a reader will not be able to do is deny that "incest" is practiced.

Most readers will probably enjoy *MF* less than some of Burgess's other books, not because it is inferior artistically, but simply because it is a devastating satire with so much of Western culture as its object. Satire that cuts in so savage and sweeping a fashion and at the same time demands too much in the way of intellectual involvement will almost always be less "enjoyable" than gentler entertainments. But just as a strong-stomached and agile-witted playgoer can find *Troilus and Cressida* or *Measure for Measure* more rewarding than Shakespeare's early romances, so a reader can find *MF* more rewarding, as well as challenging, than Burgess's lighter entertainments. (If one is repelled by *MF*, one had better avoid Petronius and Ben Jonson and Swift and Nabokov.) Like nearly all of Burgess's novels, it is a piece of linguistic wizardry that delights and never wearies. If one objects that Faber does not sound like a typical twenty-year-old university student, one is overlooking the clearly indicated fact that Faber is *not* a twenty-year-old student but a highly literate middle-aged man looking back upon his youth and remembering imperfectly the ways in which he spoke.

When Burgess wants to give us the sounds of youth, he is quite capable of doing so, as he did in *A Clockwork Orange*. If one happens to be an American and finds the directions of the satire unsettling, one may take some comfort in the fact that the objects of attack are much broader than America. One can see much of Western culture in general being satirized. One may even discern the outlines of Burgess's former residence, Malta, in the island of "Castita." Look in a gazetteer and you will not find Castita, but if you try an Italian / English dictionary, you will find "chastity." There is plenty of irony in the name, and the picture of the island and its government is not flattering. The abundant references to things Maltese and bits of "Castitan" history point strongly to that island. One might mention in particular the name "Gonzi," which the archbishop of Malta shares with the riddling, lionlike creature who attempts to trap and kill Faber.

For all its bitterness, however, *MF* does contain the seeds of Burgess's great affirmation of the power of the creative will in his next novel, *Napoleon Symphony*. Like Ben Jonson's *Poetaster*, it spares no spleen in attacking the enemies of art, but, like that comedy, it affirms the power of art itself to triumph. Faber does, after all, grow in wisdom to an understanding of the difference between art and antiart, even as the court of Augustus is enlightened by Jonson's autobiographical Horace. Jonson, however, never went very far beyond this limited affirmation to depict the divine power of a truly great artist "to imposes order on the universe." It remained for his greatest contemporary to dramatize (in *The Tempest*) the power of art informed by love. Burgess's faith in the power of art, as we see in *Napoleon Symphony*, is much stronger than Jonson's, more like Shakespeare's. Even when he produces yet another *Poetaster*-like satire against the enemies of art, in his *Clockwork Testament*, the same affirmation is implicit.

Notes

1. Anthony Burgess, *MF* (New York: Alfred A. Knopf, 1971), p. 4. All quotations are from this edition, and subsequent references will be given in the text with page numbers and abbreviation.

2. Joseph Campbell, *The Hero With a Thousand Faces* (New York: Meridian Books, 1949) p. 90.

3. Campbell, *Hero*, p. 121.

4. Cf. Lord Raglan, *Jocasta's Crime: An Anthropological Study* (London: Methuen, 1933); Emile Durkheim, *Incest: The Nature and Origin of the Taboo*, trans. Edward Sagarin (New York: L. Stuart, 1963); Sir James Frazer, *The Magic Art and the Evolution of Kings*, part I, vol. 2 of *The Golden Bough* (London: Macmillan, 1922), chapter XI.

5. Claude Lévi-Strauss, *The Scope of Anthropology*, trans. Sherry O. Paul and Robert A. Paul (London: Jonathon Cape, 1967), p. 35.

6. Lévi-Strauss, p. 39.

7. Anthony Burgess, "If Oedipus has read his Lévi-Strauss," in *Urgent Copy: Literary Studies by Anthony Burgess* (New York: W. W. Norton, 1968), pp. 260–61.

8. Interview with Geoffrey Aggeler in Stratford, Ontario, July 30, 1969.

9. *Ibid.*

10. Burgess explained: "In my novel *MF* the hero does not have his race defined at the beginning because I consider the race to be irrelevant. At the very end of the book, he defines himself as black. This is supposed to come as a surprise to the reader and the reader is intended to read the book again and see this chief character as a black man instead of white. There should be no difference. Nothing is changed. Color is an irrelevance, and what we have is a kind of synthetic person who has absorbed all the elements of culture he needs, who is totally unconscious about race and thinks of himself primarily as a human being. In other words, the book is about taxonomies, about ways of classifying things. There are true classifications and false ones. The man-woman or M-F classification is true and valid. The black-white classification is a false one, probably the falsest of all" (Interview with Geoffrey Aggeler in New York City, September 16, 1972).

Joyce's Contemporary: A Study of Anthony Burgess' *Napoleon Symphony*

John Mowat*

"In the End is the Word" is the last chapter of Anthony Burgess' *Here Comes Everybody*, whose title in the U.S.A. is *ReJoyce*, and "Rejoice" is the last word of Burgess' recent novel, *Napoleon Symphony*. Joyce is the subject of two-and-one-half critical studies by Anthony Burgess, so when Burgess celebrates Napoleon's triumphant return from Elba by creating a lettuce as the occasion for a "gratuitous earwig," or when he celebrates Bonaparte's return from Egypt with a villanelle whose archaic poeticizing reads like a pastiche of the villanelle that Stephen Dedalus writes in *A Portrait of the Artist as a Young Man*, what might have seemed like the nudge of merely indulgent allusion is justified by the seriousness of Burgess' attempt to make his own fiction a practical demonstration of what he has learned from Joyce about the possibilities of language, myth, and comedy.[1]

*From *Contemporary Literature* 19 (1978):180–95. © 1978 by the University of Wisconsin Press. Reprinted with permission.

When the Second and Third Consuls consider breakfast, they think: "Some veal kidneys might be a good idea, simmered in butter . . ." (p. 74). Precisely how good an idea Burgess has already explained in his discussion of Bloom's breakfast in *Ulysses:* "If Mulligan celebrates a parodic mass, Bloom, more classically, consults viscera" (*Joysprick*, p. 72). We are now reminded that since the titles of post-Revolutionary France parody Roman institutions, it is fitting that the Consuls' breakfast should parody the rites of the Latin haruspex. The Second and Third Consuls are like Bloom in being—to use Burgess' words—"essential gut," types of useful, unpoetic drudgery. Like him they oppose their shrewdness and their fastidiously commonplace appetites ("an exquisite herb omelette") to the famished meagerness and the megalomaniac fantasy that, in *Napoleon Symphony*, alternately inspire the imperial menus. The Emperor's taste in food runs to pills and flavored water or to banquets where the dishes are named in honor of his victories—Chicken Marengo ("sautèed in oil with crayfish and fried eggs bedded on croutons"—p. 111) being compulsory—and the meal is rounded off with ersatz tea and coffee. The banquets match the tawdry and insubstantial pretensions of Bonapartist aristocracy: a passage as naked of punctuation as Molly Bloom's soliloquy indicates that, despite the glorious uniforms, the conversation at a Tuileries ball is not of "delicate amours" but of money, whores, venereal disease, and the battlefield (pp. 249–51). The kidneys simmered in butter now appear to be the appropriate food for the minor Consuls, who never aspire to any tragic or heroic inflation of their humanity, and their meal suitably concludes their discussion and rejection of the hero's nature. Napoleon is constituted as a "machine on top of an animal," they tell each other. The "brain isn't human" (p. 73).

Napoleon Symphony also recalls *A Royal Divorce*, "Earwicker's favourite play" as Burgess notes in *Here Comes Everybody* (p. 231); this old barnstormer brings us, significantly, back to *Finnegans Wake*. A connection as elusive as the "gratuitous earwig" explains the puzzling interchangeability of Wellington and Napoleon in Burgess' novel, a puzzle without a point unless it does send us to *Finnegans Wake*. Napoleon's diseased liver is his Promethean punishment, and yet it is Wellington who complains of waking with "a damned bad liver" after drinking Austrian wine (*NS*, p. 267). Returning from Elba, Napoleon exposes his breast to the muskets of the French army, defying and escaping death and reflecting—in Wellington's words—"A near thing, damned close run" (p. 272). The interchangeability develops from *A Royal Divorce* where, in the scene depicting the Battle of Waterloo, an actor—representing either Wellington or Napoleon—enters astride what is presumably the company's only horse. Just as divorce becomes for Joyce "a *leit-motiv* representing the eternal dichotomies," so this scene becomes a symbol of the continuous process of sundering and duplication which is balanced by reunion.[2] More important is the way the whole structure of *Napoleon Symphony* has been informed by Burgess' apparent attempt to complete the design of *A Royal Divorce*. No printed copy of the play exists, but James S. Atherton, who has seen a manuscript, makes it clear that the play ends with a monologue in which the dying Josephine implies her reunion in death with Napoleon. They will "begin again." Atherton feels that the speech has suggested both the intentions and the water-rhythms of ALP's final monologue in *Finnegans Wake*, in which the cycle of life and love promises to "Finn, again!" and then start again.

If Joyce's ALP is Josephine, Burgess has been inspired to make his Josephine an incarnation of ALP, the female principle of fluidity. One verbal clue connects *Napoleon Symphony* with ALP in *Finnegans Wake* by way of Burgess' own criticism. In *Joysprick* he notes that ALP is on one occasion represented as the Greek letter Delta: "An ALP may be represented as a triangle, and an equilateral triangle is a delta. *Delta* suggests richness through its very apt denotation of a triangular alluvial . . . tract at the mouth of a river, but the very look of the letter $-\triangle-$ is, in inversion, that of the pubic mane (*Joysprick*, pp. 19–20). In *Napoleon Symphony*, Bonaparte writes to Josephine, "Oh, how I . . . hunger . . . to munch your delta of silk in the valley of bliss" (p. 3). Before the wedding Josephine's lawyer thinks, "And did not the way to the Alps lie (this was coarse, he admitted) between her legs?" (p. v). Bonaparte himself acts out the coarse metaphor. "He got his kissing mixed up the other day," one of his officers reports. "Smacked his big fat Corse smackers on the map of the Po Valley" (*NS*, p. 5). Bonaparte speaks of Genoa as the genitals of Italy: "He'll bring his lot down from Alessandria, which is the sort of inner recesses of the genitals, Italy being a woman. Right?" (p. 7).

Napoleon's crossing the Alps and abandoning his army in the Nile delta (Josephine imagines herself as a reincarnate Nile-born Cleopatra) are not merely episodes in the historical narrative. At a symbolic level which depends, magically, upon visual or verbal pun, they unite the erotic and the military aspects of Napoleon's aggression. As Joyce's ALP begins in her ending — as the waters of Dublin bay — so Josephine begins in her ending as her "delta"; and while the women in Napoleon's life seem to get progressively younger (Josephine with two grown-up children giving way to Bellitote, who arrived in Egypt disguised as a drummer boy and in turn gives way to Mary Louise, little Betsy Bascombe, and finally to an ageless young visionary with a voice as cool as "some friendly water" — p. 340) so Joyce's ALP, about to be reborn in rain, says, "you're changing . . . and you're turning . . . for a daughterwife from the hills again" (*Finnegans Wake*, p. 627). The feminine element of water persists throughout Burgess' novel: "the sea was her element, the sea was a woman, *la mère la mer*" (pp. 146–47).

Like HCE, Napoleon as man is landscape. He is also a mythic hero who is regularly exposed to disgrace by his disorderly animal nature. Fallen or stained breeches link the French Emperor to HCE in one of his historical incarnations as the Russian general with his breeches down (*NS*, pp. v, 50, 55; *Finnegans Wake*, p. 344. Cf. *Here Comes Everybody*, pp. 233–34). A head cold and language trick Napoleon into reenacting HCE's indecent exposure in the park — revealing both his "id" and his "dick" — when he greets Desaix with the words, "You are cobe id the dick of tibe" (p. 91). Apart from a fall in common, both are master builders: Napoleon is the architect of an empire and HCE combines with the builder Finnegan and Ibsen's hero and is physically manifest as Howth Castle and Environs. Napoleon, equally earthy, partakes of earth in various ways. A fortune-teller pores over "the hills and plains and rivers" of his palms (p. 240). Superimposed on the Emperor's death agonies is a campaign in the Russian adventure: "the Santon Hill nestled in his left armpit, . . . and while his stomach was a hill with a peak called the Zurlan, his whole gloriously swollen belly was the Pratzen Heights" (p. 330). Napoleon's confidence on the battlefield and love of himself (earth) and his distrust of women (water) fashion his career to fulfill an old prophecy: "She said that the earth would be my friend and the water my enemy" (p. 23). Psychologically, this prophecy corresponds to his sterility and his incapacity to love, while in his public career it represents his naval defeats, the breaking of the bridges on the Berezina, the "*l'eau*" concealed — breeches down — in Waterloo ("his own *L' eau* . . . in orthographic bo-peep hiding in the Loo") and the imprisoning Atlantic surrounding St. Helena (p. 299).

The female principle which Napoleon distrusts and which is consistently symbolized by water may be interpreted as signifying fluidity, receptive to change, flexibility, even deviousness: "Water was treacherous and, in a certain mad sense, unnatural. It could not be shaped" (p. 128). Excluded from his official personality, it continually leaks out to humiliate or betray him. He is unable to control his own body's waters: Lefebvre observes, "He can't even make water, by the way, without getting into a foul temper, and then he pisses squirt squirt all over his breeches" (p. 207). Josephine, being especially ALP-like, considers that in his lovemaking Napoleon "floods me like a river. . . . Like urine" (p. 17). His generals call Napoleon "Wet Dream" (p. 4) The unacknowledged feminine powers of his own nature conjure up disturbing dream images of bisexuality to mock him and, distrusting his own veteran troops as "prickless creampuffs," he is betrayed into a disastrous homosexual passion for the Tsar Alexander (p. 50). Conflicts between water and earth make a diagram that is always present behind the more immediate antitheses in the book between artist and conqueror, time and space, the human and the mechanical, life and reason, comedy and tragedy.

Of these, the relationship between tragedy and comedy is the most complex. Napoleon, like many of Burgess' leading characters, sees himself as the hero of a tragic situation which his creator nevertheless insists on handling as comedy. Napoleon dramatizes himself as the light-bringer Prometheus, but "Prometheus was baldish and had grown a morbid paunch. He kept going ow ow ow. 'Liver,' he explained to the audience. 'Foie gras. Rotten. Decayed. . . . Too much gross feeding. The Viennese cuisine, you know. Goulash. Bauernschmaus. Guglhupf mit Schlag. Topfenpalatschinken. Butterteigpastetchen mit Geflügelragout. Tafelspitz.' . . . One of the lengths of chain was a string of sausages" (p. 266). Burgess puts his Napoleon in the wrong more subtly when he has him answer the riddle of Stephen Dedalus, *"Is a chair finely made tragic or comic?"* with the words, "And always, remember, told this to that fool Benjamin Constant, tragedy must never have chairs on the stage. Tragic characters never sit down. Sit down and they become comic. Think about it, gentlemen" (p. 255). Napoleon considers that action is the essence of tragedy while comedy is static, thus reversing the pronouncement of the artist, for Stephen Dedalus says: "I mean that the tragic emotion is static."[3]

Restless, violent Napoleon can be only a comic figure, but the terms of comedy here are Joycean as Burgess has defined them in *Here Comes Everybody*. He finds that the "comedy of Joyce is an aspect of the heroic: it shows man in relation to the whole cosmos, and the whole cosmos appears in his work symbolized in the whole of language" (*HCE*, p. 23). In this definition of epic-comedy the cosmos, or the human society which is its microcosm, expresses its resentment of the hero through "thunder, practical jokes, gross coincidences" against which the hero opposes all that he has—"merely free will and a capacity for love" (*HCE*, pp. 23–24). As Napoleon can neither love nor change, continuing needlessly to wage war because "It's métier, trade, skill, art," he is especially unequipped for the struggle (*NS*, p. 242). But a hero of Joycean comedy he remains nonetheless, and all the more comic in his resistance to the casting. The parallel with Bloom and with Burgess' Enderby is significant, for their creators' insistence on man's viscera—his appetite, liver, wind, "essential gut"—reduces all three heroes to their grossly, and yet sufficiently, human essence.[4] What we have in *Napoleon Symphony* is, nevertheless, not a novel about the Emperor as Joyce might have written it.

First, Burgess differs most conspicuously from Joyce in his lack of sympathy for his hero (something he inherits from Waugh), for the art of Joyce still celebrates the Dublin lives whose meanness Joyce sought to escape in life.[5] At best, Burgess dislikes Napoleon, and what stature he is allowed is conferred upon him by the epic-comedy structure. Second, Joyce preferred not to write of any action more momentous than the throwing of a biscuit tin or the smashing of a chandelier: he was not interested in writing about an emperor as hero. Burgess notes that Joyce's language is too sensitive an instrument to record violence "since the thrust of fist or phallus, being a physical cliché, seems to call for a verbal cliché in the recounting" (*HCE*, p. 271). Napoleon is not a subject that Joyce could write about directly. *Napoleon Symphony* need not, and does not, therefore, attempt explicit imitation of any piece of writing by Joyce. What it does instead is to reveal the working out of aesthetic theories, attitudes, or intentions modeled upon those which—in *Here Comes Everybody* and *Joysprick*—Burgess has honored in Joyce.

These theories, attitudes, and intentions may be said to coalesce into all that follows from what Burgess calls "an ambition for artistic self-effacement more fanatical even than Flaubert's" (*Joysprick*, p. 162). One strategy to avoid spontaneous self-expression by the artist is ". . . to give / Symphonic shape to verbal narrative, / Impose on life, though nerves scream and resist, / The abstract patterns of the symphonist" (*NS*, p. 362). *Napoleon Symphony*, like *Ulysses* and *Finnegans Wake*, has an apparently random sequence of action, feeling, and expression actually directed by the logic of intellectually ordered structures based on music and myth. Both structures presuppose patterns of thought and feeling which are prior to, which transcend, which are more universal than the imagination of a single individual; and these patterns can reveal themselves unexpectedly in proverbs, puns, clichés, demotic speech, popular songs, as well as the works of other artists. What follows from this is an "opacity of language" developed through a multiplicity of parodied styles or through several different registers or levels of utterance (*Joysprick*, p. 15). As a result the language will act as a welcome veil between what is described and the personality of the artist. The language itself can become the thing described, so that Burgess can say of a passage in *Finnegans Wake* that "like music, this passage is finally to be accepted as what it is, not what it is about" (*Joysprick*, p. 152).

For Burgess, Joyce's use of parody can lead to "total objectivity," for in conjuring the parodies the artist is present only as the channel or agent of a sort of collective human imagination (*Joysprick*, p. 95). Parodies and varying levels of expression can help to exclude the oppressive personality of the creator but can also, as Lorna Sage points out, put into place an over-obstreperous subject: "[Burgess] drowns his hero's Promethean spark in a defiantly democratic (here comes everybody) stew of literary languages, as if to prove that the collective tongue absorbs all things in the end, everyone's meaning, and so no one's at all. . . . Better the collective unwisdom of the verbal stew, [Burgess] would say, that any tyrannous signature."[6] Both the imagination of the individual author and the pretensions of the subject are contained, in *Napoleon Symphony*, by the vaster ordering of Beethoven's *Eroica*, and Burgess' comments on a passage in the Circe episode of *Ulysses* show the inspiration for this.[7] In discussing the Circe passage, in which fragments of many earlier episodes are quoted and freely combined, Burgess outlines what was to be his own procedure in *Napoleon Symphony*.

> A fundamental rule of sonata-form is this: never present a tune or a theme, however lowly or fragmentary, unless you intend to repeat it at a later stage—or, preferably, transform it, develop it, combine it with other thematical material. . . . [Any detail is] a little figure, that, worked into one corner of the carpet, must eventually appear in another

corner for the sake of formal balance. Music is a sort of tapestry realised in the medium of time. Time changes things; hence the balance achieved by identical repetition of the same motif is out of place; there has to be a transformation, however slight. (*HCE*, p. 166)

Burgess admits in "An Epistle to the Reader" that to realize these principles in prose consistently is impossible: "the thing cannot be done" (*NS*, p. 363). Yet the wooden leg of the acting registrar, mentioned in the novel's first paragraph and throughout the prologue, recurs at least six times in as many variations in the course of the book.[8] Again, Napoleon, dreaming of his own *rigor mortis*, sees himself "agitating his limbs in the manner of a monkey-up-a-stick he had once had as a boy in Ajaccio" (p. 127), and this small theme achieves resolution by the end of the novel when Betsy Bascombe presents Napoleon with the identical kind of toy, the monkey caricatured to look like Napoleon (p. 296). The association is supported in the scene mentioned earlier where the Second and Third Consuls reject Napoleon for lacking a redeeming humanity (a point Talleyrand is to make obliquely later). Cambacérès says that Napoleon "has a chest like an orang-utan, have you seen him breathe in? Of course you have. He dances up and down like a monkey when he's in rage" (p. 73). At Malmaison a myopic cardinal fails to recognize the middle figure flanked by Napoleon-Louis and Charles-Louis-Napoleon, and the reader half expects this to be the greatest of all Napoleons. It proves to be an orang-utan (again), and it grabs food from the buffet as Napoleon grabs Europe.

Cambacérès, without mentioning the Emperor, draws attention to a second physical characteristic the hero shares with the monkey; "Regard the massivity of that chest," he says, adding, "And the eyes are remarkable — fierce, yet patient, closely watchful yet as though surveying great distances" (p. 224). Elsewhere Napoleon's eyes shoot bullets of charm or "double-gimlet" his critics or work like patent lamps, going out gradually or flashing "full on again" (pp. 159, 197, 201). Talleyrand concludes (a transposition of the attendant theme), "The subhuman and the superhuman are alike in that neither is human" (p. 224). The analogy and the conclusion alike reflect ironically on Napoleon's titanic pretensions ("I am sun and wind"; "I am a living spirit and a very special one as well as a military library and a craftsman and a machine as modern as a semaphore telegraph or a hydrogen balloon" — pp. 121,13). The handling of themes repeated, developed, and transposed is consciously Joycean, and since Napoleon has elsewhere resembled Humphrey Chimpden Earwicker, the choice of analogy may owe something to HCE's middle name.

It is evident in *Joysprick* that Burgess uses the term "musicalisation" to describe several different ways in which language can impose its own patterns on the artless flow of narrative. The four-part structure of *Napoleon Symphony* explicitly mimics the *Eroica* and, as in the Sirens episode of *Ulysses*, there is some direct mimicry of musical form, particularly of Part II, the funeral march. Burgess puts words to Beethoven's most clearly sounded theme:

> There he lies
> Ensanguinated tyrant
> O bloody bloody tyrant
> See
> How the sin within
> Doth incarnadine
> His skin
> From the shin to the chin.
>   (p. 125)

A reference to "the trumpeting of violets" that follows hints that the instrument entrusted with its expression is the violin. The funeral march is reprised in what could be called a feminine key, and naturally this refers to the dominant feminine presence in the book—Josephine. She appears in the song as "the re-Incarnate Cleopatra," and in her dream she feels this is "Nonsense, naturally, but rather charmingly played on flutes and oboes." This is actually the case in Beethoven's score, although there may be a bow to Joyce as well. The flute is an especially female instrument: "Body of white woman, a flute alive. . . . Three holes all women" Bloom thinks in *Ulysses*.[9] The dominant vowel in Napoleon's song was the upright, phallic "i" which becomes a vaginal "o" in the female version: "Rowers row in rows. / Posied roses interpose / Twixt the rows and the rose" (p. 142).

This conceit, which the musical form facilitates, is itself derived from Burgess' reading of *Finnegans Wake*, to which he brings a knowledge of the Cabala: "The All-Father is I and his consort is O—'Ainsoph, this upright one, with that noughty besighed him zeroine.' Introduce the dart to the egg, or the phallus to the Elizabethan 'thing of nought,' and we have IO, symbol of creation" (*Joysprick*, p. 20).[10] Such a union occurs in *Napoleon Symphony* when the parallel motifs are printed side by side (p. 156). Elsewhere Burgess will repeat a particular word as if to beat a tattoo that will constitute a bass note sounding through the ensuing scene. "From bivouac to bivouac to bivouac to bivouac" (p. 246) is such a case, and it is repeated in a social key when Napoleon is a public figure rather than a soldier—"From group to group to group to group to group" (p. 259). Similarly, at a ball an account of Napoleon's achievements is set to the rhythm of a ballroom dance, concluding, "Glance at the France that he taught how to dance. And advance. Assuming a stance leaving little to chance. La France" (p. 252).

On the whole, though, there is less direct mimicry of music than there is duplication and transformation of detail in an attempt at musical structure. This is not just an effort to honor the principle that the composer must "never present . . . a theme . . . unless [he] intend[s] to repeat it at a later stage" (*HCE*, p. 166). It relates not only to the

"musicalisation" in *Ulysses* but to the dreamlike multiplication of suggestion in *Finnegans Wake* where the two Esthers whom Swift loved become
the duplicate of another pair, the two Iseults in the Tristram story, and
both pairs can be typified by the looking-glass girl and her mirror image.
Tristram of Lyonesse is conflated with Sir Armory Tristram, the builder of
Howth Castle, and, as Burgess says, "a dream-identification of the two
Tristrams is inevitable."[11] Images split and coalesce or are superimposed;
they enter into patterns of duplication, recurrence, and inversion because
there is a mirror at the center of the dream which is history. So, too, the
many dream sequences of *Napoleon Symphony*, which are there partly to
surprise us into realization that what is called history is merely another
kind of dreaming: without art, Napoleon is told, there is only "all that
cauchemar of flesh and blood spilled about" (p. 346).

The pattern of duplication which prolongs HCE's dream—or
Stephen's "nightmare" of history—into *Napoleon Symphony* gives us, for
instance, two Cleopatras: Josephine dreams of herself in this role, which
has already been assumed by Bellitote Foures or by another of Napoleon's
Egyptian mistresses (pp. 142, 55). Josephine and Queen Louise of Prussia
have nearly identical fainting fits, the close similarity being important
because femininity and duplication are aspects of Issy, the looking-glass
girl who, Burgess tells us, "must always have her mirror to turn herself
into the two temptresses in the park" (*HCE*, p. 245). Doubling the queens
emphasizes their duplicity as Napoleon's temptresses. Again, Napoleon's
obsession with Josephine transforms the map of Italy into one of female
anatomy, as we have seen, and this is reprised on Napoleon's deathbed
when his body becomes a battlefield (pp. 6, 7, 330). During the Egyptian
campaign a soldier remarks that the corpse-filled Nile is "like a great big
meaty stew," and a conjunction of river, corpses, and food occurs on the
retreat from Moscow when the Berezina bridges become clogged with
corpses through which a path has to be cut: "What we had to do was to
hack" as if "you had a big plate of steaks and cutlets and fried eggs served
up. . . ." (pp. 35, 182). The effeminate Fighting 69th ("prickless creampuffs"—p. 50) are surely paralleled by the untrained conscripts called
"Marie-Louises" (p. 225).

Finally, in Josephine's dream of herself as Cleopatra the beauty of one
of her attendants—Thérèse Tallien—is marred by the "tiniest downy
growth on her . . . upper lip which, when stained with ferrous wine,
could glitter like a real *mustache*" (p. 144). This detail is one of the earliest
intimations of a pervasive theme of sex-reversal centering on Germaine de
Staël and her "incredibly masculine" "*longitudo clitoralis*" (pp. 96, 246,
255). In Napoleon's funeral dream she accuses him of a lack of virility (p.
246). Some reversal touches even one of the pair of feminine Maries—not
Louise but Walewska—who appears in the dying Napoleon's sex fantasy
riding in a horse-sleigh, "she with the reins and the whip, managing as
well as any man" while the conquering Emperor sits next to her as a

passenger (p. 316). Many W's (Wellington, Waterloo, Walewska) achieve duplication in the initials of a parodied William Wordsworth (pp. 299, 307–309). The doubling of artists, necessary to the pattern's intention, is achieved more subtly, but we are made to feel the presence of two Jameses: Henry James is honored with a long pastiche and James Joyce has the last word (pp. 337 ff, 360).

Napoleon's deflation, obvious enough in the novel's selection of embarrassing detail, is accomplished on another level through the symphonic structure to which his story is subservient. This arch manipulator who thinks "you could change history overnight, myth took longer" is himself manipulated by the true hero of the book (p. 160). Of Napoleon, Burgess writes in the "Epistle": "Standing behind him, though, or to one side, / Another, bigger, hero is implied, / Not comic and not tragic but divine" (p. 362). At this moment Burgess means Beethoven, but behind even this figure is a collective creative consciousness suggested by the parodies and the borrowed techniques, a presence that includes figures as various as Byron, Wordsworth, Malory, Dickens, Tennyson, James, Joyce, and W. S. Gilbert. The visionary girl Napoleon meets on St. Helena tells him the public imagination can be nourished with heroic images derived from art: "the hero doesn't have to have existed" (p. 345). The *Eroica* is a finer achievement than the man not judged worthy of its dedication. The Emperor is the deluded prisoner of the time machine which he thinks he can control, but time can be controlled and manipulated only by the artist.

The artist can stretch the novel's time span by making the reader think of poison gas in the First World War when Napoleon urges "new methods, gentlemen, for new wars," or Nazism when the prisoner Stapps is enthusiastic about "The *Volk*," or the Common Market when Napoleon advocates what he calls the Continental System (pp. 48, 134, 227). The artist can duplicate time by synchronizing it as Burgess does with dreams in Part II or as Joyce does in the Wandering Rocks section of *Ulysses*.[12] The artist can accelerate or retard time or, *par excellence*, set it to music and *beat time*. Napoleon, who conquers space but is defeated by time, contrasts with the artist who — never participating in the narrative's action — nevertheless conducts its musical rhythms. It is the contrast between Shaun and Shem, between the Ondt and the Gracehoper. Of them Burgess has said, "Shaun is revealed as the space-man, lord of solid objects. . . . Shem's task is to capture the rhythm of time, draw inspiration from the creative mother-river" (*HCE*, p. 215); and "What is the Ondt doing but filling up space with possessions? He cannot, like the artist, conquer time, the only thing worth doing" (*HCE*, p. 241). As Joyce says, "Your genus is worldwide, your spacest sublime!/but, Holy Saltmartin, why can't you beat time?")[13]

The artist is in the position of having more information than the hero, of being able to tell a subliminal story of which the fictional hero cannot be aware but which will comment on him (the irony is improved by the fact that Napoleon is historical). More than that: as master of the only medium in which the finally unreal hero can subsist, Burgess can employ his talent for pastiche not merely to display his own virtuosity but to make poetic form a criticism of content. Style is a measure of value. A representative of the Age of Reason ("I want you to grow into the light" — p. 132), Napoleon is celebrated in heroic couplets whose diction belongs firmly to the eighteenth century, with capitalized and personified abstractions like "Extortion" and "Justice" alongside "chimick" and "finny monster" (pp. 41–42). The suggestion — put more obviously in Napoleon's interview with Stapps II — is that at bottom Napoleon is a reactionary conservative (p. 235 ff). Again he regresses into the eighteenth century when he pontificates in broken-winded Alexandrines — printed as prose — which he attributes to Voltaire (p. 254). A rhythmless, prosy, doggerel mimicry of classicism is Burgess' formula for the imagination of the Empire.

Burgess uses a Joycean device — specialized language — to achieve, simultaneously, several different ends: to relate narrative to archetypal sources (*Finnegans Wake*) and to imply both a character's development and a range of possible appropriate comment on it. In this way Burgess is both extending the novel's perspective and abbreviating the explanations, analysis, stage directions, and authorial comment which, using traditional language, such an extension of the subject matter requires. Two specialized languages are made available to Josephine and both, at times and significantly, are adopted by Napoleon. That Josephine can be herself and a type of Cleopatra, a type of ALP, and a type of Issy the looking-glass girl has a precedent in *Finnegans Wake*. Incarnated as Cleopatra, Josephine uses the speech Burgess has referred to as "the fascinatingly horrible little language" of Issy (*HCE*, p. 245). The identifying vocabulary is unmistakable: "charming," "sweetly," "really beautiful," "thrilling," "perfect," "tiniest tiniest tiniest" (*NS*, pp. 142–144). Related language in *Finnegans Wake* is signaled by "my precious," "jenny-teeny," "pettest," "too perfectly priceless," "exquisite" and so, gushingly, on.[14] Napoleon is self-consciously masculine — threatening in a rage to lead the army into Paris and "make a man's town out of it" — so when his meeting with Alexander at Tilsit is described in what is apparently Napoleon's dream, but translated into the gushing "little language" of Issy-Josephine ("an exquisite little anteroom," "really delightfully appointed saloon," "exquisite" recurring *ad nauseum*), it is evident that Napoleon has fallen under the spell of Alexander's homosexual fascination (*NS*, pp. 39, 156 ff). In keeping with the shadow of Issy, the looking-glass girl ("I've two of everything up to boyproof knicks" — *Finnegans Wake*, p. 527), everything is duplicated at Tilsit: two weathercocks, two flags, two anterooms, respective national emblems and national luxuries (*NS*, pp. 156-57).

In the presence of Alexander "N was surprised but not altogether displeased to find a fire starting up in his groin: it always helped if one could feel *physically* drawn" (p. 158). Italics sprinkle Josephine's dream and hence indicate a feminine attitude. As Burgess says in *Joysprick*, italic in *Finnegans Wake* is used to represent the "obliquity" and deviousness of the artist (Shem) and roman capitals the "loud uprightness" of the self-righteous man of action (Shaun).[15] It is a formula Burgess adapts for his own ends in the scene where an outraged Napoleon speaks in capitals, Josephine in lower-case roman, and Eugène and Hortense in italics (p. 60). The effect is musical, suggesting themes and counterpoint resolved in a common chord: "*oh you are breaking our* AND LOVE they wish to break all our AND A FAMILY OF LOVING *hearts* hearts HEARTS."

The typeface, functioning to provide a condensed set of stage directions and implied analyses of the characters' motives, styles, and sincerity, is a triumph of irony and concision. Another kind of condensed allusion renders the Emperor's state of mind when he is being carried to St. Helena. Josephine, representing the usually unacknowledged feminine element of Napoleon's personality, is with him still, present in his (surely unconscious) adoption of her "Creole way of speaking" typified by her "languorous" vowels (pp. 148, ii). The vowel most appropriate to her, we know, is o, and Burgess, who has included in the novel five poems dominated by each vowel in turn, has at least two reasons for devoting an "o" poem to Josephine (p. 142). She imparts an aphrodisiac "*kissing*" prolongation to "*Divoooorce*" (p. 148). So she can be detected concealed in Napoleon's suicidal telegraphese on his way to St. Helena in the words "*thermidooooooor*," "*directooooooory*," and "*EMPEROOOOOOOOOR*" in a passage where many vowels are suppressed ("jsphn," "tlst") in view of Napoleon's noted impatience: he "eats too quickly" and as a lover is "always so quick about everything" (pp. 273–74, 78, 10).

Finally, an understanding of Napoleon's stage army completes a justification for all the pastiche, parody, musical form, and opacity of language. It is there to remind the reader, *passim*, that we are not sharing in a re-creation of actual historical experience, which would include seeing thousands suffer horribly and unnecessarily. There is, in any case, no possible breaking through the veil of language; experience cannot be created truthfully on the page—only in the dogma of the proto-Nazi Stapps I is "the truth . . . above language" (p. 137). We are watching a version of Earwicker's favorite play and the troops are a stage army who, as soon as they are killed, put on different uniforms and fight again. There are always twenty-one of them and their fictive, histrionic status is signaled to us by names familiar in the French cinema — Carné, Jean-Louis Barrault, Pierre Brasseur — and these same figures are capable of reappearing as Paris citizens (pp. 9, 11, 26, 76, 118). A critic of Napoleon actually mentions stage armies: "Enter left half a million, cross stage, then exeunt. Enter from right ten thousand, cross stage, exeunt. That is, I suppose, funny" (p. 203). Napoleon's infant son is as prodigal with his lead soldiers as his father is with flesh and blood. Throughout the novel we are aware that both hero and writer are directing a stage army but that, to identical materials, hero and artist impute contrasting modes of existence. To Napoleon, as to his child, troops are like toys and limitlessly expendable because endlessly replaceable; to the artist this random list of names becomes an irreducible pattern, recurring with the haunting persistence of dream images or of a theme in music.

Such devices, and the use of anagram, acrostic, and wordplay (to which we have not referred), challenge the reader to decode meanings which can operate on a quite superficial level (for instance, Napoleon's vanity) or on a deeper level which is still relevant to the psychology of the novel's hero (his noughty zeroine, as a principle of obliquity, never forsakes him). They can suggest, too, the artist's ironic contemplation of the illusory play of action which is all the participants know of history. Burgess continues to write a traditional novel whose interest remains, after all, individual moral responsibility within a universe we cannot fully decipher. Like Joyce he cherishes the commonplace. His imagination is democratic and his chosen pseudonym — Burgess — means *bourgeois*: or "boor Joyce" in one of his own puns.[16] In *Napoleon Symphony* he has availed himself of Joycean devices which have often seemed to exclude all but professional readers, and he has used them to communicate the novel's common concerns with heightened wit, density, concision, and pleasure. The innovative deployment of Joycean techniques that still leaves Burgess' originality unquestioned makes the present novel the crown of an achievement that already includes the felicities of *The Malayan Trilogy* (1956, 1958, 1959) when read *in toto*, the imaginative re-creation of *Nothing Like the Sun* (1964) and the brilliance of *The Wanting Seed* (1962).

All this should make Burgess worthy of more than the modicum of critical attention he has so far received.[17] That his present acclaim is largely ephemeral is indicated by recent interviews with Burgess which pay exaggerated attention to his association with Stanley Kubrick's notorious film of *A Clockwork Orange*.[18] We have in Burgess an artist who may be of far more significance in that he is frequently capable of finding paradigms for both metaphysical insight and those historical accidents that have produced the times in which we live, all rendered in a language ceaselessly alive.

Notes

1. Burgess discusses Joyce in *Here Comes Everybody* (London: Faber and Faber, 1965), published in the U.S.A. as *ReJoyce* (New York: W.W. Norton, 1965); *A Shorter Finnegans Wake* (London: Faber and Faber, 1966); *Joysprick* (London: Andrė Deutsch, 1973). For Stephen Dedalus' villanelle see Harry Levin, ed. *The Essential James Joyce* (London: Penguin, 1963), pp. 226, 228. Page references to *Napoleon Symphony* refer to the Alfred A. Knopf (New York) edition, 1974.

2. James S. Atherton, *The Books at the Wake* (London: Faber and Faber, 1959), p. 162.

3. *The Essential James Joyce*, pp. 220, 213, Cf. *Here Comes Everybody*, p. 63.

4. *Inside Mr. Enderby* (London: Penguin, 1966); *Enderby Outside* (London: Penguin, 1968); *The Clockwork Testament or: Enderby's End* (London: Hart-Davis, MacGibbon, 1974).

5. Bernard Bergonzi, *The Situation of the Novel* (London: Pelican, 1973), pp. 210–11.

6. Lorna Sage, "Decomposing," *Observer Review*, 29 Sept. 1974, p. 31.

7. James Joyce, *Ulysses* (London: Penguin, 1971), pp. 254–90.

8. For example, pp. 42, 50, 119, 188, 226, 257.

9. *Ulysses*, p. 284.

10. James Joyce, *Finnegans Wake* (London: Faber and Faber, 1964), p. 261; or Anthony Burgess, ed., *A Shorter Finnegans Wake* (London: Faber and Faber, 1966), p. 136.

11. *A Shorter Finnegans Wake*, pp. 12–13.

12. *Ulysses*, pp. 218–54.

13. *Finnegans Wake*, p. 419. There is even a parallel contrast between Shem-James and Shaun-Jaun. The "Juan Dyspeptist" of *Finnegans Wake* (p. 453) whose name, Burgess points out, "has liverish overtones of a great lover" is an implied presence in *Napoleon Symphony* when Burgess celebrates his liverish hero in a pastiche of Byron's *Don Juan* (pp. 90–91). Cf. *Here Comes Everybody*, p. 243.

14. *Finnegans Wake*, pp. 458–61.

15. Anthony Burgess, *Joysprick* (London: André, 1973), p. 18.

16. Anthony Burgess, *Inside Mr. Enderby* (London: Penguin, 1966), pp. 105, 106, 110.

17. Carol M. Dix, *Anthony Burgess*, published for the British Council by Longman Group, 1971; Julian Mitchell, "Anthony Burgess," *London Magazine*, 3, No. 11 (Feb. 1964), 48–54.

18. *Paris Review*, 14, No. 56 (Spring 1973), 119–63; *Playboy*, 21, No. 9 (Sept. 1974), 69–86.

The Musicalization of Fiction: The "Virtuosity" of Burgess' *Napoleon Symphony*

David McNeil*

Anthony Burgess' *Napoleon Symphony* is the most daring novel to date in that category of fiction which is characterized by the use of a musical paradigm as a basis for narrative form. Earlier examples include the "Sirens" episode in *Ulysses* and *Point Counter Point*. Whereas Joyce and Huxley were content to imitate a general "fugue" structure, however, Burgess is concerned with fictionalizing a specific musical masterpiece: Beethoven's Third Symphony in E Flat Major, more commonly known as *Eroica*, and originally dedicated to Napoleon. Composed in and around Beethoven's personal crisis in 1803 — a crisis caused by the realization that

*From *Mosaic* 16 (1983):101–15. © 1983 by *Mosaic: A Journal for the Interdisciplinary Study of Literature*. Reprinted with permission.

he was going deaf — the *Eroica* is generally considered to be the first major expression of romanticism in the symphonic mode, constituting a break from the classical forms which had been fully explored by Mozart and Haydn. *Napoleon Symphony* is equally revolutionary, approximating the *Eroica* not merely in its use of a four-part structure to reflect the four movements of Beethoven's work but also in its use of such unconventional techniques as verse sections, fluidity of point of view and rhythmic language.

As the author of *MF* (1971), an experimental novel based on the structuralist principles of Claude Lévi-Strauss, Burgess had previously demonstrated his capabilities as an experimental novelist. But specifically what qualified him for the task of musicalizing fiction is his own expertise in the field of music. In addition to three full-length symphonies, he has composed a number of concertos and sonatas for various instruments — a situation which has led him to regret that no one ever refers to him as a composer who writes novels but rather as a novelist who happens to compose music.[1] For the same reason, he must also regret that, despite the substantial amount of criticism concerned with his work,[2] no attempt has been made to determine how successful *Napoleon Symphony* is as a piece of musicalized fiction.

My objective in the following essay is to provide such an assessment. After first examining the symbolic appropriateness of the general scheme itself, I will then go on to examine in detail each part of the novel in conjunction with the corresponding movement of the *Eroica*. But lest this sound as if I am proposing the kind of analysis which an early reviewer debunked in advance — "even if someone comes up with a list of every correspondence between Burgess and Beethoven, it will prove only that the critic has worked hard and that Burgess is ingenious"[3] — let me immediately emphasize that I see Burgess' musical method as possessing two dimensions: a narrative imitation of the score and a thematic interpretation of the essential feeling of Beethoven's symphony. Nor are the two dimensions always distinguishable, since Burgess frequently resorts to symbolism and allusion to accomplish the more technical part of his project. This overlapping of the two dimensions, however, is also a chief characteristic of music itself in the sense that it is as difficult to distinguish between score and melody as it is to separate the "mathematical" and the imaginative components of a composer's mind.

• • •

The best introduction to the virtuosity of *Napoleon Symphony* is contained at the end of the novel and called "An Epistle to the Reader." Here Burgess comments on the tradition of musicalized fiction and gives the reader an autobiographical sketch of how he came to write his own contribution to the genre. He whimsically passes off *Point Counter Point* and the *Four Quartets* as reluctant to go "the whole hog" with musicalization and calls Joyce's "Sirens" episode "The most ambitious effort the world knows / Within this manic field. . . . Designed to show that the thing cannot be done."[4] As a composer and musician, Burgess is well aware that music is the perfect fusion of form and content, something that literature can never be. We hear and feel music directly, while with literature we must get through the language first. Furthermore, whereas music is often polyphonic (two or more parts may be played simultaneously), prose cannot escape the monody of narrative. Still, in his humorous tone, Burgess describes how he has always felt the urge to try what ultimately remains an "impossibility":

> I was brought up on music and compose
> Bad music still, but ever since I chose
> The novelist's métier one mad idea
> Has haunted me, and I fulfill it here
> Or try to—it is this: somehow to give
> Symphonic shape to verbal narrative.
>
> (p. 348)

Although the literary virtuoso can never make verbal narrative convey the esthetic experience of music, he can make it approach a symphonic structure and delight readers through the ingenuity of the resemblance. The vital principle of Burgess' virtuoso talent is "comedy" (p. 348), not just slapstick (although *Napoleon Symphony* is very funny) but the reconciliatory kind. The historical figure of Napoleon is harmonized with the artistic ideal of Beethoven's symphony. At least this is the impression that Burgess tries to create in his novel. To accomplish it, he must make frequent mood modulations; he must alter the tempo, develop, recapitulate and either narratively or thematically make the fiction fit the symphonic paradigm to which he is wholeheartedly committed. Therefore, according to the Epistle, Napoleon "robs and rapes and lies and kills in fun / And does no lasting harm to anyone" (p. 348) because, as Burgess' hero, he really represents the spirit of Beethoven's symphony.

The Epistle next relates the well-known story of how Beethoven originally composed his Third Symphony in E Flat major for Napoleon but ripped the dedication page off the score when Napoleon declared himself Emperor, giving it the new title, *"Sinfonia eroica per festeggiare il souvenire di un grand' Uomo"* (Heroic Symphony to celebrate the memory of a great man). Within the context of the *Eroica*, this act symbolizes the passing of Napoleon, the man, into Napoleon, the myth. Fittingly, Beethoven uses his old Prometheus theme in the *Finale*, just as prophetically, the myth of Prometheus—chained to a rock while eagles eat out his liver—fits the popular theory that Napoleon was slowly poisoned while on St. Helena. In his novel, Burgess makes the transition from man to myth figuratively. The disastrous Russian campaign is Burgess' fictional correlative for Beethoven's *Marcia Funebre*.

Beethoven's own recovery from the despair of going deaf has probably more to do with the heroic theme of the symphony than does Napoleon. What makes the *Eroica* such an enduring part of the symphonic repertoire is the remarkable grandeur with which it portrays this theme. In each of the four Movements, and in the symphony as a whole, a familiar pattern emerges: the will asserts itself, then seems to succumb to a greater force, but finally returns in a new and triumphant shape. The pattern corresponds to the basic sonata (or First Movement) form in music, the Christian myth of the fall and redemption, and the form of comedy.[5] It can also be located in a standard romantic phenomenon: vision-disillusion-recovery. Hence, there is an organic connection linking Napoleon to Beethoven and both to Burgess. Napoleon is the romantic icon. Nobody dreamed that some obscure Corsican lieutenant could rise to become ruler of Europe. But for millions (including Beethoven) Napoleon was the great-liberator-turned-terrible-tyrant. Nevertheless, the ideals of the French Revolution were spread throughout Europe as a consequence of his actions. Beethoven is the romantic composer who achieves some renown in Vienna only to discover that he is going deaf. How tragicomic! The sounds of the world are lost to his ears, but in his composer's mind he is able to isolate and express the most profound feelings of humanity, which he does in his subsequent works. Both Napoleon and Beethoven are extremely passionate men and represent the age of rebellion. Napoleon overthrows the aristocrats of Europe, Beethoven the classicism of Mozart. Finally there comes the composer-novelist, Burgess, who has this "mad idea" about musicalized fiction. Comedy replaces the romantic resurrection and Burgess does give "Symphonic shape to verbal narrative." Music's perfect fusion of form and content is impossible, but choosing the *Eroica* to serve as a model for Napoleon's life is a clever way of simulating such a union.

Turning to *Napoleon Symphony* itself, one notices that a curious little section precedes Part I. It is obviously meant to represent the orchestra tuning up. Several of the characters, who will figure prominently in the subsequent action, are assembled in a room waiting for Napoleon to arrive for his wedding: Tallien, Calmelet, Barras and, of course, Josephine. Witty conversation, involving many numerical images and Republican references, occupies their time. Then each character begins to improvise, in verse, on the subject of "the acting registrar's wooden leg" (p. 12). *"Lui"* strides in, tells the registrar to get his wooden leg away from the fire (the Promethean image), gives Josephine two love-pinches ("one on each lobe") and cries "Begin!" (p. 12). Robert Morris associates the love-pinches with the two opening chords of the *Allegro*,[6] but I am more inclined to think that they simply represent the director tapping the podium. They come at the end of the introductory section and not at the beginning of Part I proper, where one finds the two verbs "throbs" and "frets" (p. 15) suggestive of the chords. The "Begin!" section is hardly original (being copied from the "Sirens" episode in *Ulysses*), but its symbolism is interesting. Napoleon is the director, the person who will control and orchestrate all of the parts of Europe. An association might be made between Josephine and the oboe, the instrument which the first violinist — here it would seem to be Calmelet — signals to harmonize the orchestra around the standard A-note (pitch 440) before the director enters. This Josephine-oboe association is strengthened in Part II which follows the *Marcia Funebre*. Thematically, Burgess gives us the first hint that the male entity must stabilize itself around the female.

• • •

Part I of *Napoleon Symphony* is formally divided up into the four conventional segments of the First Movement form (Exposition-Development-Recapitulation-Coda). To what extent Burgess tries to match up his own narrative with the numerous episodes in each of these segments remains open to question. He has said that a strict correspondence exists between the bars of the symphonic score and the pages of the novel,[7] but it is difficult to determine whether or not this strictness is consistently maintained. A comparison of the first four scenes in Part I with the first fifty-five bars of Beethoven's *Allegro* will give you some idea of how Burgess adapts the score. The novel opens with a monologue spoken by Napoleon which corresponds to the opening expression of the first subject played by the cello and basses. This melody is the heroic spirit which appears in various shapes throughout the symphony, and one is immediately struck with how distant literature seems when compared to music which speaks directly to the heart. As the rest of the strings enter in the score and are followed by the winds, so Napoleon's subordinates enter the narrative. The statement of the first subject is interpreted by Burgess as Napoleon's passion for Josephine, embodied initially in his thoughts, then in the conversation of his subordinates. The strongly accented chords (sf), which fall between bars 25 and 30, may well be represented by the list of officers that appears just before Napoleon's first military victory (p. 19). Romain Rolland describes the radical change to a charming series of three-note phrases on the woodwinds as "the regrets of the tender and weary heart."[8] Burgess transposes this change by abruptly shifting his narrative from the military campaign to Josephine in bed with her lover Charles.

So far so good, but from here on the correspondence becomes fuzzy. Much of the difficulty stems from the fact that Beethoven's *Allegro* deviates so much from the so-called "rules" of the classical First Movement form. George Grove, for example, points out that the second subject (bars 83 to 89), as "beautiful" as it is, is never used again until the Recapitulation.[9] This melody might have been the basis for Burgess' narration of the incident at Lake Geneva when a bomb lands near Josephine's carriage. The incident is framed by two passages which depict Josephine in a semiconscious drowsiness, and this sleep or dream motif is not used again before Burgess' own Recapitulation. To pursue a match-up analysis, however, is futile — and also unnecessary since we have already touched on the greater "comic" and thematic significance of Burgess' exercise.

An excellent critical statement of the essence of Beethoven's *Allegro* was made by Richard Wagner: "The *First Movement* embraces, as in a glowing furnace, all the emotions of a richly-gifted nature in the heyday of unresting youth. Weal and woe, lief and lack, sweetness and sadness, living and longing, riot and revel, daring defiance, and an ungovernable sense of Self. . . . Yet all these feelings spring from one main faculty — and that is *Force*."[10] This emotional storm is exactly what Burgess tries to reflect in his hero. As far as themes are concerned, however, Burgess can probably be called more conventional than Beethoven in following the First Movement form because he gives the reader two distinct subjects in Part I (War and Love). The most obvious mood modulations in Burgess' narrative occur when the scene shifts from the battlefield to the bedroom. Napoleon's passion vacillates rapidly and frequently between the extremes of hate and love. While Napoleon is in Italy, Josephine remains in Paris with her lover. This contrapuntal structure may symbolize the association of love and femininity with the woodwinds and of war and masculinity with the strings. But in a paradoxical and symphonic world opposites always threaten to merge, as Napoleon himself says, "It is in some way . . . an emblem of love, this engaging of armies. . . . the quality of the beating of the heart, which is the same for both love and war" (p. 20). Transitional or bridge passages from the battlefield to the bedroom are represented by having Napoleon address his emotions to Josephine in his mind at the end of the first scene and Josephine read the same in a letter at the beginning of the next (pp. 20, 33). One of the revolutionary aspects of the *Eroica*, according to Grove, is the "continuous and organic mode of connecting the second subject with the first" (p. 50). Hence, as Burgess' battle scenes are loaded with references to love, so the love scenes are sprinkled with battle images (see pp. 29, 33). The suggestion is clearly that the two passions of love and hate stem from the same force.

Many musicologists have commented on the effect of the odd C Sharp in the main theme of the Exposition. It is a stroke of genius on Beethoven's part, because it withholds the heroic spirit from its complete expression and thereby retains a sense of yearning. In the words of Rolland, "this burden itself is its destiny, is a part of its essence; it accepts it with a sigh, and abandons itself to the stream" (p. 55). Therefore, within the first few bars of the *Allegro* we find the embryonic pattern that grows throughout the entire symphony: vision-disillusion-recovery. Burgess transposes this C Sharp "burden" into the first section of his own Part I. Napoleon asserts his strength and then that strength is undercut by doubt or fear. When he takes the bridge at Adda by "impossible gambling," Napoleon's delirious, orgasm-like feeling of victory is at once swept away by the panic produced by the discovery of the broken glass in his miniature of Josephine: "It means she is very sick or very unfaithful. Oh God God God" (pp. 23–24). Burgess' section continues just like Beethoven's Exposition; the heroic spirit gains strength and momentum, yet at times it ominously hesitates.

As mentioned, the officer-lists are modeled on the successions of strongly accented chords. At bar 102, the strings break into a quick run and Burgess keeps up the pace in his own narrative by using heroic couplets. This particular verse passage describes how Napoleon chases Wurmser with extra zeal after the latter has frightened Josephine: "Mark how the Alexander of our age / Bids soldier's skill fulfill a lover's rage" (p. 31). Again the two passions of love and hate, as well as two conquering heroes (Alexander and Napoleon), are brought together. The couplets relate the basic events briskly. Their rhyme and rhythm create a marching-like, musical effect. Later, Burgess speeds up the narration of the battle in the Osteria gorge with another verse section. This one contains footnotes which do not follow consecutively and do not seem to have any literal connection to the verse — nor are they meant to, as Burgess makes clear in an interview: "a battle is set up in the form of a poem of notes, so the terrain and the position of the figures referring to footnotes is not numerical; it varies according to position so that you can tell by reading the poem, by moving around, exactly where they are and when they're conducting the battle" (Bunting, p. 506). This is an ingeniously compli-cated way of compressing the stages of a battle, but the reader might have a problem figuring out the system of references for himself. Of course, Burgess probably intended the narrative confusion to reflect the confusion of battle. In the final scene of the first section, the word "Egypt" curiously appears and represents Beethoven's bridge passage from the Exposition to the Development; the Development is Burgess' model for the Egyptian campaign.

Early critics of the *Eroica* tried hard to link it with Napoleon's life, and it was suggested "that Napoleon's army had arrived in Egypt by the time the Development had been reached since one of its episodes was a theme of 'decidedly Oriental colouring'."[11] More recent critics tend to ridicule this approach and argue that the *Eroica* owes more to Beethoven's crisis about going deaf than to Napoleon's career. Nevertheless, Burgess exploits the Egyptian theory in spite of its dubious nature and shows that his novel is based not only on the heroic myth behind the *Eroica* but also on the critical myth which grew up around the symphony. In other words, Burgess' Napoleon is a fictional incarnation of the heroic spirit as it has been popularized by the critics as well as an evocation of the spirit permanently embodied in the music itself. After all, critics are largely responsible for making and breaking heroes.

According to the First Movement form, the Development is supposed to explore the material presented in the Exposition. The heroic spirit is still present, but it is softened and distant. Burgess simulates this effect in the second section of Part I by using a rank-and-file soldier as narrator. Suddenly, the reader sees the dark side of Napoleon's will as it meets with frustration. Unlike the 1796 Italian campaign, Egypt provides no surging victories. Its culture and climate are foreign; for a moment the heroic spirit seems as lost as it does in Beethoven's Development.

Of course Burgess is hard pressed to recreate Beethoven's magnitude and range. Thematically, he does expand the two basic subjects of his opening section, war and love. Because this two-fold expansion accords with the classical expectations for the Development where the *Eroica* does not, Burgess' mode of musicalization may again be said to follow a more conventional form than Beethoven's music. The second section of Part I emphasizes the horror of war through the use of grotesque descriptions and echoes of the holocaust. After a battle, the Nile is said to be full of Mameluke corpses: "Like a great big meaty stew" (p. 44). Burdened with thousands of prisoners, Napoleon orders a mass execution and imagines a day when an army might rid itself of such undesirables "by a simple pumping device, of some venomous inhalant" (p. 56). Burgess' intent is obviously to remind the reader of the Nazis' Final Solution. Only after Auschwitz could the idea of a "pumping device" reverberate with horrific implications. Chronology is irrelevant in the mythologizing process. Heroism has overreached itself, and the horrors of war are always the same. Innocent victims always rank high among the casualties; mass slaughter is always justified by political ends.

The love theme is also treated to a few shock waves. Napoleon must finally be told of Josephine's unfaithfulness because everything has come out in the British press. The news makes Napoleon explode into a fit of rage and obscenity. This is the dark underside of the human will when disillusion smacks it in the face. Later on, after a tremendously emotional scene — narratively presented as a three-part fugue (pp. 66–67) — the reader sees the reconciliatory power of love, and the couple is reunited. This three-part (Napoleon, Josephine, Eugène) fugue is based on Beethoven's famous fugal episode that begins at bar 240 and breaks down into a storm of passion. Eighteenth-century decorum gives way to romantic chaos.

The drudgery of a desert march is effectively reproduced in a verse section packed with repetition and hypnotic rhythms. Another verse section strikes a chord of alarm as Napoleon returns to France and plots to overthrow the Directory: "O shake yourself awake and take your lance, / Triad of virtues shamelessly asleep, / For Bonaparte has kissed the soil of France" (p. 65). It is a portentous signal that looks ahead to the death knell of Part II (based on the *Marcia Funebre*). Despite the warning, Napoleon proves to be too quick. But so are Beethoven's horns at the end of the Development. They begin the main theme in the tonic, while the violins are still in the dominant key. Needless to say, the boldness and daring which this unusual move conveys is completely appropriate to the mood of the symphony.

In the Recapitulation section we see Napoleon strut across the familiar ground of Europe for the second time. Now, however, he carries with him the greater experience of victory and defeat. Burgess follows the form, both in terms of theme and narrative, by using scenes which are close imitations of those he used to approximate Beethoven's Exposition. There are similar officer-lists, strategy sessions and addresses to the troops. Some slight, but important, differences do occur. Napoleon speaks more eloquently; he is more confident and self-assured. This shift away from the undermining self-doubt of the first section reflects the fact that in the Recapitulation Beethoven allows the main theme to harmonize more naturally after the C Sharp. As the battle at the Adda bridge was central to the campaign outlined in the Exposition, so the battle at Marengo is the climax of the campaign in the Recapitulation. There is also another moment of orgasm-like victory (pp. 99–100), but this time Napoleon is in complete and unquestioned control. Moreover, the bedroom scenes now show Napoleon carrying on the extra-maritial affairs. Josephine, on the other hand, becomes desperate about bearing an heir. As a conqueror and lover, Napoleon has fully realized his physical potential. All the other characters refer to him simply as *"Lui"* and this pronoun designation is suggestive of his archetypal status as hero. By the end of the Recapitulation, *Lui* has risen to a glorious height — First Consul for life.

But there is still the Coda to come and Burgess' is almost as impressive as Beethoven's. Napoleon dozes off into a little nightmarish dream about water seeping into his carriage while *en route* to see a performance of Haydn's *Creation*. In the *Eroica*, the Coda commences quietly in E Flat. (One might well remember how the E Flat chord came to a drowsy Wagner and became the basis for his incredible opening to *Das Rheingold* which symbolizes womb-water or primeval existence. Burgess connects the heroic archetype, the subconscious dream, and the life-giving — or threatening — water with the E Flat keynote of the *Eroica*.) Suddenly, after the music comes to rest in E Flat, Beethoven shatters the lull with a resounding D Flat chord. And so a cart blows up in the *rue de la loi* as Napoleon's carriage rides by, an assassination attempt: "The street exploded" (p. 104). Napoleon escapes physical injury, but his end has been prophesied. French soldiers apprehend a suspect who is not even on French soil — a hint that the heroic will has gone beyond its proper bounds. The reader moves quickly over narrative leaps and stripped dialogue as Louis Antonine is raced through a mock trial to his inevitable doom. The rest of the Coda section builds toward the Coronation, a fitting conclusion which sees Napoleon at the *forté* of his glory. There is a long catalog of faithfuls, then a Byronic (ABABBCDCC) verse passage describing the ceremony.

• • •

In Part II Burgess makes elaborate use of a dream structure. Beethoven's curious utilization of basses in the *Marcia Funebre*, where one would normally expect to find drums, may have suggested the practice since the basses create a muffle-effect. Yet Burgess could also have been prompted by one of the *Eroica*'s critics, Rolland, who cites a dream in relation to the *Marcia Funebre* in which the "dreamer saw the dead man, and, in the same moment, he was the dead man: he was at the same time stretched out in the coffin and floating above it . . ." (p. 313). This is exactly Napoleon's situation as he dreams of his own funeral procession which marches right into the English channel. In any case, Part II of *Napoleon Symphony* depicts an underworld in which the descent of the archetypal hero recalls the inexorable course of Shakespearean tragedy.

For Burgess, the process of restoring Napoleon to the symphonic score of the *Eroica* involves a large amount of literary synthesis. Unlike music's self-contained expressiveness, musicalized fiction must use multiple forms to convey depth or richness of content. Hence, one is invited to remember Shakespeare's Antony when Napoleon (now referred to as "N") is warned by a prophetess about the unfavorable element of water: "She said the earth would be my friend and the water my enemy" (p. 33). This Napoleon-Antony association is appropriately reinforced in the Development or Egyptian section of Part I (p. 62). Water, an uncontrollable fluid, is identified with the female entity: "The damned Seas, the accursed woman-element, the immutable boundaries of his Empire" (p. 168); whereas land, the malleable solid, belongs to the male: "You [Napoleon] created, in your Promethean manner . . . your men out of clay, though to create woman you had no power" (p. 330). Burgess enlarges his symbols at every opportunity in an attempt to imitate the sheer profundity of Beethoven's melodies. To represent the melodies narratively, a more verbal and poetic correspondence is required. The verse passage, used to represent the main theme of Beethoven's *Marcia Funebre*, illustrates both of these processes as N becomes a Shakespearean Macbeth and the meter a syllabic equivalent of the music:

> There he lies
> Ensanguinated tyrant
> O bloody bloody tyrant
> See
> How the sin within
> Doth incarnadine
> His skin
> From the shin to the chin.
> (p. 127)

The last line reaffirms the comic vision, and indeed the bringing together of history and art or of myths in their varied forms can be viewed as a comic reconciliation.

Josephine dreams of riding down a river in a rose-decked barge as Cleopatra (p. 142). In Beethoven's *Marcia Funebre*, the solemn and dignified main theme is first played by the violins, bars 1 to 9, and then immediately repeated by the oboes, bars 9 to 17. Once again we find the

male-strings / female-woodwinds associations, but there is no strict correspondence between the episodes in the *Marcia Funebre* and the narrative
of the Part II dream sequence. In contrast to the listener who hears the
woodwind repetition right after the opening by the violins, the reader is
first given N's dream, the Stapps flashback and N's subsequent fall back
into dream, before he is presented with Josephine's dream-flashback-
dream sequence. This breakdown in simultaneity (as per the *Eroica*
model) is accentuated by a chronological breakdown (as per history)
insofar as the individual dreams occur three years apart. N is dreaming in
October of 1812 or in the middle of his disastrous march back from
Moscow, while Josephine is dreaming in December of 1809 just after her
divorce from N. The Russian campaign, in which only 50,000 men
survived of the 650,000 who set out, was Napoleon's real military collapse,
and his divorce from Josephine to marry the daughter of the Austrian
Emperor the corresponding collapse in love. Thus just as the first two
Movements of the *Eroica* trace the physical rise and fall of the heroic
spirit, so Parts I and II of Burgess' novel show the worldly achievement
and undoing of Napoleonic belligerence and ardor.

The climbing notes of the *Marcia Funebre*'s second subject (bars 37 to
39) serve to counteract the gloom of its main theme and are also
transcribed into verse passages: "O Deutschland arise / Light is arising in
the / Deutschland skies" (p. 132). N and the Grand Army may be
marching to a slow death, but the German *Volk* is only beginning to rise.
The suggestion here is that N's politics produced a reaction of Germanic
patriotism that would ultimately culminate in the horror of the Third
Reich. These are the excesses of the human will which eventually must
lead to the grave.

More important is the remarkable key shift from C minor to C major
which alters the mood from the horrible to the comic. Beethoven's
expression of the hero's death includes the *danse macabre*, since it is the
true spirit in which the hero meets the inevitable. N's nightmare returns
when the C minor march returns. Burgess has said that the crossing of the
Berezina River corresponds to Beethoven's majestic double-fugue: "Two
bridges. Two actions at the same time, occasionally converging."[12] From
this it can be seen that Burgess interprets the score in whatever way he
finds most appropriate. It could be in terms of narrative form, the
thematic mood, or — as in this case — the actual physical action of the
army. If one particular mode of interpretation were followed throughout,
then the whole exercise of writing musicalized fiction would be too
mechanical.

Once more the reader is given the perspective of the rank-and-file
soldier and then a section of light verse describing Marshal Ney's quick
escape from the Russian army. Both passages are rather facetious, considering the horrible subject matter. For Burgess, as for Kurt Vonnegut and
Joseph Heller, grotesque humor seems to be the only way of dealing with

the terrible absurdities of war, or as N himself remarks, "Always important to remember that a very narrow compartment indeed divides the sublime from the ridiculous" (p. 198). The inevitable and cyclical nature of myth lends itself to the comic, and Beethoven — as we shall see — seems to suggest a vision along these lines in the last two movements of the *Eroica*. As far as the *Marcia Funebre* is concerned, one thing is certain — Beethoven does not allow us to wallow in grief. There must be some resurrecting power and this was precisely what Wagner identified: "Out of grief there springs new Force, that fills us with a warmth sublime . . . we will not succumb but endure" (p. 223). And so at the same point that Beethoven shifts key from the elegiac C minor to the joyful A Flat major, Burgess shifts from the horrors of the Russian campaign to a low domestic comedy in the Napoleon household. At the end of Part II, both N and Josephine are back in their respective dreams. This time, however, their verse passages appear together. Simultaneity is restored, but time has faded completely into myth. We are prepared for N's transition into archetype: "It's the mind that counts, the mind will prevail" (p. 238).

• • •

After the solemnly slow *Marcia Funebre*, we feel as if we cannot go any further, but Beethoven then gives us his breathlessly fast *Scherzo* which breaks headlong into a volley of frolicking jubilation and carries us with it. It is within this accelerated rhythm that the hero N merges with his mythic counterpart, Prometheus, to become "Promethapoleon" (p. 351). Part III presents a closer narrative imitation of Beethoven's music than either Part I or II. Here the incredibly fast tempo of the *Scherzo* is simulated by the short, regular beat of the flowing prose. Promethean fire and motion are implied in the opening sentence: "From bivouac to bivouac to bivouac to bivouac and all the way it was torches . . ." (p. 241). Long rhythmic sentences catalog the dignitaries present at N's anniversary celebration. Lists of comments, descriptions and even the names of the foods served begin to whirl and whirl as the orchestra strikes up "another waltz" (p. 243); the minuet by this time is as *passé* as Mozart. Burgess even brings N's long-time aid, Berthier, into the action because his reputed stutter is a means of narratively reflecting those bustling triple-time notes in Beethoven's *Scherzo*. Berthier organizes a rabbit hunt that backfires when the rabbits, being tame, run toward their baffled hunter — N. The idea of the hunt comes from Beethoven's famous use of hunting horns in the Trio (middle segment of *Scherzo*). The unexpected smothering by the rabbits foreshadows the third section of Part III (based on the third, or repitition, segment of the *Scherzo*) in which N is smothered by Captain Randon's men when he returns from Elba. The festive mood comes from an awareness of mythic patterns which transcend the physical. Wagner said of the "buoyant gaiety" in Beethoven's *Scherzo* that "we have before us now the lovable glad man, who . . . looks laughingly across the meadows" (p. 232), and so it is, if by "meadows" we mean the rolling epochs of history.

After the celebration, N rides through cheering Paris crowds to the theater to see Enuiluban's mythological dramatization of Prometheus. "Enuiluban" is "Nabuliune" (Napoleon's original name) spelled backwards. This alphabetic reversal reflects N's role in rewriting the last act, since of course, only true heroes can mold history. Identifying himself with the fire-stealing Prometheus, N rejects the notion of having to be saved by Hercules, a god, and orders an improvised ending to the play—Prometheus freeing himself. But when the curtain rises on the second act, N has actually become Prometheus and the rock is Elba. The stage is now Europe, and each major country (Prussia, England, Austria and France) figures in the negotiating game—similar to the film *Oh What A Lovely War!* Reality has moved into the play, into the historical myth. Tightly structured verses summarize N's life and accomplishments up to Elba. Vienna, the capital of music and home of Beethoven, is alive with the waltz and the 1815 Congress. Deals whirl and whirl around the table, Talleyrand calls for a better prison—Elba being too close to the continent. The others pay no attention. The last sentence of the middle section (modeled on the Trio segment) beautifully expresson how the Congress representatives, preoccupied with their own scores, receive the news of N's escape: "Then the news came through and the orchestra stopped (heard the last of old) dead" (p. 260).

The third section of Part III covers the 100 Days or N's attempt to regain his former power. Comebacks are famous for making heroes, but N's is not that successful. If the reader expects some grand Waterloo, then he will surely be disappointed. In Morris' words, Burgess "speeds up the battle of Waterloo in the manner of Sennett's Keystone Cops" (p. 88). This acceleration is the basis of the comic-mythic because the patterns and hilarity of life emerge only when life is seen in fast-time. Therefore, dance imagery, specifically the waltz, dominates Part III of Burgess' novel. One must also remember that Beethoven was the first to introduce the jocular *Scherzo* (which is the Italian word for "joke") into the symphony. Moreover, Beethoven attaches a short coda to the *Scherzo* in the *Eroica* which creates the sense of a false ending. The final note is held back for twenty bars while the orchestra pours out a final *presto*. It is as if Burgess saw the coda itself as a symbol for N's 100-Day escape, his exile to Elba also being a false ending.

• • •

In the Fourth Movement, Beethoven draws upon all the aspects of the heroic spirit expressed thus far. Here the human will asserts itself, dies and recovers enough to climb to heaven. Here humor and dignity go hand in hand. For Burgess' story, there is still St. Helena—the rock from which N will not escape. And yet from St. Helena N can see how the ideals of the French Revolution have taken hold in Europe. In Part IV, Promethapoleon is synthesized with yet another archetypal hero—Jesus Christ. N first makes his analogy himself: "I am removed from the European scene as a personage but now may enter the world as a principle. . . . I showed the world that a resurrection was possible. . . . But you may say that the four extremities represent those victorious allies that are hammering in the nails. . . . they dare not affix a mocking inscription. INTERFECIMUS NAPOLEON REGEM IMPERATOREM. The thought of my martyrdom frightens them" (pp. 273–74). The INRI (*Iesus Nazarenus Rex Iudaeorum*) initials appear throughout Part IV and symbolize the first theme in Beethoven's *Finale* which is played by the woodwinds (bars 20 to 23). The theme rises, then falls, then rises again, and Burgess has said that it "sounds a bit like a cross" (Aggeler, p. 226). Divine incarnation and martyrdom epitomize the arch-hero, who is of titanic strength and who sacrifices himself to save others. Perhaps it is the heroic quality of mankind that constitutes God's image, in which man is made in the Christian sense.

The opening section of Part IV contains some bizarre italics which include syncopated words, such as "Jsphn" for Josephine (p. 273), and the INRI initials. Looking at the opening of Beethoven's *Finale*, we find that Burgess is imitating the *pizzicato* strings which play an outline or base of the Promethean theme. The *Finale* may contain Beethoven's ultimate statement of redemption, but it begins with a joke.[13] The joke seems to be that reduced to its simplest form heroism may be more awkward and silly than anything else.

As Beethoven goes on to improvise on his Prometheus theme, so Burgess improvises on the literary styles of the nineteenth century. This theme-and-variation structure is a fitting way for Beethoven to close his symphony, because it reminds us that the essence of the heroic spirit can be derived only from its multiple manifestations. Conversely, the structure can also represent the Promethean notion of the hero as progenitor. However one interprets the form, it is organically connected to the content. Burgess' first literary variation, or perhaps it is more accurate to say imitation, is an extremely subtle passage modeled on Henry James. Then comes the stilted dialogue of Walter Scott, some Wordsworthian blank verse, and a Dickensian scene. Each of these sections deals in its own way with Napoleon or the theme of the hero. Burgess even writes a prose improvisation on Tennyson, full of emotional intensity and classical allusions. Hopkins' sprung rhythm is also represented, and the dichotomy between natural wilderness and artificial creation becomes a dominant motif. There are several echoes of Voltaire's "We must cultivate our garden" (p. 281), maybe hinting that the better part of the Enlightenment will rise again to control the wild abandon of revolution—as wisdom tempers youthful energy.

Interspersed between the variations of Part IV are ridiculous scenes at N's bedside in which the Corsican physician, Dr. Antommarchi, argues incessantly with his English counterpart, Dr. Arnott, about N's treatment.

Burgess may be able to capture Beethoven's humor, but he cannot approach the latter's heavenly *poco andante* episode, which Grove describes as "the very apotheosis of the Hero" (p. 80). The terribly abstract and drawn out conversation that N has with Betsy Bascombe about the "heroic image," Beethoven's rescinded dedication and the quality of essence (pp. 329–33) does not come near the beauty and profundity of the music. Burgess' final flourish, however, is more impressive and closer to those surging notes, so typical of Beethoven's exits — one last expression of the glorious N racing and leaping into triumphant, cosmic myth. The INRI initials are again worked into the narrative and the closing words recall the modern progenitor of musicalized fiction: "all the flowing wine of the world rejoice. Rejoice. And again I say rejoice. And I say aga INRI ng bells bells bells bells and rejoice. Rejoice." (p. 343).

• • •

The *Eroica* was not only a new road for Beethoven after the gloom of the *Heiligenstadt* statement; it also marked the beginning of a new era in music. Musicologists have explicated the romantic elements in each of its Movements, although they tend to emphasize the *Allegro* and *Marcia Funebre*. What perhaps is not stressed enough is the harmonious relationship between the Movements — not just the appropriateness of the funeral march after the opening *Allegro*, but of the speed of the *Scherzo* which carries us to another plane, and of the joyful *Finale* which is a celebration of the whole. But of course the beauty of the *Eroica*, as with any great musical work, is that the listener can feel its harmonies without specialized knowledge.

In contrast, reading *Napoleon Symphony*, with or without a knowledge of its model, can be a laborious task. Yet the rewards are great for those who can appreciate literary virtuosity. As an example of musicalized fiction, *Napoleon Symphony* may not achieve music's form and content but it does succeed as a grand synthesis of art and history. The dazzling and inventive manner in which Burgess follows his symphonic paradigm renders his novel almost as unconventional as the *Eroica* was in 1803. He ultimately creates an imaginative fiction that portrays what the listener of the *Eroica* feels: the striving, the joyous triumphs, the grotesque discords, the sorrow, the humor, the elegant resurrections and the festive spirit. Furthermore, although *Napoleon Symphony* may exaggerate the humor of the *Eroica*, this is desirable since laughter — the real music of humanity — possesses the power to unite, in heroic fashion, the roughest incongruities of mankind. Even though Beethoven ripped up his original dedication, posterity demands a comic reconciliation between the *Eroica* and Napoleon. Burgess delivers. Bravo!

Notes

1. See *Life*, 25 October 1968, pp. 87–97.
2. Geoffrey Aggeler deals with the way in which the novel comments on the role of the

artist, but he does not concentrate on musicalization (*Anthony Burgess: The Novelist as Artist* [University, 1979], pp. 208–32); Samuel Coale focuses on Burgess' concern with myth in *Napoleon Symphony* (Anthony Burgess [New York, 1981], pp. 125–34); for a discussion of Joycean elements in *Napoleon Symphony*, see John Mowart, "Joyce's Contemporary: A Study of Anthony Burgess' *Napoleon Symphony*," *Contemporary Literature*, 19, No. 2 (1978), 180–95.

3. Jonathan Raban, "What Shall We Do About Anthony Burgess?" *Encounter*, 43 (1974), 86.

4. Anthony Burgess, *Napoleon Symphony* (London, 1974), p. 349. Burgess' comments on Joyce's "musicalisation" appear in his critical work *Joysprick* (London, 1973), pp. 82–92; his comments on the simpler musicalization of *Point Counter Point* can be found in his study, *The Novel Now* (London, 1967),p. 211.

5. Northrop Frye associates the "*mythos* of comedy" with both the "ternary form" in music and the central Christian myth; see *Anatomy of Criticism* (Princeton, 1957), pp. 171, 185.

6. Robert Morris, "With Flourish of Hautboys," *The Nation*, 219 (3 August 1974), 88.

7. See Charles T. Bunting, "An Interview in New York with Anthony Burgess," *Studies in the Novel*, 5 (1973), 505.

8. Romain Rolland, *Beethoven the Creator*, trans. Ernest Newman (New York, 1964), p. 55.

9. George Grove, *Beethoven and His Nine Symphonies*, 3rd ed. (New York, 1962), p. 61.

10. *Richard Wagner's Prose Works*, Vol. III, trans. William Ashton Ellis (London, 1894), p. 222.

11. Anthony Hopkins, *Talking About Music* (London, 1970), p. 47.

12. Anthony Burgess, quoted by Alex Hamilton, "Roll Over Beethoven," *Guardian*, 5 October 1974, p. 8.

13. For a lively discussion of Beethoven's humor at the beginning of the *Finale*, see Anthony Hopkins, *The Nine Symphonies of Beethoven* (London, 1981), pp. 92–96.

Faust in the Labyrinth: Burgess' *Earthly Powers*
Geoffrey Aggeler*

It seems hardly coincidental that the most significant attempts in postwar western fiction to explain twentieth-century history are novels with Faustian protagonists. Unquestionably the greatest of these is Thomas Mann's *Doctor Faustus*, in which, through the characterization of Adrian Leverkühn and his friend Zeitblom, we are made to see how all of the impulses and ideals which had produced the greatness of German culture were inextricably bound up with the forces which had produced Nazism. Very nearly on the same level of achievement and equally large in scope is Malcolm Lowry's *Under the Volcano*, mirroring in its drunken protagonist the world itself on the brink of war in 1938.[1] Both of these

*From *Modern Fiction Studies* 27 (1981):517–31. © 1981 by Purdue Research Foundation. Reprinted with permission.

novels embrace within their depictions of the Faustian quest the forces which had but recently threatened and were still to some extent threatening the very survival of western civilization. To an extent, both of them reflect Spengler's thesis that the spirit of modern Europe and America is Faustian, that civilized western man is aging and wasted, effete, infirm, and defenseless, yet still hopeful of achieving everything, including the impossible.[2] But both novelists, influenced by events Spengler did not live to see, go well beyond him in emphasizing the vulnerability of civilized Faustian western man, his vulnerability to the powers of evil.

Now we have Anthony Burgess' *Earthly Powers*, perhaps the most significant attempt since Mann's *Faustus* to explain history in Faustian terms. The novel's original title was *The Affairs of Men*. Then it became *The Prince of the Powers of the Air* and finally *Earthly Powers*.[3] The second title was taken from Hobbes's *Leviathan*, Part IV, "Of the Kingdom of Darknesse":

> *Besides these Soveraign Powers*, Divine, *and* Humane, *of which I have hitherto discoursed, there is mention in Scripture of another Power, namely, that of the* Rulers of the Darkness of this world, the Kingdome of Satan, *and the* Principality of Beelzebub over Daemons, *that is to say, over Phantasmes that appear in the Air: For which cause Satan is also called* the Prince of the Power of the Air: and (*because he ruleth in the darkness of this world*) The Prince of this world: *And in consequence hereunto, they who are under his Dominion, in opposition to the faithful (who are the* Children of the Light) *are called the* Children of Darknesse . . .[4]

Burgess quotes this passage in full in *Earthly Powers*, as it is being read by the narrator-protagonist, Kenneth M. Toomey, on his way to a visit with the other protagonist, Don Carlo Campanati. Toomey reads further in Hobbes concerning: "*a Confederacy of Deceivers, that to obtain dominion over men in this present world, endeavour by dark and erroneous Doctrines to extinguish in them the Light, both by Nature, and of the Gospell: and so to disprepare them for the Kingdome of God to come*" (*EP*, p. 397).

At this point there is no explicit linkage of Don Carlo with the Son of the Morning. Indeed Don Carlo has defined himself primarily in terms of his role as a defender of man against the powers of darkness. But a careful reading of the novel as a whole suggests that the nature of his relationship with the Devil is more equivocal.

For our perception of Don Carlo we are dependent upon Toomey, an eighty-one-year-old homosexual novelist-playwright modeled deliberately on W. Somerset Maugham. The ubiquitous references to Maugham himself and the obvious parallels between Toomey's career and Maugham's make the identification virtually explicit. But the reader may still wonder why Burgess chose to narrate his Faustian drama from such a point of view.

To some extent, one may conjecture, he must have been influenced by some of Maugham's ruminations in such works as *The Summing Up*, *Looking Back*, and *Don Fernando*. In the last named work, Maugham discusses the psychology of the homosexual in general terms with specific reference to the case of El Greco:

> Now it cannot be denied that the homosexual has a narrower outlook on the world than the normal man. In certain respects the natural responses of the species are denied to him. Some at least of the broad and typical human emotions he can never experience. However subtly he sees life he cannot see it whole. If it were not for the perplexing sonnets I should say that the homosexual can never reach the supreme heights of genius. I cannot now help asking myself whether what I see in El Greco's work of tortured fantasy and sinister strangeness is not due to such a sexual abnormality as this. . . . I should say that a distinctive trait of the homosexual is a lack of deep seriousness over certain things that normal men take seriously. This ranges from an inane flippancy to a sardonic humour. He has a wilfulness that attaches importance to things that most men find trivial and on the other hand regards cynically the subjects which the common opinion of mankind has held essential to its spiritual welfare. He has a lively sense of beauty, but is apt to see beauty especially in decoration. He loves luxury and attaches peculiar value to elegance. He is emotional, but fantastic. He is vain, loquacious, witty and theatrical. With his keen insight and quick sensibility he can pierce the depths, but in his innate frivolity he fetches up from them not a priceless jewel but a tinsel ornament. He has small power of invention, but a wonderful gift for delightful embroidery. He has vitality, brilliance, but seldom strength. He stands on the bank, aloof and ironical, and watches the river of life flow on.[5]

In some respects, but not in all, this is an accurate picture of Burgess' protagonist. Not being a homosexual himself, Burgess may well have relied upon Maugham's insights into the homosexual psyche. And what seems to have interested him especially were Maugham's remarks upon the ways in which a homosexual artist's vision is limited by his condition. Whether or not Maugham was intentionally drawing in this passage a rather masochistic self-portrait we can only wonder. Certainly he had no illusions about his status as a writer, though he attributed critics' neglect of his work largely to the fact that he had never been a propagandist.[6]

Burgess' protagonist, too, has a sense of his limitations, but he is resentful that the highest honors have gone to others he regards as less deserving: "As for the Nobel, I did not write inelegantly or tendentiously enough. I was not, like Boris Dyengizhdat, in political chains—which, I felt sure, he would break soon enough when the dollar royalties had mounted sufficiently. I did not, like Chaim Manor or J. Raha Jaatinen, belong to a gallant little nation that, possessing no strategical resources, had to be compensated with a great writer. I was, they had always said, cynical, not given to deep feelings or high thoughts. But I still sold well enough" (*EP*, p. 19). Such remarks of course belie his assertion that he is "not at all bitter." What he says about "Boris Dyengizhdat" inevitably reminds one of Burgess' own remarks about Solzhenitsyn,[7] but we should resist the temptation to take this or any of Toomey's other ruminations as expressions of Burgess' own feelings. At times, such as when he is lecturing at an American college on the craft of fiction, we may strongly suspect that he is speaking for Burgess. But his rather condescending attitude toward Joyce, whom he meets in Paris, hardly resembles Burgess' view of Joyce, and with regard to the crucial issues of the novel, such as the question of human freedom, he is clearly expressing his own point of view, a point of view shaped and limited by his sexual makeup, his Catholic upbringing, and his observations of human experience.

One gathers that Toomey would agree with Maugham when, in the conclusion to *The Summing Up*, he offers an answer to the question: "When then is right action?" His answer is an aphorism of the sixteenth-century Spanish theologian, poet, and teacher Fray Luis de Léon: "The beauty of life is this: it is incumbent upon every man to act according to his nature and his occupation."[8] For Toomey, however, such a saying would have a somewhat different meaning than it probably had for Fray Luis and, perhaps, for Maugham. Toomey has throughout his long life acted in accord with his nature and his occupation as a writer. Where it has gotten him is clearly revealed in what he himself calls the novel's "*arresting opening*": "It was the afternoon of my eighty-first birthday, and I was in bed with my catamite when Ali announced that the archbishop had come to see me" (*EP*, p. 7).

Especially suggestive in this first sentence is the word "catamite," evoking as it does an image of refined decadence and pagan luxury in a quasi-Olympian setting. Generally acknowledged "greatness" as a writer has eluded Toomey, but he has achieved a kind of Olympian eminence of fame, wealth, and the freedom of fleshly indulgence that goes with wealth. The Ganymede (L. *Catamitus* altered [*Ganymedes*] Gr. *Ganymēdēs*, Ganymede) he keeps, however, is no downy-chinned little Greek boy but a fat, sadistic drunkard of a man named Geoffrey Enright, who may be modeled on Gerald Haxton, one of Maugham's secretary-compan-ions.[9] As we soon see, the freedom of fleshly indulgence is also the bondage. Enright is only one of a line of lovers who have made Toomey pay for their favors with more than money. To escape the pain of loneliness, he has had to endure repeatedly humiliation, spite, and treachery.

The fact that Toomey's pederastic play is interrupted by a visit from an archbishop is also significant, foreshadowing much that is to come in the novel. Religion has always gotten in the way of Toomey's pleasures to some extent. Unlike Maugham, he is burdened with a Roman Catholic conscience. As a young man he had felt compelled to leave the Church because he could not refrain from homosexual activity, yet he was convinced that it would damn him, and he had no doubts whatever about the reality of Hell. Unable to reconcile the notion of a God making him as he is, yet forbidding him to act according to his nature, he was driven toward dualism: "But, since God had made me homosexual, I had to believe that there was another God forbidding me to be so. I may say also that I had to believe there were two Christs—one the implacable judge of the Sistine fresco, the other the mild-eyed friend of the disciple John" (*EP*, p. 52). Later, this dualism develops into a kind of Manichaeism. But heterodoxy cannot save Toomey from his Catholic conscience. Even when he is trying to justify pederasty in an outrageous rewriting of the Book of Genesis, the result, in the words of Ford Madox Ford, "smells of unfrocked priests" (*EP*, p. 171).

Catholic guilt and the attractions of Manichaenism are familiar themes to Burgess' readers, especially of such novels as *The Worm and the Ring* and *Tremor of Intent*. What is interesting in this new novel is how he relates them to larger themes, sometimes in rather subtle and provocative ways. For instance, when Toomey is setting up the frame story for his rewriting of the Book of Genesis and he is depicting transports of homosexual passion with a lyrical relish and vitality that James Baldwin might envy, he inserts a classical fragment that gives the attentive reader a perspective of the scene and the fable in relation to what the novel as a whole is saying about the human condition and the problem of evil in the modern world. In the frame story, a youngster who is in the process of being fellated by his lover moans out the words "*Solitam . . . Minotauro . . . pro caris corpus*," words which his lover supposes are "the memory of some old lesson, of some ancient attempt at seduction in that Jesuit school library he had spoken of" (*EP*, p. 166). Earlier in the novel, and much later in his life, Toomey is watching over his sleeping catamite Geoffrey and is amazed to hear him snore out the same words. Along with the Latin fragment, Geoffrey emits "a ghastly odor . . . of gross decay" that is somehow "remotely familiar" to Toomey. The sleeper becomes for him an image of the human condition, and this prompts a somewhat Augustinian reflection: "Man does not ask for nightmares, he does not ask to be bad. He does not will his own willfulness" (*EP*, p. 38).

The Latin fragment is from Catullus LXIV, a poem describing the wedding of Thetis and Peleus, on whose marriage bed is a coverlet decorated with pictures of various heroes, including Theseus. The lines in which the words occur are as follows:

> Cecropiam solitam esse dapem dare Minotauro.
> quis angusta malis cum moenia vexarentur,
> ipse suum Theseus pro caris corpus Athenis
> proicere optavit potius quam talia Cretam
> funera Cecropiae nec funera portarentur. . . .
>
> Cecropia was wont to give as a feast to the Minotaur
> chosen youths, and with them the flower of unwedded maids.

Now when his narrow walls were troubled by these evils, Theseus
himself for his dear Athens chose to offer his own body,
rather than that such deaths, living deaths, of Cecropia should
be borne to Crete.[10]

In other Burgess novels, notably *The Worm and the Ring* and *Inside Mr. Enderby*, the Minotaur is described as a Greek mythic analogue of Original Sin, and Theseus is seen to be analogous to the heretic Pelagius, who denied Original Sin and asserted that man was capable of achieving perfection without the aid of divine grace. The poet Enderby's *magnum opus* is a long allegorical piece about the Minotaur and about how the labyrinth houses not only the monster but Cretan culture itself " — university, museum, library, art gallery; a treasury of human achievement; beauty and knowledge built round a core of sin, the human condition."[11] Then Theseus, who is characterized as "the Pelagian liberator, the man who had never known sin, the guilt-killer," enters the labyrinth and leads out the monster on a string. Humanity then seizes the monster, reviles, buffets, and crucifies it, whereupon the labyrinth collapses, burying Cretan culture. The poem's argument, as Enderby's homosexual fellow poet Rawcliffe sums it up, is "Without Original Sin there is no civilization" (p. 55).

The reader of *Earthly Powers*, even if he happens to be familiar with the words of Catullus and Enderby, may feel that this is a rather overly subtle way of introducing the Pelagian versus Augustinian theme that becomes a central concern of the novel, as it is of so many of Burgess' others.[12] Why must we take such a roundabout and difficult detour through Catullus? The answer is, I believe, in what Catullus' poem contains besides the reference to the Minotaur. It relates how the wedding of Achilles' parents was an event attended by the Olympian gods, who were wont in days of yore, before religion was despised, to visit the homes of heroes. Since that time, men and women have sunk to such a level of depravity, are guilty of so many unnatural sins, including fratricide and incest, that the gods will no longer visit them. The poem is also about the betrayal of love, containing, in its description of the abandoned Ariadne and her lament, one of the most moving passages in Latin poetry. Her lover-betrayer is also guilty, by reason of his thoughtlessness, of his own father's death. As the poet presents these betrayals, they completely overshadow the hero's achievement in overcoming the monster.

I am suggesting that Burgess includes this repeated fragmentary reference to Catullus LXIV because it effectively mirrors the main thematic concerns of his novel. And he places it in contexts which further emphasize the same themes. In the first that Toomey happens to recall, his sleeping catamite, who has just spent an evening humiliating him and causing him to have a heart attack, becomes a mirror of the fallen human condition — depraved and vicious but pathetic in his helplessness, in need of sustaining love human and divine. In the second, Toomey is introducing his revision of the Biblical description of the consequences of the fall, according to which man was deprived of his prelapsarian condition of homosexual bliss and cursed with the burden of heterosexuality. Those who are "blessed" with a homosexual nature are able to "remake in their lives the innocence of Adam . . . and their embraces call back the joys of Eden" (*EP*, p. 170). Just how little of this Toomey himself really believes is shown in the scene of cruel, bestial buggery he writes to close his frame story in this work, which he entitles *A Way Back to Eden*. There is no escaping guilt if one is to remain human. Indeed one who seeks to escape it is likely to become less than human. Man is capable of heroic activity, of overcoming monsters, but until he learns to love and not merely to gratify his appetites in the name of love, he will be overcome by the monsters within him.

That there are monsters abiding within the labyrinth of the human soul is something both Toomey and Don Carlo believe. For Toomey, one of Burgess' "Augustinians," the monsters are the forms of badness that are part of fallen human nature. His own personal monster is his homosexual nature, which he has managed to overcome only once, through the experience of a love that is utterly unlike anything he has ever felt and called by that name. While sojourning in Malaya as a young man, he meets another young man, Doctor Philip Shawcross, whom he soon learns to love, and he recalls how he "marveled at the mystery of a particular nonphysical love apparently driving out generalized physical desire" (*EP*, p. 242). His love for this man, which is as inexplicable and mysterious as the operation of grace itself, is potentially an avenue of regeneration: "There was nothing remarkable in Philip's body or brain; I had to resurrect and dust off a concept long discarded by the humanists whom I believed I had joined, namely the *spiritus* of the theologians, the entity you could define only negatively and yet love positively, more, love ardently, with and to the final fire. So, however reluctantly, a man may be brought back to God. There is no free will, we must accept, with love, the imposed pattern" (*EP*, p. 243). The death of this man, which is the result of diabolical machinations, in effect deprives Toomey of a grace bearer, indeed the only source of grace in his life, leaving him prey to the monster of his own nature and the monstrous relationships his nature demands.

For Don Carlo, on the other hand, the monsters within are all intruders who have come from the kingdom of darkness. Because man is God's creation, he is perfect. Evil is wholly from the devil, who taught man how to be evil and is still teaching him. God permits this because He will in no way abridge human freedom. Don Carlo even goes so far as to assert that God, "in His terrible love, denied Himself foreknowledge, imposed upon Himself a kind of human ignorance" of man's fall in Eden, which, if he had foreknown it, would have been predestined, "and where there is predestination there is no freedom of will" (*EP*, p. 149). Man is still totally free to choose, and his choice is a clear one "between the kingdom of good and the kingdom of evil." Moreover, he has the capacity to negate the consequences of the fall: "God made man without flaw, but also free to become flawed. Yet the flaws are reversible, the return to perfection is possible" (*EP*, p. 151). Mankind has only one enemy, the enemy of mankind's Creator.

It is these beliefs that shape Carlo's theology and his career. Toomey emphasizes and reemphasizes their importance in his thinking. Initially, they lead him into prominence in the field of exorcism, an activity which Toomey regards as "a lot of nonsense," until he sees Carlo in action in Malaya, in combat with the devils who have been summoned to destroy his friend Doctor Shawcross. A short time later, Toomey sees him in action again, this time in Chicago, attempting the formidable task of exorcizing a bunch of Italian mobsters who have murdered his brother Raffaele. It is the Prohibition era, and in Carlo's view such evils simply demonstrate that "This country has gotten the devil in it" (*EP*, p. 272). Wherever the devil is at work, it seems, he may expect to encounter Carlo.

While Carlo sees himself as Satan's enemy and a champion of mankind against the powers of darkness, it is suggested early in the novel that he is himself vulnerable to these same powers, and the reader must be attentive to these suggestions if he is to accept some of the later developments in the novel as plausible. The genuinely heretical nature of Carlo's beliefs in human perfectibility is first suggested to Toomey by Carlo's adoptive mother, Concetta Campanati: "I think what Carlo believes may not be quite orthodox. But orthodoxy may be a matter of strength of will. Carlo thinks you can will anything. Oh, with a bit of grace and prayer as side dishes" (*EP*, p. 278). She has casually but accurately defined him as a Pelagian heretic. A short time later, Carlo himself says to Toomey, "I have never known the impossible to be much trouble. You start off with the impossible, and that is a blank sheet on which the possible may be written" (*EP*, p. 314). This rather Faustian statement is uttered as he is trying to persuade Toomey to publish under his own name a book setting forth his plans to bring about a reunification of the Christian churches. Essential to the achievement of this end are drastic alterations in orthodox Catholic doctrines with regard to the role of the Pope, the Real Presence in the Eucharist, and other matters. The liturgy of the mass, he argues, should be malleable enough to be altered in harmony with local customs and cultural traditions, and the example he gives of how this might work, which becomes important later in the novel, is the African mass, in which dancing and chanting would replace "the imposition of organ voluntaries or Western hymns." "Here," as Toomey describes it, "was the terrible ecumenical strategy set out in clumsy single-spaced typing, and I, who considered myself to have lost my faith, was appalled" (*EP*, p. 316).

Predictably, the treatise goes on to argue in defense of Pelagius himself and for acceptance of his teachings, "as more consonant with the True Reformed premise of the goodness and dignity of man than the

Augustinian doctrine of his natural depravity" (*EP*, p. 319). What especially worries Toomey, who, largely because of his own nature and experience, inclines toward Augustinianism, is the virtual absence of any discussion of sin, Original or other: "Dangerous this denial of original sin, though it was not expressed in so many words. You could blame yourself for lack of moral judgement, but not for the dynamic, which animated your acts of evil. Original sin was original weakness, not being sufficiently clever, or Godlike, to spot the machinations of the fiend" (*EP*, p. 318).

At this point, the reader will perceive, if he has not already perceived, that the model for Carlo is Pope John XXIII, the most beloved pontiff of modern times. As with the characterization of Toomey, Burgess has made the character larger and, in some ways, more heroic than the model. But he has also, as with the characterization of Toomey, made him a good deal less attractive than his model. Eventually he develops into a very sinister figure indeed, one who seems to have acquired his earthly powers by means of a Faustian bargain. Why, we may wonder, does Burgess do this? Why diminish John XXIII? The answer, I believe, is in the passages I have just quoted. Burgess is not diminishing Pope John himself so much as what he and his ecumenicism seemed to represent, a revival of the Pelagian heresy and a willingness to achieve the reunification of Christianity at the cost of abandoning the very essence of Catholicism. Pelagianism is an attractive heresy, but, as Burgess suggests in the secular contexts of *The Wanting Seed* and *A Clockwork Orange*, it inevitably breeds "DISAPPOINTMENT," which in turn causes people to become extremely Augustinian in their thinking, which in turn may lead to evil consequences. Pope John XXIII, he seems to be suggesting, may have set in motion processes which his successors might not be able to control.

Whether or not Burgess is correct in his thinking about John XXIII is a question to be discussed outside the context of a critical exegesis of *Earthly Powers*. Personally I think he is wrong, but that does not prevent me from appreciating his Faustian characterization, which is both reminiscent of other great Faustian protagonists and highly original. He is indeed a much more absorbing character than Toomey, who tends to become rather wearisome after a while. We see so much of Toomey, too much of him. His sexual problems and humiliations arouse sympathy but also disgust, and this, I suspect, will be the reaction of any reader, no matter what his or her sexual makeup happens to be. His preoccupation with his own importance, or lack of it, as a writer is also wearing. Carlo, on the other hand, is a richly developed character whom we can visualize clearly but who retains elements of mystery which stimulate and free the reader's imagination.

A crucial event in Carlo's development is the discovery that he is adopted. This has been foreshadowed in a kind of epiphany Toomey experiences as he compares Carlo physically with the other Campanatis: ". . . Carlos was physically gross in comparison with that pared and elegant family. In a flash I saw him as a changeling, a goblin baby dumped in a Campanati pram" (*EP*, p. 156). The passage is worth quoting because it in effect suggests the possibility of enchanted, even demonic origins. As it happens, Carlo finds out that he can never be certain about his origins, and the effect of this on him is initially devastating. In the process of coming to terms with this fact, with the anesthetizing aid of strong drink, he is prompted to engage in what turns out to be a conjuring. By means of cursing and blasphemy, he succeeds in summoning either the devil himself or a phantasm of him in the form of a large rat, "whose sleek fur and bright teeth Carlo admired extravagantly in various languages, including, I think, Aramaic" (*EP*, p. 332). What follows is a kind of monologue-dialogue with the devil, reminiscent of the demonic dialogues of Adrian Leverkühn and Ivan Karamazov. Wisely, Burgess does not try to imitate these celebrated dialogues, even as Virgil wisely eschews imitating certain episodes in Homer that cannot be surpassed. What he gives us, however, is powerfully evocative:

> In the tones of an upper-class Englishman he said, "For the moment you are in the ascendancy, old boy, what, rather. I see your large clean fangs grinning at my temporary failure. *Salut, mon prince, votre* bloody *altesse*. You and I are alike in not possessing a mater, old boy. Even God forced himself into a filial situation. But will prevails, don't you know. There is never any failure of the will. We are what we make ourselves, old chap. Let's see you now as a serpent, your first disguise. Very good, that's really a most remarkable cobra hood, old fellow. I've never been much afraid of snakes, don't you know. The colonial experience, so to say, *mon brave*. But you bore me rather, you tire me somewhat. A little shut-eye is indicated, wouldn't you say? Rather." (*EP*, p. 332)

Significantly, Toomey reports this without any skeptical comment, though he himself has not actually seen the apparition, except through Carlo's eyes.

Having overcome the shock of discovering that his parentage is unknown, Carlo apparently undergoes some changes in personality, and the reader can only infer that his meeting with the devil, whether real or imagined, has had something to do with these changes. He now despises the family that had adopted him, regarding them all as "failures," whose only admirable qualities can be accounted for in terms of weaknesses or folly. Though he professes to be "brimming" with compassion, we can see that a hardness and a coldness have set in and along with these qualities a growth in pride and ambition. He reveals to Toomey his intention to "make Pope." No longer despondent about his mysterious origins, he likens himself to Oedipus, a "son of the goddess Fortune," who is free to make what he will of her gifts to him. Above all, he intends to "survive," like the Church itself, all the ephemeral forces of destruction in the modern world.

Neither he nor the Church will be what he calls contemptuously a "victim."

Actually, he has more in common with Oedipus than he realizes. His contempt for victims and failures and his complete confidence in himself manifest what Toomey rightly suggests is an attitude bordering on *hubris*. Much later, after he has learned humility from perhaps the only one who can teach him, Carlo recalls his earlier conversation with Toomey about Oedipus and Greek tragedy. Having been shown by the devil himself, during an abortive exorcism, the limits of his powers, he admits in effect that he has been guilty of *hubris*. What he does not realize is that he, like Oedipus, is a man whose illusions of freedom and power will blind him as he is caught up in the process of fulfilling a strange, terrible fate. The devil sees to it that he will remain blinded. As he is in the process of casually breaking the neck of the possessed victim, he hails Carlo as *"Sancte Pater."*

Before Carlo's humiliation by the devil, which appears to be instrumental in leading him to make a Faustian pact whereby he becomes indeed *Sancte Pater*, Carlo is able to maintain the illusion of his own power against the forces of evil. And his Pelagian belief in the essential goodness and perfectibility of man does not abandon him, even when it is tested by spectacles of the Nazis in action. During the Nazi occupation in Italy, he, as Bishop of Moneta, becomes a heroic figure in the resistance movement, and when an SS officer named, significantly, Liebeneiner, falls into his hands, he reassumes his old role of exorcist and undertakes the formidable task of driving out the devil Hitler. Eventually, through force and persistence, he succeeds, at least to the extent of disillusioning the man and removing his former beliefs. But the whole effort, albeit finally crowned with a degree of success, reveals that the root of the problem is an evil that does not come from the Kingdom of Darkness outside of man.

The episode of Liebeneiner's conversion, one of the most memorable passages in the novel, effectively illuminates the limitations of Carlo's understanding imposed by his Pelagian view of human nature. The man is, Carlo believes, "a new type of human being" produced by Nazi Germany, one who is "capable of putting the abstraction of a political system before the realities of human life" and willing, when ordered, "to perpetuate the most ghastly enormities without remorse" (*EP*, p. 416). Carlo's explanation for this, as for all human evil, is that "The devil got into" Liebeneiner and his people. In Liebeneiner's particular case, there was "a kind of vacuum" to begin with, and the process of saving his soul is made difficult for Carlo by the fact that it is "not much of a soul." What Carlo does not grasp is that Liebeneiner is not merely a representative Nazi but a representative of the fallen human condition in the modern age — fragmented, capable of utterly separating his sense of duty from his humanity, in desperate need of grace secular or divine. He is indeed a "vacuum," a living embodiment of the privative concept of evil, revealing, like Shakespeare's Iago, an essential emptiness. As his very name indicates, he is without love, and this is the vacuum the Nazis have filled with devotion to the German state. Carlo in effect imposes irresistible grace upon him and forcibly achieves his regeneration.

Immediately following this episode in the novel, and in effect juxtaposed with it, is Toomey's own view of the same triumph of evil. He relates how he was sent, at the end of the war, with a parliamentary delegation to visit Buchenwald. Viewing the horrors, he, like Carlo discovering Liebeneiner's inhumanity, thinks first of "The Prince of the Power of the Air," but then he quickly rejects this explanation: "No. This was no Luciferian work. The intellectual rebel against God could not stoop to it. This was pure man, pure me" (*EP*, p. 426). His revulsion and disgust carry him beyond even Augustinian pessimism: "Man had not been tainted from without by the Prince of the Power of the Air. The evil was all in him and he was beyond hope of redemption" (*EP*, p. 427). He does not, like Carlo, believe that the Nazis had produced "a new type of human being." Indeed, in his view, they had produced nothing essentially new but had merely exploited on a vast scale the evil that men have always found within themselves: "The Nazis had, in a quantitative age, exploited the horror of surfeit: that was their sole new achievement . . . I wanted to have Carlo with me there to smell the ripe Gorgonzola of innate human evil and to dare to say that mankind was God's creation and hence good. Good, that's what I am, sir, it was the devil made me do it. Man was not God's creation, that was certain. God alone knew from what suppurating primordial dungheap man had arisen" (*EP*, p. 427).

As he recalls this bitter meditation, Toomey relates how he had discovered a scrap of paper clinging to his foot. On it was the same Latin fragment: "*Solitam . . . Minotauro . . . pro caris corpus.*" It is never explicitly identified in the novel, but to the reader who recognizes it in context it becomes progressively more meaningful. We are being led in effect ever further into the labyrinth of the human soul, and the monsters are becoming ever more threatening.

By juxtaposing Carlo's and Toomey's contradictory views and explanations of the Nazis, Burgess does not seem to be suggesting that one or the other is wholly correct. He suggests rather than both views are to some extent partially correct, but both are also significantly limited. Viewing the spectacle of twentieth-century history, Toomey would attribute the triumphs of evil wholly to innate human depravity, while Carlo would credit them wholly to the devil. In fact, as Burgess' depiction of events suggests, there is an interaction, a cooperation between the demons that are a part of man's nature and the devil himself. Failure to recognize the existence of both may lead to dreadful consequences.

The demons within Carlo which lead him in effect to become the instrument of his enemy are pride and ambition, the very demons that led man into the fallen condition Carlo refuses to recognize. His Faustian pact with the devil is never actually shown in the novel. Indeed it may not be *consciously* made, but it is strongly suggested, nonetheless, by the events that follow his ascendancy to the papal chair which was linked to his reign. He does indeed "make Pope," becoming a beloved pontiff who is recognized as a champion of mankind against the devils of social injustice. He also initiates changes that threaten to transform the Church beyond recognition. When he dies, he becomes a candidate for sainthood.

Crucial to Carlo's canonization is the verification of a miracle attributed to him, and it happens that Toomey is the only witness. When the two men had been visiting Carlo's dying brother Raffaele in a Chicago hospital, they had seen a child dying of spinal meningitis, and somehow Carlo, "through the fierce gentle compassion of his presence" (*EP*, p. 271) had managed to bring about a complete cure. As it turns out, this miracle is ultimately responsible for bringing about one of the most ghastly triumphs of evil in recent history. The child survives to become "God Manning," a fanatical religious leader modeled obviously on the late Jim Jones. Burgess transfers what is obviously Jonestown and the horrible events there from Guiana to the Mojave Desert in California. In linking Carlo with them, Burgess appears to be suggesting that Carlo's role as an instrument of the devil actually began long before he became Pope. While Carlo firmly believes that good can be wrought out of evil, his miracle effectively shows how the powers of darkness are able to use what is essentially good for their own purposes. There is also the suggestion of Carlo's direct connection with other evils, including the destruction of two of the most attractive characters in the novel, who apparently become sacrificial victims in an African mass of the kind Carlo had advocated.

Carlo's Faustian identity is made explicit near the end of the novel, when a priest asks Toomey to tell him what Carlo had said to his, Toomey's, sister when she visited him near the moment of his death. Carlo had professed his love for her, a love like that of Dante for Beatrice. Hearing this, the priest utters the most famous line in Goethe's *Faust* and asks Toomey to quote it in the original: "*Das Ewig-Weibliche zieht uns hinan*" (*EP*, p. 600). The line doesn't seem to be all that relevant because Toomey's sister has not, like Gretchen in *Faust*, played any vital role in Carlo's Faustian progress, though she may, as the only human being he seems truly to have loved, serve potentially as a grace-bearing agent of his salvation. On the other hand, it may be a bitterly ironic allusion, like the epigraph from *Faust* that introduces Malcolm Lowry's drama of damnation, *Under the Volcano*.

There is a great deal to discuss in *Earthly Powers* besides the Faustian drama of Carlo Campanati. What needs to be discussed in a larger essay than this one is how Burgess integrates all the many parts of this vast and demanding novel. I do not doubt that the connections between Toomey's accounts of social, literary, and political history will be worked out in future critical exegeses. Burgess is clearly in command of his material, and it remains for us to appreciate critically what he has achieved. I tend to agree with those who call it his "masterpiece," though it is certainly not without flaws. Parts of it are, as I have said, wearisome, and the language is occasionally pedantic. The flaws are, however, minor and unavoidable in a work so large and ambitious. Overall it is a magnificent performance, what we have been waiting for from Burgess.

Notes

1. "On one level, the drunkenness of the Consul may be regarded as symbolizing the universal drunkenness of war, of the period that precedes war, no matter when. Throughout the twelve chapters, the destiny of my hero can be considered in its relationship to the destiny of humanity." "Preface to a Novel," trans. George Woodcock, *Malcolm Lowry: The Man and His Work* (Vancouver: University of British Columbia, 1971), p. 14.

2. See Oswald Spengler, *Form and Actuality*, Vol. I of *The Decline of the West*, trans. Charles Francis Atkinson (New York: Knopf, 1926). See also H. Stuart Hughes, *Oswald Spengler: A Critical Estimate* (New York: Scribner's, 1962).

3. Letters to Geoffrey Aggeler: 2 November 1971; 22 April 1977; 11 July 1979.

4. Quoted in Anthony Burgess, *Earthly Powers* (New York: Simon and Schuster, 1980), p. 397. All subsequent references to this edition will be given in the text in parenthesis.

5. W. Somerset Maugham, *Don Fernando or Variations on Some Spanish Themes* (Garden City, NJ: Sun Dial Press, 1950), pp. 245–247.

6. Maugham, *The Summing Up* (New York: Signet, 1964), Chapters 58, 59, 60.

7. During recent talk show interviews with Dick Cavett and others, but see also *The Novel Now* (London: Faber & Faber, 1967), pp. 175–176.

8. *The Summing Up*, p. 191.

9. See Ivor Brown, *W. Somerset Maugham* (London: International Textbook, 1970), p. 76 for a brief description of Haxton that virtually fits Enright.

10. *Catullus Tibullus and Pervigilium Veneris*, trans. F. W. Cornish, J. P. Postage, J. W. MacKail (London: Heinemann, 1968), p. 103.

11. Anthony Burgess, *Inside Mr. Enderby* (London: Penguin, 1966), pp. 16–17.

12. See my article "Pelagius and Augustine in the Novels of Anthony Burgess," *English Studies*, 55 (February 1974), 43–55.

INDEX

1985, 18
Nothing Like the Sun, 10–11, 12, 15, 16, 33, 37, 89–103, 105–9, 121n, 181, 197
Novel Now, The, 52, 102n
One Hand Clapping, 3, 4
ReJoyce, 27, 102n, 167, 185, 186, 189, 192, 193, 194
Right to an Answer, The, 6–7, 11, 15, 16, 40, 58–62, 65
Shakespeare, 44, 103n
Time for a Tiger, 1–2, 16, 72
Tremor of Intent, 12, 15, 16, 45, 98, 111, 128, 152–58, 158–72, 179, 217
Vision of Battlements, A, 1, 9, 15, 32, 50, 54, 84, 102n, 105–9, 123, 182
Wanting Seed, The, 3, 6, 9, 11, 15, 18–19, 34, 61, 62–65, 111, 123, 128, 140–51, 172, 180, 182, 183, 197, 221
Worm and the Ring, The, 3, 5–6, 15, 16, 46, 61, 123, 172, 217, 218

Burgess, Liliana, 102n
Butler, Samuel, 36, 41
Byron, Lord, 4, 33

Calmelet, Jérôme, 201, 202
Calvin, Jean, 105
Campbell, Joseph, 176–77
Cancer Ward, 38
Canticle for Leibowitz, A, 151
Carné, 196
Cary, Joyce, 29
Catharism, 44
Catullus, 217–18
Chaika, 31
Churchill, Thomas, 102n, 121n
Coale, Samuel, 120n, 121n
Coffin for Dimitrios, A, 152
Comedians, The, 43
Condorcet, Marquis de, 141
Confessions, 156
Conrad, Joseph, 68–69, 86, 88
Creation, 206
Cullinan, John, 138n

Dante Alighieri, 12, 225
Das Rheingold, 206
Davenport, Guy, 13
Defoe, Daniel, 41–42, 153
DeVitis, A. A., 15–16, 98, 103n, 124, 131
Diaghilev, Sergei Pavlovich, 107
Dickens, Charles, 3, 11, 46, 55, 83, 125, 194, 211

Diderot, Denis, 153
Dix, Carol M., 15, 131
Doctor Faustus, 38, 213, 222
Doctorow, E. L., 154
Don Fernando, 215
Don Juan, 33
Don Quixote, 29
Dos Passos, John, 33
Durkheim, Emile, 177
Durrell, Lawrence, 48

Edward, Black Prince, 33
Edward III, King of England, 33
Einstein, Albert, 76
El Greco, 215
Eliot, T. S., 24, 57, 59, 79
Elizabeth I, Queen of England, 164
Ellison, Ralph, 41
Ellmann, Richard, 103n
Enright, D. J., 11, 92, 102
Eroica (Beethoven), 32, 190, 191, 199, 200–213 passim
Essay on the Principle of Population, An (Malthus), 141–44

Faust (Goethe), 225
Field, Andrew, 81
Fielding, Henry, 42, 153
Finnegans Wake, 26, 27, 51, 179, 180, 186–87, 188, 190, 193, 195, 196
Fitzgerald, F. Scott, 41
Flaubert, Gustave, 26, 51–52, 190
Fleming, Ian, 12, 153
Fleming, William, 159, 165, 167
Ford, Ford Madox, 36
Forster, E. M., 3, 23, 47, 68–69
Four Quartets (Eliot), 199
Fourier, Charles, 141
Frazer, Sir James, 177
Freud, Sigmund, 135–36, 155

Galsworthy, John, 14
Garis, Robert, 56
Gilbert, W. S., 194
Godwin, William, 141
Goethe, Johann Wolfgang von, 225
Goldsmith, Oliver, 92
Graham, Virginia, 48
Graves, Robert, 120n
Greene, Graham, 16, 36, 43–44, 81, 85
Grove, George, 202, 212

Hamlet, 87–88, 90, 92–93
Handful of Dust, A, 36, 70